NIGHT VOICES

Night Voices

Heard in the Shadow of Hitler and Stalin

HEATHER LASKEY

McGill-Queen's University Press
Montreal & Kingston · London · Ithaca

© McGill-Queen's University Press 2003
ISBN 0-7735-2606-4

Legal deposit third quarter 2003
Bibliothèque nationale du Québec

Printed in Canada on acid-free paper that is 100% ancient forest free (100% post-consumer recycled), processed chlorine free.

McGill-Queen's University Press acknowledges the support of the Canada Council for the Arts for our publishing program. We also acknowledge the financial support of the Government of Canada through the Book Publishing Industry Development Program (BPIDP) for our publishing activities.

National Library of Canada Cataloguing in Publication

Laskey, Heather, 1936–
Night voices: heard in the shadow of Hitler and Stalin/by Heather Laskey.

Includes bibliographical references.
ISBN 0-7735-2606-4

1. Ałapin Rubiłowicz, Stasia. 2. Poland – History – 1945-1980. 3. Jews – Poland – Biography. 4. Poland – Biography. 5. Polish Canadians – Biography. I. Title.

DK4435.A26L38 2003   943.805'4'092   C2003-903134-9

This book was typeset by Dynagram inc. in 10.5/13.5 Sabon.

For those whose stories remain untold

Contents

Acknowledgments ix
A Guide to the Pronunciation of Polish Names xi
Introduction 3
1   Stasia's First Life   11
2   Mietek, Peter, and Alina Tell Their Stories   113
3   Stasia's Second Life   201
Postscript   239
Selected Bibliography   253

Acknowledgments

This book was made possible primarily through the unstinting cooperation of Dr Stanisława Ałapin Rubiłowicz, the late Dr Mieczysław Rubiłowicz, Peter Ałapin, and "Alina."

The author's thanks go to many other people. Eric Bednarski shared the results of his research for his MA thesis on the "Soviet Destruction of the Polish Home Army: 1944–45," pointing her towards many of the books with particular relevance for this project; he also tracked down extra material for her in Warsaw. Geoffrey Turnbull, for many years the executive producer of CBC Radio current affairs in Halifax, gave her invaluable advice and help on structure. Colin Stuttard provided much assistance in transposing and setting up the manuscript from computer discs.

The late Dr Cyla Zak supplied crucial documentary and other information about pre-war, wartime, and post-war Poland, and the generosity of the late Zdzisław Domaszewski made possible the author's visit to Albinów.

Thanks also to Dr Norman Pereira, professor of Russian history at Dalhousie University, to Sheila Fischman, the eminent translator of French Quebec literature, and to Dr David Jones, Russian military historian and book collector. Further thanks to Christene Hirschfeld for her advice and to the author's daughter, Minga O'Brien, for her stern supervision of syntax and style.

Appreciation is expressed to the Canada Council for the Arts for an Explorations grant which, among other things, enabled the author to make the journey to Poland and Denmark.

A Guide to the Pronunciation of Polish Names

The pronunciation of Polish names is often confusing for the English reader. The following is an approximate guide.

C on its own or followed by an *e* or *o* sounds like *ts*. Thus Jacek sounds like Yatsek, and Gecow like Getsov. The *ci*, as in Babcia (grandmother), is pronounced as a *ch*. Sz is pronounced *sh*; so the Polish name Janusz sounds like Yanush, and Staszewski like Stashevski. Cz is pronounced like *ch*; thus General Moczar's name sounds like Mochar. The *i* in Irena is short, as in "it." There is no *j* sound in Polish; the letter is pronounced as the English *y*. Thus the name Jan sounds like Yan. W is pronounced as a *v*. Thus the personal names Ewa, Władysław, and Wictor and the place names Albinów and Iwaniska sound like Eva, Vladislav, Victor, Albinov, and Ivaniska. The *z*, as in the names Jerzy and Rożański, sounds like the *s* in "measure" or "treasure."

Mietek is pronounced M'yetek. Stasia and Lusia sound like Stasha and Loosha, and the city of Szczecin (Stettin in German) sounds like Schechin.

NIGHT VOICES

Introduction

It must have been in 1984, not long after they came to live in Halifax, that I met Stasia and her husband, Mietek. Introduced to them by Stasia's son, Peter, I noted with interest the reserved, polite man and the slight, fair-haired woman in her mid-sixties with a practised, wary charm. A few years later, after we had crossed the first barriers of acquaintance and I had made a short CBC radio documentary about her memories of the last days of the Second World War, Stasia asked me to work with her on what were first intended to be her memoires. It became a close but not an easy relationship – with Stasia, nothing was ever simple. We started with formal interviews. Then, as I began to see the lines of development, she also wrote copious notes in answer to some of my questions. I had agreed to the project possibly out of a sense of duty, of something being owed, because she was a Jew who had survived the war in Poland, and I, also a Jew, had never had to hear the stamp of approaching jackboots. But if my motives had initially arisen from a sense of obligation, they quickly changed to curiosity.

I had assumed that Stasia's story would essentially be that of a life caught up in the maelstrom of the Holocaust, the individual subsumed by the enormity of events. What was emerging was more complex. Her memories were all intensely personal, to do with her milieu as much as with a cataclysmic situation that had left her with the immovable weight of "survivor guilt." She would, for example, frequently emphasize that her family were not only middle class but "assimilated," distancing herself from what had been the Yiddish-speaking culture of most Polish Jews. During the war, she had not only worked in the Warsaw ghetto as a doctor and been rescued from a Gestapo prison, but she had gone off with the Red Army. There was the role of her ambitious, glamorous mother, who had become famous as one of Poland's leading actresses, and there were Stasia's own turbulent romantic involvements.

And another issue presented itself: Mietek had been a colonel in the Bezpieka, the Security forces that were Poland's equivalent of the Soviet KGB, albeit as a medical adminstrator, and both he and Stasia had been committed communists. It became increasingly clear that I was getting an unusual insight into the story of the Jews who became part of Poland's new, Soviet-imposed establishment as it took shape at the end of the war. It was this aspect that led me to extend the field of my research through interviews with Mietek, Peter, and Alina, a close friend of theirs, and to gather whatever relevant material came my way. And also to understand that I was venturing into sensitive, controversial territory.

For a few years after the end of the war, Jews were visible in the "upper echelons" of the Soviet-installed governments of Hungary, Romania, and Czechoslovakia, as well as in Poland. But after those few years they disappeared from view or, as in the famous case of party leader Rudolf Slansky in Czechoslovakia, were hanged after being the central exhibit of Stalinist show trials.

Then in the late sixties, news reports came out of Poland about a government-sponsored anti-Semitic campaign pressuring the remaining Jewish population to leave the country. For many of us in the West, it was a surprise to hear that there were any Jews still in Poland. One learned that many of them were communists, and thus there was a reluctance on the part of Western countries to receive these unwilling emigrants, the principal exceptions being Denmark and Sweden. They could go to Israel, but party doctrine had long been furiously anti-Zionist, and these people were not Zionists. Nevertheless, the Polish government insisted that, on paper at least, Israel had to be the emigrants' official destination. Their forced departure was, in effect, the end of 1,000 years of history.

❧

Poland was once known as the "Paradise for Jews." During and after the centuries of the Crusades and of the Black Death in Europe, the country became a sanctuary of relative safety for refugees from the mass slaughters, persecution, and deportations of long-established Jewish communities in Germany and Bohemia. Polish kings and landowners tolerated and sometimes even encouraged Jewish settlement, according the growing communities formal status and varying degrees of self-government. As the Jewish population increased, a new language, Yiddish, and a distinctive culture evolved in a society parallel to and, in varying degrees, coexisting with its Christian Polish neighbours.

By the end of the eighteenth century, an estimated 800,000 Jews, at that time the largest Jewish demographic concentration in the world, were living in Poland. But in 1795 Poland, as an entity on the map of central Europe, disappeared; Prussia, Russia, and the Hapsburg Empire carved it up among themselves, all imposing their own autocratic styles of governance on their new subjects, the czarist fist being the most harshly oppressive. During the later years of the nineteenth century, when millions were emigrating from central and eastern Europe in the hope of escaping from extreme poverty and land shortages created by expanding populations, the Jews among them also saught freedom from the endless pogroms, inequities, and persecution encouraged and promoted by the czarist regime.

For Poles, the idea of a sovereign Poland remained unextinguished during the century and a quarter of the Partitions, despite four brutally repressed major insurrections. In exile in France, poets, playwrights, and musicians nurtured the flame of a romanticized, martyred Polonia. However, when Poland returned into being in 1918, it was almost by default; the chaos following the defeat of Germany and the Austro-Hungarian Empire created a power vacuum and shifting frontiers in central Europe, the Bolsheviks having already withdrawn from the battlefield to force their revolution on Russia.

Two men whose lives had been dedicated to the cause of an independent Poland, but with sharply different visions of its nature and how to achieve their purpose, were ready to lead their reborn country. What they represented informs much of the thinking of the people in this book. Józef Piłsudski's name has joined the pantheon of Poland's heroes. A larger-than-life personality born into the Polish gentry, he was schooled in the conspiratorial politics of socialist revolution; he had known imprisonment and banishment and, as a soldier, had led his volunteer Legionaries against the czarist army during the war. For Piłsudski and his followers, the main threat to Polish independence came from Russia, which he described as "that Asiatic monster covered with European veneer."

Anti-Semitism was as profoundly alien to Piłsudski as it was fundamental to the views of Roman Dmowski, the leader of the National Democrats – referred to in this book as the "Endeks," from their Polish acronym. His ideas owed much to the ideology of nationalism and statism developing in Germany in the late 1800s, though paradoxically, he saw Germany as the main enemy of Polish interests. Dmowski was anti-socialist, but above all he and his followers wanted a Poland free of other races, most specifically, its Jews, on whom he laid the burden of blame for most of Poland's misfortunes, past and present.

It was the charismatic figure of Piłsudski, whether in the foreground or behind the scene, who dominated the Polish political landscape in the first years of the country's independence. As Poland laid claim to its borders under the fiat of the Versailles Conference of 1919 or through force and by soundly routing a Bolshevik invasion in 1920, the role of the military, led by Piłsudski, was central. In the two decades of Poland's independence before the Second World War, and with uncertainty over the stability of its borders with Germany and the Soviet Union, the military had great status, consuming a large slice of the state budget. In terms, however, of its strategy, training, and equipment, it failed to modernize: the Polish officers loved their horses.

In the reborn state, overwhelming problems faced a confusion of successive governments and a fragmented body politic representing multiple viewpoints and interest groups with no experience of conducting parliamentary democracy. The country, wrested from its three previous rulers, had inherited different forms of administration, and its infrastructure and economy had been devastated by the 1914–18 war. There was labour unrest, hyperinflation, a lack of capital for investment, persistently high unemployment, acute poverty, both urban and rural, and hostility from the Germans, Ukrainians, and Byelorussians who found themselves within the new frontiers.

In 1926 Piłsudski – excluded from direct power in the first constitution, disgusted with parliamentary bickering, corruption, and upheavals and with the interference of politicians in the affairs of the army – led his followers in a *coup d'état*, pre-empting another coup being planned by Dmowski and the extreme right. Poland was subsequently ruled by Piłsudski and an inner group of his supporters, dominated by his old Legionaries. Although the regime was increasingly authoritarian and politically repressive, an avant-garde art, literary, and theatrical scene and a vibrant café society were able to flourish, despite times of great economic difficulty. This milieu of the arts and the intelligentsia included a growing number of assimilated Jews who wished to be part of mainstream Polish society, rather than of the Yiddish-speaking minority.

The 1930s Depression hit Poland exceptionally hard, and the acute hardship and unemployment were most extreme among its Jewish population. In the years immediately before the Second World war, between a third and a half of Poland's 3.5 million Jews, then constituting over 10 per cent of its total population, were dependent for survival upon charity, money sent mostly from the Jewish community in the United States. Conditions in the Jewish-occupied slum areas of a city such as Warsaw were considered to be among the worst in Europe. The depth of Jewish destitution owed much to the government acceding to pressure from the Endeks, the anti-Semitic right, increasingly vigorous after the rise of Hitler and his Nazis in Germany and after Marshall Piłsudski's death in 1935. The colonels and generals of the ruling Junta introduced laws excluding Jews from public office and public employment; industries previously dominated by Jews, such as the manufacture of spirits and tobacco, were nationalized, and their Jewish employees lost their jobs after Saturday – their Sabbath – was made into a compulsory work day. Jewish traders and craftsmen, already burdened by a discriminatory tax structure, were subjected to a boycott promoted by the Endeks and supported by both government and the church. The boycott appealed to the traditional antipathy of many Poles towards their non-Christian neighbours, who were often conspicuous through their lack of fluent Polish and, in the case of orthodox Jews, their appearance. The Polish government openly pressured its Jewish population to leave the country. Zionism had been a growing movement in the country since the late 1800s, but Britain was permitting only a trickle of immigrants into Palestine, and before the Depression, even the United States was no longer opening its arms to newcomers. The Jews of Poland, though they could not know this, were trapped.

If Jews were conspicuous in the ranks of the regime that imposed a communist state upon Poland in 1945, then at least some of the explanation must be found in their pre-war experience. Marxist-Leninist theory promises the goal of a classless society, which, when the "masses" are sufficiently educated and enlightened, would ensure justice for all its citizens, whatever their race. Other explanations for communism's early attraction to a relatively large number of Jews include the strands of messianism and universalist idealism in traditional religious interpretation: redemption should be found, and justice – including social justice – should apply, in this world; thus the kingdom of heaven could be created on earth. Communist theory can be interpreted as a form of secular messianism to be achieved by revolution. It was, however, a theory that had appealed to only a small fraction of Poland's Jews – an estimated 5 per cent voted for communist-front parties in the 1930s; most were strongly opposed. Nevertheless, within the small, underground pre-war communist movement, Jews were always overrepresented, particularly in its leadership.

Marxist theory was also internationalist – patriotism and nationalism were condemned as "bourgeois diversions," and it was the refusal of communists to acknowledge aspirations for Polish national independence that was to condemn its advocates in the eyes of many Poles. When the Bolshevik Red cavalry stormed westwards into Poland in 1920 to raise the flag of the international proletarian revolution, it had been welcomed by the tiny but vocal communist groups and their sympathizers. This fact was not overlooked by Roman Dmowski and his Endeks; they eagerly spread his label "*Zhydokomuna*" ("Jewish-communist conspiracy") to cover all Polish Jews. The Nazis eagerly appropriated it when they invaded Poland in 1939.

In the years following Hitler's rise to power, the rapid growth of the German war machine, in contravention of the terms of the Versailles Conference of 1919, was obviously met with inadequate response by France and Britain. But Poland, Germany's most geographically vulnerable potential victim, was least prepared for the onslaught to come. Not only had the military waited too long to advance its technology and training from the glory days of 1920, but its foreign policy adjusted too late to the Nazi threat. Politically, the Junta risked antagonizing France, the Poles' old ally, by dallying with the Nazis as well as with Mussolini, and when Germany annexed the Sudetenland from Czechoslovakia, Poland used the opportunity to grab a part of the country. It was only in early 1939, when Hitler's intention to invade was clear, that the Junta obtained from the British government an agreement to guarantee Poland's independence, a promise that could not be fulfilled. The Junta refused to negotiate with its old enemy, Russia (now operating as the Soviet Union), and on 23 August 1939 the USSR signed the Pact of Non-Aggression with Germany, providing once again for the partition of Poland. The Second World War began on 1 September with Germany's invasion of Poland; on 17 September, the Red Army moved in from the east. The alliance stood until June 1941, when Hitler was ready to invade the Soviet Union. Poland became the charnel house of Europe: by May 1945, six million Poles, of whom over three million were Jews, were to lose their lives.

Poland's post-war Jews, a tiny fraction of what the population had been, had survived the Hitler years against all odds. The Red Army had liberated them from their death sentence, and many of those who stayed in the country, driven by a desperate and doomed desire to salvage something good out of the ashes of the Holocaust, placed in communism their hopes for a just society, free of anti-Semitism.

The stories I was told by Stasia, Mietek, Peter, and their friend Alina opened the door for me into the closed, secretive milieu of the privileged class in a communist state. I learned of the bitter disillusionment of decent people who realized that they had been Stalin's pawns, and I heard the insiders' view of a revolution that devoured its own children. And reluctantly, they led me to the case of Jacek Rożański, a man whom they had all known and whose name became synonymous with the worst abuses of Stalinist rule.

This book is centred on Stasia's life; the other interviews and material were used to give depth and context to the wider story of her times. Both Stasia and Mietek would often tell me that it was impossible for someone who had not been there to write about and understand the times they had lived through. For that reason the story is told mainly through the voices of those who were there. Mietek and Peter were endlessly generous with their time and knowledge. I interviewed the family's close friend Alina in Denmark. All had led lives that could have been the focus of the book; all tried to help me to get the feel of a society and a world of which I had no personal experience. Their lives had been caught in the same mesh, and what they told me dictated the shape of the following story. Between them, they recreated a different era, they populated it, and they provided new insights into lives lived in the shadow of Hitler and Stalin.

Stasia and I often met for lunch or for coffee. Always attentive to her appearance, she dressed stylishly from a large wardrobe to which she was constantly adding. Through her seventies, she still had a good figure, and people often commented on how attractive she was. "No," she'd say, pleased, "I look awful. Such an old woman!" And she would give a sparkling little laugh. On most occasions she would sit up straight, facing the world with that look of middle-European hauteur assumed by women of her era and class. But sometimes, when she was in a certain mood, she would hunch over her food, eating fast, almost desperately.

One day she was bent in silence over a cappucino and a rich chocolate cake in a downtown Halifax café, the tables around us crowded with provincial civil servants. Behind us a couple of men were talking about a sailboat someone had just bought. She did not look at me when she suddenly spoke. "I repel and disgust myself. Why am I alive? Why didn't I go with them? Everyone must think that I did something wicked to have survived. People like myself are not normal. We must in some sense be abnormal. We are marked. Stamped. It all comes back at every opportunity and without opportunity. It comes back and back as a nightmare in our sleep, as a nightmare when we are awake. The people who survived, survived in their bodies but not in their souls. The Nazis did not succeed in killing only those who died. They also killed us, the ones who survived."

Then she straightened up, wiped the corners of her mouth with a napkin, and started to talk about her dog, a miniature poodle, which she said needed to be taken to the dog parlour for a grooming. It was a nervous little creature, demanding and receiving constant attention from her, just as she demanded, and received, constant attention from it.

One

In which Stasia tells the story of her "first life," which she wished to be prefaced by these two quotations:

In our sort of life, everybody gladly falls for illusions or seeks some belief that gives a sense of reality. If the life around you is illusory, you take refuge in illusory activity, entering illusory relations with others, embarking on illusory love affairs – you must have something to hang on to.
> Nadezhda Mandelstam, *Hope against Hope*

The natural inheritance of everyone who is capable of spiritual life is an unsubdued forest where the wolf howls and the obscene bird of night chatters.
> Henry James to his sons, Henry and William

My Inheritance

Today, as I often do, I took my little dog for a walk through the park. The streets of this quiet Canadian city are lined with trees, and there are wild, overgrown places where the trees jostle one another for light. In the park, joggers in bright colours run past, parents play with their children, and young lovers stroll by, absorbed in each other. Others, like me, walk alone with dogs chasing scents and scolding squirrels. Strangers nod and smile at me – the people here are friendly. I am always glad that others are nearby; I do not like to walk alone through the trees.

My dog runs off after a scent, along a footpath. As always, I glance over my shoulder to see if I am being followed, then I walk after him.

I am back on the path through the forest at Albinów. Moist air, the odour of rotting leaves. She is lying there, her skin white against the black stockings and garter belt, brown hair against the brown of the sodden leaves and pine needles, the eyes in the young face staring at the canopy of branches. My heart is racing. I can't move. Who is hidden there, watching me?

Then my little dog comes running back, barking at me, and I am here in the park. We walk on.

❦

If we have the keys to our abandoned homes, these are only phantom keys – memory keys, thought keys, toy keys, keys of non-fulfillment, keys that cannot open anything any more. The keys to abandoned homes get lost on the way, and there is no way of finding them again.

One of the first struggles of a small child is to stand up and then to keep itself steady on its feet. It is a struggle that accompanies you through childhood and adolescence and into adult life, only to intensify again in old age. If the ground is firm under your feet, it can be quite easy. But if the ground shifts and quakes, then you can lose your balance, even be sucked under. Events have made it difficult for me to keep my balance, and sometimes I have lost it.

Warsaw, 1919. There was nothing before.

We did not hear anyone knocking, just the shot outside. Old Zawadzka, the housekeeper, opens the door. Watching from behind her long skirts, I see the man's body on the threshold, lying there on his back, blood on his head, a revolver by his side.

He was an extremely handsome man. During the years to come, this fact about him seemed the most important to me, as my mother's beauty was the most important fact about her. (I am told that I am unusually concerned about people's looks.) He was a German army officer, a married man, a bank director in civil life in Berlin. That day old Zawadzka was expecting him to come with tickets for my parents and himself to go to the horse races. My mother had once taken me to a seaside resort, and he too was there.

Old Zawadzka closed the door quickly so that I would not see him, but it was too late. She called the police, who came and took away the body. When my mother arrived home, she was hysterical. That night, in the bed in the corner of the room, I stare, paralyzed with confusion and terror, as she throws herself on the floor, screaming and crying. My beloved, my adored father puts his arms around her, trying to calm her. Again and again she violently rejects him. "Leave me alone … go away … leave me alone …" Finally he left. They completely forgot that I was there. Neither of them was ever to know that that night accompanied me through my life, through long sleepless nights. It seems to me that, after that event when I was four, I was never again a child.

Even when she was old, my mother was beautiful, but in her youth she was the most beautiful woman I have ever seen – beautiful to the point that passersby would stop just to look at her, and people often commented on her beauty. "Goodness, Irena!" a woman once said to her when we were walking along a street. "Doesn't your little girl look like you!" "What, this ugly child?" said my mother, hurting my feelings because of course I wanted to look like her. She had grey-green eyes and luminous, porcelain-white skin untouched by cosmetics, black hair, a wonderful figure and legs. Always elegantly dressed in perfect taste, she had a great sense of style, spending much time on her appearance.

She did not like my father's surname, Grynbaum, or his business in import-export. (He had intended to be a lawyer but was expelled from law school after he took part in the 1905 student protests against czarist rule.) It was to please her that he left this work and, instead, set up movie houses, importing films, so he was dealing in a milieu that she considered to be more artistic, less petit bourgeois. And less associated with Jews. She also made him try to change his name and was furious with him when he was unable to do so.

She married my wonderful, my unique and perfect father when she was eighteen and he eight years her senior. His mother, my Babcia (Grandma) Sara, said that my mother determined to have him as a husband because all the other girls in her town were after him. I, Stanisława, their only child, was born in 1915, when she was twenty-one years old. I think my father was always very much in love with her, and it seemed to me that she neglected and betrayed him. Because I adored my father, I resented – sometimes even hated – her for the suffering she caused him.

She had little interest in me as a child; her concen was in her looks, in establishing herself in the career that she had chosen, and then in the man who was to become her new husband – Karol Adwentowicz, one of the most famous Polish actors and producers of his time. I don't know when it started, but when he visited her, he would bring me chocolates. The door to her boudoir would shut behind them, and old Zawadzka would give a knowing smile. I would never dare to enter her room unbidden; I was frightened of her temper and intimidated by her sharp tongue, her cleverness, and her beauty. My mother had artistic ambitions; she wanted to become an actress, a profession unacceptable for a married woman of a "good" bourgeois family. Probably she was suffocating in our home on Śliska Street.

For some years, until my parents' divorce, we lived in a lovely, large, old-fashioned fourth-floor flat, approached by a clanking lift operated with a brass handle by the janitor. Of course, it was not in a Jewish quarter of the city – that would have been totally unacceptable to my mother. The rooms were spacious, with high ceilings; a long balcony connected my mother's boudoir and my father's study – separate bedrooms, as was then the fashion. Although my mother's pretty boudoir was forbidden ground where no one could enter without her permission, I explored it when she was not at home, carefully replacing anything I picked up. I would often open the drawer in her escritoire, where I had discovered that she kept her photographs. Among these I would find and inspect the picture of the handsome man who had shot himself on the doorstep of our earlier home. If old Zawadzka or Babcia Sara saw me in the room, they would make a fuss and persuade me to come out, but they never betrayed me.

I slept in a small room overlooking the courtyard at the back of the flat, a room with bare walls and no toys except one doll given to me by distant relatives who had a toy factory. They had allowed me to choose her – she had fair hair in braids, pink cheeks, and blue eyes – and I kept her for years. Frequently the room was shared by Babcia Sara, whom I dearly loved. She showed me how to embroider and crochet when I was five and taught me some German, her native tongue. She encouraged me to study and made me special little sandwiches to take to the kindergarten school, where an older cousin of mine was the teacher. Babcia would not permit my mother to smack or shout at me. Old Zawadzka slept in another small room off the kitchen. I felt safe and protected when I was with them. The two old women sit with me at the kitchen table, smiling, watching me eat a dish they have prepared specially for me. "Will you stay here with me for ever and ever?" I ask them. And they nod and smile.

My mother would not socialize with most of my father's relations, except his fair-haired, Polish-looking brother, Franek, who was his business partner, and Uncle Franek's wife, Aunt Genia. She also accepted Aunt Barbara, "Basia" (everyone in Poland has several short forms of their name), Babcia Sara's cousin. Aunt Basia was a lady with impeccable manners and the style of a "grande dame." She paid great attention to her appearance – she was always elegantly dressed – and to manners, which had to be faultless. When we dined with her or she with us, we always had chicken, and each time she instructed me on how to eat it. "Pay no attention if somebody tells you that one may pick up chicken with one's fingers. That is truly dreadful! It shows that whoever behaves in such a manner has not had a proper upbringing. Like every other meat, chicken can be managed perfectly well using both your fork and your knife. Now, Stasia, watch me." And then she would demonstrate, disposing of her chicken as she preached. "Voila!" she'd say, gesturing to the clean bones on her plate.

Social life was conducted in the formal dining room, with its long table, high-backed chairs, and a buffet in which, when my mother forgot to lock it, I would find sugar-covered almonds, handmade chocolates with crystallized violets, nougat, nuts, dried fruit, chocolate wafers, candies, and cake – I have always loved sweet things. In this room my mother surrounded herself with and entertained writers, poets, painters, musicians, and actors, Warsaw's artistic, bohemian milieu, with which she wanted to be identified. Among them, I'm sure, almost no Jews. I loved one of the guests, Bruno Winawer, the novelist, poet, and short-story writer. He was tall, thin, and angular like Don Quixote, and he used to draw pictures of animals for me.

Otherwise we lived like a typical middle-class Polish family, and I was brought up as a good Polish girl. At Easter we painted eggs. Christmas was celebrated as in any Polish middle-class home with gifts waiting under the candle-lit pine tree and a big dinner with a glazed roast ham. And on All Saints' Day we visited our dead in the cemetery – the Jewish cemetery. For that is where they lay.

Our family was so well assimilated that there was never the slightest sign of the Jewish religion in my upbringing. I knew nothing about it. I never saw anything to do with Jewish holidays or traditions, nor did I ever hear anyone speaking the Yiddish language, and I never knew any of them, not even Babcia Sara, to pray, talk about religion, or go to synagogue.

My favourite place to be was in my father's room. It was furnished with modern leather armchairs, the divan on which he slept, his writing desk, bookshelves, and a windup gramophone. Sometimes my mother would put on a record of the Charleston, the shimmy, or the foxtrot and dance to it. My father, though, listened to opera. Always very slim, he had long, slender hands and dreamy grey eyes. He was a man of natural charm and gentleness, and had unusual sensitivity towards the feelings of others and an extraordinary probity of character. Everyone loved him, and he thought the best of everybody. In the afternoon, after the late Polish lunch for which he would come home, he used to put on a record and stretch out on the divan, and I would curl up at his feet. He would question me about issues arising from the books he had given me to read – never children's stories but authors like Tolstoy and Victor Hugo. Questions such as "Was Jean Valjean wrong to steal food to feed his starving children? What do you think?" Then it was my duty to read to him until he dozed off; I would cover him with a blanket and tiptoe out, closing the door without a sound.

One afternoon Uncle Franek arrived unexpectedly. "Shhh," I whispered. "Papa's sleeping." But he ignored me and went in. He found my father sitting at his desk with a revolver in his hand. They talked for a long time, and soon after that I was sent away to boarding school.

❦

The Sara Höniger school was in Germany, in Lower Silesia, and its rules were based on Prussian standards of discipline: up at 6:30, run in single file across the grounds, gymnastics, cold showers, and then breakfast, though I had little appetite. Everything was so different. I was not fluent in the language, I hated the regimentation, and I felt abandoned and lonely away from the old flat, from my father, from Babcia Sara, from old Zawadzka and the friends from my kindergarten. The children were from all around the world and mostly, like me, from well-to-do but broken families. I used to dream about some tragic end for myself. Maybe, I thought, when I die, they will pay some attention to me.

After a few months my father came to visit me, bringing me a pineapple, a very rare and expensive treat at that time. I begged him to take me away, and he promised he would do so as soon as he could. "Be patient, my darling," he urged me, but patience does not come easily to an eight-year-old child. Then the year ended, and at last he came to take me back with him. But when we returned to Warsaw, my mother had gone, old Zawadzka had gone, Babcia Sara was living with her daughter, my Aunt Ola, and our home on Śliska Street had gone, along with everything that had been in it. My father had given my mother whatever she wanted – everything except me. I can see now that a child would have been a nuisance for her. She was young and beautiful and at the beginning of her career as an actress, and she had a new man. But it upset me then, and for a long time after, that she had let go of me so easily.

After my father brought me back to Warsaw, the two of us lived in rented rooms and ate in restaurants – a strange life for a child, but we were together. He must have worried that I was not getting a normal family life, and he often had to go away because of his movie-house business, so sometimes I stayed with his sister, my darling Aunt Ola. Old-fashioned, plain, and tiny, she looked funny beside her husband, a big, rough-mannered bear of a man, whom I liked because he was so straight-spoken. Although he owned a small factory, he was a communist, which meant that he was in danger from the police. This odd-looking couple had two daughters, one a year older than me, the other, Irka, a beautiful auburn-haired girl who was born deaf and was dependent upon Aunt Ola for communication with the world. Aunt Ola, with the help of speech therapists, had taught her to speak, but only those close to Irka, like me, could understand her. I loved them all. Because of my uncle's political activities and his giving money to "the cause," and also, I suspect, because he ran around with other women, it was a turbulent household with money difficulties.

At one point my father found a couple who were looking for a suitable companion for their daughter, a girl the same age as me. I lived with them for a while, my father paying for my upkeep. But I did not like the girl, who was stupid and only interested in religion, and the family, which was Catholic, was determined that I go to church with them, which I did not want to do. So I went back to my father again and the rented rooms.

My best friend, Lena,[*] and I both went to the same school. Her family, who lived in a shabby street in the outskirts of Warsaw opposite the Jewish cemetery, were working-class. Her father was a foreman in a fish cannery, and they deprived themselves to give their children a good education. Lena was embarrassed by their poverty and their speaking Yiddish. She liked to spend as much time as possible with me wherever I was living, to study and to play. She was very gifted, particularly at drawing and mathematics. My dear father, who was so thoughtful, always brought back presents for both of us from his business trips, and when we were older, he once brought each of us a pair of silk stockings, which delighted us because we were the first girls at our school to have them. At the weekends and on school holidays, we would spend afternoons at his movie houses with free tickets, watching our favourite film stars time and again – Charles Boyer, Frederick March, Maurice Chevalier, Greta Garbo, Danielle Darieux. There was Rudolf Valentino in the *Sheik of Araby*, Marlene Dietrich in *The Blue Angel* – I adored romantic melodramas.

---

[*] Her name has been changed from her real name, Irena, to avoid confusion with Stasia's mother.

Stasia, age eight, in Dresden, Germany, with "Grandfather" David Schwartz; her mother's half-sister, Theja, is in the centre

I was on my way home from school when the gunfire started. It was the military coup of 1926, when Marshall Piłsudski, who had led Poland to independence and whom we all called "Dziadek" (grandfather), again took over the government. On the streets people were running in all directions. I didn't feel frightened – it was like being on a giant movie set – and I joined a group rushing towards the Vistula and then went with them in a ferry boat to the other side of the river, to Praga, the suburb where Aunt Ola lived. I ran to her home, and when I got there, she telephoned my father, who had been frantic with worry at my disappearance. After he came to fetch me, he kept questioning me, asking why I had not gone home. But I couldn't answer him. I think I had liked the excitement, the adventure.

In the spring of the year that I was fourteen, I went on my own to Germany to visit my other grandmother, Franciszka Schwartz. She lived in Dresden with her second husband, David, whom I called

"Grandfather," although he was not, and my mother's half-sister Theja. A handsome, rather aloof woman with cold blue eyes, my grandmother had remarried after the death of her first husband in Poland. She had taken only her son, my Uncle Wicek, with her to Germany, leaving my mother to be brought up by her grandmother. Grandfather Schwartz had made a fortune in the tobacco industry, which he later lost through bad investments. At that time they lived in a beautiful, elegantly furnished twelve room house in which everyone had their own large bedroom, most, like Aunt Theja's, with their own bathroom. In my grandparents' bathroom was the wonder of a sunken marble bathtub, along with every imaginable luxury. Their Polish housekeeper reigned in the huge kitchen, and outside there was a lovely large garden in which Grandfather Schwartz had planted fruit trees, now all in blossom, and where I played with Uncle Wicek's young son, Bob. It was Passover when I was visiting, and Grandfather took me with him to synagogue, the first of the few times in my life I have been inside one.

After the divorce, my mother at first lived in the city of Łódź, finding work in minor roles in the theatre. I once visited her there but did not enjoy myself. She was too busy to have time for me, and I saw her more at the theatre than at her flat. Karol Adwentowicz, for whom and for a different life she had left my father, was twenty-two years older than my mother. A tall, handsome, distinguished man, he was very self-contained, and unlike my father, he was the dominant figure in a relationship in which my mother deferred to him. Already twice married, Karol had left his second wife for her, and he and my mother were living together before his divorce came through. Sometimes they appeared together in the same productions, in which, after a while, my mother took leading roles. She had got what she wanted. In my opinion, she was a good actress but not an outstanding one, although she was aided in her career by her outstanding beauty. Karol, however, was a truly great actor, though for years I was resentful of him.

To marry Karol, my mother had converted to Catholicism. I know that she was not a believer, but this gesture was part of her achieving her desire to lose her Jewish identity, an identity incompatible with her wish to be thought of as Polish. She changed her name by deed poll, taking her mother's maiden name, Stange, which didn't sound Jewish. For the stage, she took the name

Stasia's mother, Irena Grywińska, in 1939

Grywińska, and with marriage, she also had Karol's name, Adwentowicz. So she was covering her tracks.

She pressured me to convert to Catholicism so that I would become more Polish, or perhaps so that I not be a source of potential embarrassment for her, and she was furious at my refusal to do so. But I followed the example of my father, whose attitude, although he was not religious, was "I was born a Jew, and I shall die a Jew." (And indeed, a special Jewish death was reserved for him.) "That curly Jewish hair of yours," my mother would say to me. "You ought to do something about it." Or "How did I come to have a daughter with such a Jewish nose!" She created in me a distaste for anything Jewish, an ambivalence about myself – who I am, where I belong – which I think I have never resolved. In truth, many of us in one way or another had that ambivalence. Many Polish Jews would have understood, even if they did not share it. Even Jacek – Jacek Rożański – would have understood.

I was thinking of him last night. Thinking of that time after the war when I went to see him, overcoming my fear. The gates of the

Security building closing behind me and the guard taking my identification papers and party card, examining them slowly, looking carefully at my face and at my photographs on the documents. He speaks into a telephone and then tells me to go through an entrance. I ring a bell. Another guard opens the door. We climb stairs, walked down corridors. He opens a door into a large room with a big window, blank walls, a round table in the centre, nothing on it. Behind a large desk sits Jacek, as always very good-looking and charming. He greets me, offers me a chair opposite him, his manner calm and informal. "So, Stasia, why do you want to see me?" "It's about the case of Jerzy Sawa." Jacek's eyes black and penetrating. "And why should this case concern you? Take your time," he says. "Tell me everything."

Jerzy Sawa. He was the husband of Mira Sawa, my classroom and French teacher at school. When I told Mira that my parents were divorced and that I was living with my father, she and Jerzy, themselves childless, virtually adopted me. Her mother was French, and Mira was an excellent teacher, very demanding. I did not fear her, but many of the girls did, and since I had become special to her, some of the fear they felt for her, in some strange way, they also felt for me.

The school was private and secular, belonging to the teachers' union. After I left the boarding school in Germany, it was the only one I attended until I went to university. We were educated in the Polish culture, Poland's history and literature, in the works of its great romantic and patriotic novelists and poets – Słowacki, Mickiewicz, Krasinski, Wyspiański, Sienkiewicz, Orzeszkowa, Reymont, Żeromski – all of whom I felt were mine. We were imbued with pride in Poland's tragic yet heroic past. We knew that the spirit of Poland had never died during the years of struggle and martyrdom against Prussia, Austria-Hungary, and Russia, during the more than one hundred years after they had divided up our beloved country among themselves and inflicted despotic rule on it. Naturally, we were brought up to be intensely patriotic: when "Dziadek" (Marshall Piłsudski) died in 1935, we all wept. Why? Probably because we saw him as the personification of the all-powerful, loving father figure who could protect us from danger. With him gone, suddenly we felt left by ourselves in the wilderness, unprotected, vulnerable, orphaned. Anyway, this was the feeling inspired by our school, and it was general in the country, particularly among Jews because he would not permit official anti-Semitism. But we were all moved by his death to a greater or lesser degree, and being very emotional, I was especially affected by the feeling.

Both Mira and Jerzy were deeply patriotic, and their attitudes and values had a strong influence on me. Jerzy was a notary and lawyer, a tall, slim, fastidious man with an analytical mind, a great sense of humour, and a stock of the latest political jokes. Mira was a quick-moving, energetic woman, practical, well organized, and erudite. Both were religious Catholics, not so much in formal observance as in their deep Christian beliefs. On their summer vacations, they sometimes took me with them, treating me as their own daughter. I went to their flat for Christmas, Easter, all the big Polish holidays. It was the same even when I grew up: a week would not pass without my seeing or telephoning them. Jerzy and Mira never tried to convert me, although, like my father, they tried to instill ethical values in me. My mother, however, insisted that I take Christian religion classes at school, so I became familiar with the catechism and prayers. What she could not foresee was that, if nothing else, this knowledge was to save my life when Stefa Kunowska wanted to finish it.

Stefa was the class below mine, a blue-eyed girl with straight, blonde hair and a rather angelic expression. She knew me, as did everyone in the school, because I was an outstanding pupil and at recreation time my Polish and French essays were often read to the entire school. Many of the girls were my friends, some even competing for my friendship. But because of my academic success and because most of the teachers liked me, others hated me. I had nothing to do with Stefa, but I knew her.

It was 1943. I know it is her and she knows it is me when our eyes meet as I am crossing the courtyard at the back of the building where I am living. Stefa gives no sign of recognition, but I know she has placed me. I go in the entrance, run up the staircase, and then look down from a window into the courtyard. She is knocking at the concierge's door. He comes out. Stefa's white skin is flushed. She is talking vehemently to him, gesticulating, pointing to where I had gone in, making her point clear, wanting him to understand what she is after …

Girl in a Red Beret

Bolek, swimming out to sea. He swims and swims, farther and farther away, until I can no longer see him. I fear that he has gone too far, that the endless waters will claim him, that he will never return ...

Bolek and I had rented a cabin by the sea at Jastarnia on the Baltic. He was so young and strong, so full of energy and of ideas, so interested in everything that life had to offer, so intense, so untiring. He was too fast for me. I lagged behind, never able to keep up with him.

Bolek used to say that he would always remember me as the girl in a red beret walking down Marszałkowska Street, carrying a bunch of flowers. I was nineteen and with Gregory, a friend of mine – actually, a boy I'd had a crush on at the boarding school when I was nine years old and whom I had run into again years later in Warsaw. This time he was the one who was infatuated. I noticed a good-looking young man approaching us from the opposite direction. He stopped in front of us. "Hello, Gregory," he said. Then "So what about introducing me to your friend?" "No," said Gregory bluntly. "All right," said the young man. "I'll introduce myself." There was nothing poor Gregory could do about it, and he joined Gregory and me, walking back the way he had come. He said he was Bolesław – "Bolek" – Ałapin, a medical student, and we got talking about this because I was about to enter medical school and he was already in his third year. He asked for my address, and after a few days he had managed to transform our acquaintance into an "I am here to stay" relationship. Within a few weeks we knew each other well. I could talk about everything to him, and he understood everything. Bolek was in love with me. I was not in love with him, but after a few months he had become indispensable to me.

I hadn't wanted to study medicine but the arts, the subjects in which I had done best at school, at which I had a natural aptitude, and which I loved. My mother also wanted this; she didn't want her daughter in a profession that was not only bourgeois but identified with Jews. I had thought of becoming an actress, and Mira encouraged me in this idea, but my mother was utterly opposed. She didn't want me to be an actress like herself. As Irena Grywińska, she was already well known in Poland, playing romantic roles such as Anna

Bolek Ałapin in 1937

Karenina, and she didn't want it known in theatrical circles that she was old enough to have a grown-up daughter. If not an actress, then I wanted to be a journalist or a poet, but my father, who was determined that I should be able to support myself, pressured me to become a physician. Writers, he said, lived from hand to mouth, and he saw medicine as a way of ensuring that I could be independent from any man, a condition he thought necessary for women because "All men are pigs." "How can you say that, Papa? You aren't a pig!" "Me too." As I always wanted to please him, I reluctantly agreed. But by now it was extremely difficult for a Jew to enter medical school.

When "Grandfather" Piłsudski died, it was the end of any protection Jews had against anti-Semitism. The atmosphere and the situation were not too different now from what was going on in Nazi Germany; there were posters up telling people not to buy from Jewish-owned shops, and frequently one heard of pogroms. With the exception of the communists and socialists, all political parties opposed Jews having equal rights under the law, and under the *nu-*

merus clausus rule, Jewish students were permitted to take only 10 per cent of places in medical schools. Although my examination marks were very good, it was only through my father's influence with one of the ruling colonels – the governing regime – whose brother was under some obligation to him, that I was able to get a place.

Before I went to medical school, I had been insulated from anti-Semitism. It had not confronted me personally. I thought of myself as a Pole, not as a Jew, and I certainly didn't identify myself with those Yiddish-speaking people who behaved differently from us, sometimes dressed in their long traditional garb, and lived in self-imposed Jewish districts. If I thought of it at all. We were assimilated; we were Poles. And besides, I had my studies and my first love affair.

He was a handsome young cadet at the army engineering school. Of course, not Jewish – a Jew could not be an officer.* I was nearly seventeen, and it was carnival time, the weeks from New Year's Eve until Ash Wednesday when it seemed that all the upper- and middle-class young people in Warsaw went to a constant stream of parties and balls. I was a good-looking girl and had already begun to find that I could attract any boy I wanted. That night I was wearing a long, décolleté black silk dress, a gift from Grandfather Schwartz, who had let me choose it myself when I was on a visit to Dresden. Lena, my old school friend, and I had gone out with a couple of boys we knew, who had managed to get invitations to the military engineers' student ball. I met Jan there. We danced all night, fell in love, and when he was taking me home in a fiacre, I had my first kiss. He was my boyfriend until he had finished studying at the engineering school, when the army posted him away from Warsaw. He wrote to me for a while. Then he stopped and did not reply to my letters. Without telling anyone except my friend Lena, I decided to go to see him. I arrived without warning, and "it" happened there for the first time. He wanted me to stay, but how could I? I had to go back and finish my school. So I took the train home to Warsaw. He still sent no letters, but for a long time I continued to write to him and still thought of myself as being in love with him and promised to him.

---

* This statement is incorrect. It was difficult but not impossible.

I told Bolek early on about Jan, that I was still in love with him and that, although by then he had not written to me for months, I considered myself engaged to him, and for this reason could not be his, Bolek's, sweetheart.

"But he'll never marry you because army officers aren't allowed to marry Jewish women."

"He doesn't know I'm Jewish."

"You didn't tell him? That's worse."

Bolek would listen patiently, almost stoically, while I poured my heart out to him about Jan, and he would dry my tears when I cried. The fact that he was the only one to whom I could talk freely brought us even closer.

Bolek was also from a Jewish "non-Jewish," assimilated background, and he too was interested in literature, the theatre, art, ideas, ideals – socialist ideals – everything I was interested in. We would meet nearly every evening, spend hours together, go to one of Warsaw's many coffee houses, where there would be a pianist playing modern sentimental songs, a romantic atmosphere, candlelight, other young couples holding hands. We would talk and talk and never have the feeling that it was all we had to say to each other. With Bolek there was never such a thing as being bored, and that was what was so good about it. We spent so much time talking to each other late into the night that inevitably we became lovers. It was not difficult because, since I was fifteen, my father had rented separate rooms for me, at first in someone else's flat and later on my own.

It was uncommon for someone from my kind of background to have a premarital relationship, but we considered ourselves free of petit bourgeois values, as leftist and progressive. I think now that the ease with which I was able, both then and later, to ignore social conventions may not have been simply a matter of intellectual principle but something in my psyche, a protest, perhaps, against my childhood experiences, a subconscious imitation of my mother's behaviour. Anyway, it was that summer that, unknown to our families, we went on our vacations together, renting the cabin on the beach at Jastarnia.

After we were back in Warsaw, Jan arrived at my door without warning. I told Bolek that I could not see him because of this. Janek and I spent the day together, and then he went away again. Bolek was dreadfully upset. "If you don't marry me, I'll kill myself," he told me again and again, threatening to throw himself out of a window. Every time he said that, I was overwhelmed by another image, of the shot outside the door, of my mother's lover lying there with blood on his head, the revolver by his side, my mother crying and screaming.

I was so young that I believed him, and he was so persistent that finally I agreed. My father had to give his consent because I was under twenty-one, and when I told him that we wanted to marry, he had no objections. "I have nothing against you marrying this boy. I think you suit each other well, and he comes from a very good family." By "good," he meant solidly bourgeois with no scandals attached to its reputation. Bolek's father was a dermatologist, his older brother a surgeon, and his uncles medical specialists. We, however, insisted that none of his family be told. We did not want a big traditional wedding; as leftists, we opposed spending money on such things. My mother did not approve of the marriage, and refused to attend. She said that I was too young, but I think she did not want me to marry a Jew or anyone in a bourgeois milieu. Although Bolek objected strongly on principle, we had to be married by a rabbi because the law required a religious as well as a civil wedding. After the ceremony my father took us to a restaurant with Uncle Franek and his wife, Aunt Genia. Then we went to tell Bolek's mother. She knew me and liked me, so after getting over her surprise, she felt pleased and got out some champagne. And that was that. It was April 1935.

Bolek's family were rather rich because his father was an eminent physician, but he wouldn't accept any money they offered us. As well as studying, he worked as a medical orderly, which students often did then, and he also coached me through the first two years of medical school. He was very good at maths, physics, and chemistry, subjects in which I was weak. I often wanted to abandon medicine, but Bolek made me stick at it. In fact, he was very bossy – everything had to be done as he wanted, his way, according to his wishes. When my father bought me a lovely fur coat for the winter, Bolek would not permit me to wear it. "My wife does not need a fur coat," he pontificated. "It is petit bourgeois, it goes against all my

Stasia in 1936 or 1937

principles, and I won't have it." He was immoveable, and the coat languished there in the closet unworn. I think that it was not just principle with the coat but that he was also jealous of my adoration of my father and because I did look gorgeous in it.

I hated dissecting cadavers in the anatomy classes. Other students did not seem to mind it; some even ate their sandwiches in the room. But it made me feel sick. That revolting, awful smell of formaldehyde – it invaded my mouth and throat, turning my stomach, making me choke. I could not get used to it and wanted to leave the faculty. But my father was so upset when I mentioned the idea, that using all my willpower, I kept at it. Years later I would remember that smell when I was again engulfed by it.

We lived in rented rooms in a fashionable area near Bolek's parents. You could probably call us "salon socialists" or "salon communists" because, in practice, we did nothing political except talk, although at one point Bolek stored communist leaflets at his parents' home, where he knew the police would never think of searching, and later we used to keep them at our own apartment. There were people we knew who were more active, four of my cousins – it was one of them who made Aunt Ola cross because she was always getting money for "the cause" from Aunt Ola's husband. And there were others, such as Jacek Rożański – that was not his name then.

I first met Jacek at the home of Ida, my best friend at the university. She and I often studied together at her place or mine. Apart from Lena, who had been my closest friend when I was at school, Ida was the only person I knew who lived in the Jewish area of the city. Her mother, a widow, made luxury bedspreads for the top stores in the city. They were a lovely, warm family, and I always felt comfortable with them. Ida's older sister, Anka, was finishing law school. Jacek, Anka's boyfriend, also a law student, was often at their home. Anka, so I was told, was a member of the Communist Party, and it was understood that Jacek, even then, was seriously involved with this clandestine organization, a fact that somehow gave him an air of romantic mystery. He was very good-looking – tall with black hair and dark velvety eyes that looked at one as though they could see everything going on in one's mind, though the truth was that he did not give a damn about anyone, certainly not about us "kids." Nevertheless, when we met again years later, when so much had happened and so much had changed, he recognized me immediately.

Bolek and I believed in the ideals of liberty, equality, justice, the international brotherhood of man. The awful poverty in Poland, the unemployment, ignorance, and squalor, the medieval condition of the peasants, the extreme nationalism, the chauvinism, and the anti-Semitism – all were contrary to our socialist theories and under socialism would clearly be resolved. We were not Zionists; we were Polish patriots – this despite the government encouraging Jews to leave the country. It never occurred to us to want to go to Palestine, although many of the unassimilated Jewish students were involved with the Zionist movement. We did not mix with them. In fact, most of our friends were Jewish, but they were like ourselves and shared our viewpoint. It was not until then, at university, that I realized that we so-called assimilated Jews were left in the cold, in a no-man's land, neither here nor there – Jews living like Poles, rejecting a Jewish life, but in turn rejected by the Poles.

There were always a few Poles who stood – literally – with us, but very few. In 1937 I was in my fourth year at Warsaw University when "ghetto benches" were introduced under pressure from the rightist, pro-fascist students. They were supporters of the violent ultra-nationalist party known as the Endeks. By then there was not even a 10 per cent quota for Jews, and it was nearly impossible to get into medical school. At lectures we were to sit on the left, on the so-called ghetto benches, and "Aryan" Poles on the right. Enforcing their rule with knuckle-dusters, clubs, razors, fists, and knives, the Endek students boycotted all liberal and Jewish professors. I was in a delegation that went to professors to ask that they refuse to lecture to divided classes, but none of them supported us. Two professors who objected to the division had already stopped lecturing.

Officially, the students were divided into two organizations: the Brotherhood, exclusively for the "Aryan" students, and another for the Jewish students. But Bolek and I would not join the Jewish one because, apart from anything else, it had Zionist overtones, and any form of nationalism was distasteful to us. My student identity card was given a stamp reading, "Sit on the left side," which, according to the university authorities, was supposed to reflect membership in the Jewish organization. So I went to the dean to complain that my stamp was contrary to the rules. He hemmed and hawed, obviously embarrassed – he himself was probably not a bigot but was acting under pressure – and finally he ordered his secretary to erase the stamp on my card. There was some moral satisfaction in exposing their hypocrisy but nothing more.

A group of us Jewish students would not bend. We stood during the lectures, and of the other a hundred and eighty or so non-Jewish students, there were four who, on principle, stood there with us. Most of the rest were not Endeks; they were simply indifferent. And this, both then and later, was the situation with the Polish population in general: most were indifferent to Jews, some were actively hostile, and a few held to their moral convictions. The four who stood with us were leftists, and they were among our friends.

Because of the violence, Bolek used to escort me to my classes in the morning. One day the Endeks had put up a poster at the entry to the anatomy lecture room reading, "Jews sit on the left side." Bolek tore it off, and I went in, but soon after, I could hear a commotion outside. Someone called me out, and there was Bolek, his face covered with blood, but still on his feet. Some Endeks had put up another poster, and he had torn it down again. Then a gang of these heroes attacked him. They had broken his nose – he managed to break one of theirs too – and by the time I got him to hospital, he was faint from the loss of blood. Being Bolek, he swore he would do it again if need be.*

Bolek never gave up. In February 1939 we were with a group of friends at the Adria nightclub for the medical faculty's Carnival Ball. There was a good band, and we were dancing and enjoying ourselves when suddenly there was an announcement – everyone must leave that room because "an important Italian guest and his party are visiting the club." We knew that Count Ciano, Mussolini's son-in-law, the Italian foreign minister, was on an official visit to Poland; the government had already welcomed top German Nazis, and some of the right-wing press had been praising the fascist system, calling for closer ties with Italy. As we were going into another room, Bolek recognized Ciano coming in and shouted, "The fascist Italians are occupying this room like they've occupied Abyssinia!" We managed to get him out of there and into another room, but then I realized I had left my purse at the bar. Bolek insisted on going back to get it, but he wasn't allowed in. Over the uproar I heard him shouting, "These fascists have stolen my wife's purse – just like they stole Abyssinia!" Before I could get over to quieten him, some Polish plainclothes police grabbed and arrested him. When they were taking him away, I started to make a fuss, so they arrested me too. We were both taken to a police station, though they let me go when I told them I had to go home to nurse my baby – Peter had been born three months before – but Bolek was charged with communist conspiracy and put in prison.

Our worry was that he would be sent to Bereza Kartuska, the notorious prison for political prisoners. Since Piłsudski's time it was mostly for leftists, both communists and socialists. But Bolek's mother was able to hire a very expensive lawyer, well connected with the government – he charged 5,000 zlotys at a time when a kilo of sugar cost 1 zloty. Arguing that Bolek's outburst was no more than a drunken student's mindless eruption of high spirits, he got the charge altered to one of disturbing public order, an administrative, not a political, offence. Bolek was in prison for only a

---

* In an article written after the war, Bolek identified the man whose nose he had broken as Bolesław Piasecki, the leader of the Falangists, a fascist group. Piasecki re-emerged after the war as a leading communist propogandist.

month, and when we all went to bring him home in a *dorozka*, a horse-drawn carriage, he was laughing, telling us that it had been a good extension of his education because he'd learned a lot of useful things, such as how to open any lock without a key.

Being young, we laughed a lot of things away, but the atmosphere in the medical school was not pleasant. There was a constant sense of social alienation, and scarcely anyone spoke to us. In truth, our only friends were Jewish students of like minds and the tiny minority of leftist Polish students.

There was an embarrassing situation when the school authorities refused to permit Jewish students into the dissection rooms unless Jewish cadavers were made available, but the city's Jewish religious governing body refused, on theological grounds, to supply corpses. Several of us picketed their offices, demanding corpses, and finally they permitted the bodies of newborns to be used. It was all so embarrassing.

Then there was the humiliating incident at a student ball. I was an attractive girl, and one particular fellow, a good-looking and really nice young man, kept dancing with me. In the middle of a fox-trot or quickstep, I became aware of a small group of people making their way towards us through the other couples on the dance floor. I didn't take much notice of them until their leader, a woman medical student, came up to my partner and tapped him on the shoulder. A narrow, prim, expressionless face, sharp nose, thin lips. On her blouse, the green Endek ribbon. "You realize that you're dancing with a Jewish woman?" He didn't reply. Her eyes small, cold. "If you don't stop, you'll have to face the consequences, and they could be unpleasant!" He was perplexed and obviously embarrassed, but I could see that he was frightened. He apologized to me, but he obeyed her. I was hurt, painfully humiliated.

We ourselves were to blame, Bolek and I. None of the other Jewish students had gone to the ball, but we did not want to give in to the pressure of anti-Semitism – it was our private struggle against it. We were young, idealistic, obstinate, and so sure of ourselves. We thought we could push through the wall of prejudice, false accusations, and hatred. But it was too thick, too strong to be penetrated. It was impossible to change anything.

I had grown up seeing myself as totally assimilated, identifying myself only as a Pole, knowing and caring nothing about Judaism, seeing nothing Jewish in the behaviour of my family. Yet I was now being treated and judged as a Jew and discriminated against as a Jew. How was I to remain a patriot of a country where the majority of the citizens simply did not want us? How were we supposed to behave? Ineluctably and with difficulty, we were having to face the reality of alienation within our own and, up to now, beloved country. Finally, all that was left was shame and humiliation.

⚜

I went on standing at the lectures right through my pregnancy until Piotr – my son, Peter – was born in November 1938. Up to then my marriage to Bolek had not been going well. It was my own fault, but I hadn't really wanted to marry him. I was not in love with him; I felt no passion for him, though in every other way he was the perfect husband for me. We were never bored with each other; we had similar opinions, the same interests; and we spoke a common language. But I wasn't ready yet for a compromise. I was still subconsciously looking, still unsettled. I was not a good wife. When Jan, my first love, turned up in Warsaw for a day, I went out with him. And there was a tall, blonde, and very handsome student from the military medical school who started to accompany me when Bolek wasn't around. Then there was the incident at a party we gave in the first little apartment we rented. A Polish friend (later murdered in a Nazi camp) brought a friend who was studying to be a diplomat – tall, very handsome, with beautiful dark eyes. We both got a bit drunk and just disappeared from the party and went for a walk. Nothing serious, but so humiliating for Bolek – though I didn't see it like that then. And each time he forgave me.

It must have been the summer of 1937, after his finals, that Bolek told me he was going on an organized trip to Bulgaria. I couldn't go because I was in hospital recovering from the removal of my tonsils. I was angry with him because not long before that I'd had an abortion – Bolek didn't want children; he said it was egotistic. When I recovered, I didn't see why I should stay alone in our little apartment, so I went to a seaside resort near to where I knew Jan was posted. I wrote to him, and it started again. He was so tall and handsome in his army uniform, and on the beach we were the best-looking couple. Then Bolek arrived back from his trip when I was out all night. I told him about Jan and said that I wouldn't go back to him, that it was Jan I wanted. When I returned to Warsaw, I rented a room for myself, and Jan, who had now introduced me to his family as his fiancée, continued to visit me for a while until, without any warning, he stopped coming. He sent a letter saying we would have to break off the relationship. I think he'd found out that I was Jewish, though I'd also heard that Polish officers were not allowed to marry divorced women. Who can know?

Probably I was bad, but I was upset and called Bolek. We began to meet each other again. He wanted me back, and I agreed to try again. As a reconciliation celebration, we went on a journey abroad together for several weeks, to Yugoslavia, Berlin, and Paris, and it was then that my Peter was conceived. Bolek still refused to have children, but I longed for a baby, so I pleaded with my gynecologist, and he agreed to tell Bolek that I could not have any more abortions. I adored Peter from the moment he was born.

We moved into an apartment bought for us by my father and Bolek's mother (his father had died by then) in an elegant old house in the very centre of the city, at Marszałkowska 108. It had three rooms, a kitchen, and bathroom. As in my childhood home, we didn't have a common bedroom – this too we considered petit bourgeois – and in the same way, our rooms had a common door. I furnished Bolek's room like my mother had furnished my father's, and mine like hers, only realizing the similarity after I had done so. When Peter was born, his crib was in my room, where I could hear him, attend to him, and talk to him. I rarely "visited" Bolek, and this made him cross with me. He would complain that he had no wife, but really I just couldn't cope with his passionate intensity and his need to be constantly near me. I needed room to breathe and move. Perhaps it was the shadow of Jan that made me keep my emotional distance, but that was fading, and surely all that was required was time and my maturity. Or so I now believe.

Bolek and I. In those last months before the war, we were awash in a sea of talk, of study, of work, of new parenthood, of our emotions, of energy and youth, of entering the world of adulthood, of talk and more talk. We were not aware, or perhaps we did not want to be aware, that the time was one minute to midnight.

On a warm evening late that summer, we were in a new nightclub in the centre of the fashionable district. We had gone there at about

10:30 to meet up with Lena, my old friend. She was now an architecture student and was with her latest boyfriend, a Yugoslav, whom she was madly in love with. Bolek was making jokes about the nightclub's name, Pod Kogutem (Under the Rooster), because H., our well-known professor of neurology, lived in the apartment above the club and had a reputation as a womanizer. Bolek did not know that for the last year Professor H., twenty-two years my senior, had been courting me, sending me roses, taking me out to dinner in private rooms at the best restaurants when Bolek was on night duty. I was flattered and liked the attention of a sophisticated, adoring, eminent older man. But it was not serious, so why should Bolek have known.

The nightclub was charming – art deco style, intimate atmosphere, candle-lit tables with flowers. Lena's new love had eyes only for her; she was radiant and relaxed. A gypsy girl came round with roses, and both the men bought us one. The dinner was delicious, and we drank champagne, joked, made funny toasts, laughed, and talked about everything – everything but war.

We were dancing and singing along with the band, Bolek holding me very close, when suddenly the music stopped. Everyone on the floor stood still. A man had come up to the microphone: "The mobilization order has just been given. From now on, no more alcoholic drinks will be sold."

Of course, it had been predicted, but for us it came as a shock. We had simply not been expecting it. Nor had we any idea that it was the end – the end of our way of life, of our naive insouciance, of the very essence of our youth. The end of our marriage, which we had so recently begun to put on a firm foundation, of moments such as the one we had been enjoying, of everything we knew of the world.

All were gone forever.

Crossing the River

One of the recurrent scenes that play before my eyes. Bolek and I are standing by the window in the courthouse, looking down at the street below. The building has entrances on either side; one door leads back into the ghetto, the other to the Aryan side. The women who clean the courthouse are all from the Aryan side, and we have bribed one of them to take Peter out. At the door to the Aryan side stands a German soldier with a rifle in his hands. When she leaves, will he remember that when she went in, she had no child? She comes out onto the street; beside her, his little hand in hers, is our son. They walk down the road and out of sight. Then Bolek and I go down the stairs and out into the ghetto. And we walk away, each in a different direction ...

※

I was in a train with Peter when I first saw the bombers. After the German invasion, not wanting us to be separated, I'd immediately gone to fetch him back from the rented cottage in the country where Bolek's mother was looking after him, away from the heat of the city. The little steam train had been chugging along, stopping at every small station, when we heard the airplanes coming. It screeched to a halt, and a guard ran along outside the carriages shouting at us to get off and lie on the ground. I lay with my body over Peter's under the trees by the track while a string of bombs fell, exploding too far away to hurt any of us.

Warsaw seemed to be defenceless. A few days after we got back, there was an announcement on the radio that the government of Poland had gone into exile and that all men of military age should leave the capital and go towards the east, where a new defence line would be established. It was then that Bolek left us. On the day he went, Peter, who was ten months old, had found that he could stand up. He was on his feet, clutching the side of his cot, delighted at his achievement and laughing at Bolek, who turned his head and looked at his son as he went out of the door. As he closed the door behind him, we did not know that our marriage had ended.

For days, a rain of bombs and mortar shells fell on Warsaw. I was holding Peter in my arms when one of the windows broke, showering glass onto us, but we were not injured. There was no water, no gas, no electricity, no food. For a while I stayed with Bolek's mother and his uncle Herman Ałapin's family, going every day to the university's maternity hospital. The universities were not functioning, and I had yet to complete all my final medical examinations, but I was allowed to work unpaid at the hospital. One morning I was walking to the hospital when the airplanes roared overhead. A bomb fell in the road ahead of me, making a crater, gushing flames. I waited in a doorway for a few minutes and then went around it. Another bomb fell not far behind me, yet although thousands were killed or injured, I wasn't hurt on that occasion or in any of the constant bombardments that we endured in the weeks before Poland's final capitulation. I am not a brave person, and now I cannot understand why I didn't panic, why I went out to the hospital every day.

At the hospital there was no water because the bombs had damaged the water mains, so we couldn't wash our hands properly – this was before disposable gloves came into use – and there were no facilities for sterilizing needles and instruments. All we had was a small amount of alcohol, but this ran out. We kept expecting infections, but amazingly, nothing happened – women gave birth and we had no complications. The professor had given me and another Jewish woman doctor permission to work there, but his immediate subordinates, two doctors married to each other, were virulent anti-Semites and would not teach us anything, though some of the other physicians went on instructing us.

Finally the bombing stopped. Poland was defeated. It had all happened so quickly, and now men in Nazi uniforms were occupying the city. Meanwhile, within a couple of weeks of the German invasion, the Soviet army had invaded Poland from the east. The country, reunited and independent only since 1919, was divided and occupied yet again. The west of Poland was absorbed into the Reich, the German state; the Nazis also ruled an area that had Warsaw at its centre under the name of the "General Government," and the east of the country was occupied by the Soviets.

My father was trapped in the city of Łódź, now part of the Reich. He had remarried not long after my marriage and was living there with his wife, Lilka, a nice woman, also divorced, and her thirteen-year-old son, Janek. They were all smuggled over the border into the General Government by some of his employees from his moviehouse business, at the risk of their own lives. He was such a good and charming man that they were fond of him. The three of them came to stay with me and Peter back at the Marszałkowska Street apartment, in a city whose inhabitants began to hear rumours that the Nazis were killing Jews.

A man arrived with a message from Bolek. It said that he was in Lwów (Lvov), in the Soviet-occupied zone; the man was to take us to him. My father, Peter, and I went with the guide, while Lilka and Janek were to follow later. At the border we were stopped by some German soldiers. They were not unpleasant, but they searched us and took all the money and jewellery they could find, including some banknotes my father had hidden in his socks. "Are you a Jew?" one of them asked my father, who was very Jewish-looking. He thought they would kill him, so he answered, "I was born a Jew, but I've been baptized ... I've changed my religion." They thought that very funny. "Jude bleib Jude!" (A Jew is always a Jew), said one of them. But they did us no physical harm. Fascinated with the soldiers, Peter chuckled and grabbed at one of their rifles with his little hands. I pulled him back quickly, frightened that the man would strike out at him, but the soldier laughed and played with him. Perhaps he had a baby at home. They didn't try to stop us leaving. In fact, they seemed to find it amusing that we wanted to go to the Soviet sector. "So you want to go to the communist paradise?" said one of them. "Well, go on – there are enough Jews here. Over there you'll live happily ever after!"

It was dusk and a chilling mist was rising off the water while the group of people we had joined were being rowed over the Bug River, the frontier between the German and Soviet sectors. By the time we were all across, it was black night, the moon and stars blotted out by the damp vapour swirling around us. With Peter heavy in my arms, I became lost in the marshes and the mist, separated from the others, separated from my father, going in what direction I did not know, struggling to pull my feet up through the sucking mud, stumbling on and off patches of firm ground, crying and calling for help. "Ratunku! Ratunku," my voice absorbed by the moist air. Silence and impenetrable darkness.

After struggling for endless hours, I saw a light glimmering through the mist and made my way towards what turned out to be a lamp shining dimly through the window of a little peasant hut. I knocked and they were friendly. I told them what had happened – though not, of course, that I was a Jew – and that we were trying to escape from the Germans to go to my husband. The man said that he had a pair of horses and that "in the morning, with God's help, I'll take you to the railway station and you can go directly to Lwów." They gave Peter milk and put us in a bed, and when I explained that I had nothing to pay them with because the Germans had taken everything, the man said that I was not to worry. "Rest," he told me. "Sleep."

Before dawn there was a knock on the door. It was the guide, looking for me with a note from my father and insisting that I go with him because my father was desperate and had said that unless he could see me, he would not believe that I was alive. Loving my father as I did, I went with him. Perhaps if I hadn't, my life would have been different. Perhaps.

When we found my father, some Russian soldiers were standing by him. They ordered us to return to the General Government. My father, who spoke fluent Russian, implored them to let us stay. He told them that the Germans were killing Jews, that we wanted to live under Soviet rule, that we wanted to work and to contribute to society. But nothing helped. They were good-humoured but said that they were under strict orders to send back anyone who was found illegally in the zone. "But I must go to my husband," I pleaded. They laughed, "Oh, you've lost your husband? Don't worry, you'll find another!"

Back in Warsaw the terrorizing and humiliation of Jews came upon us fast. One day when my father was walking in the street, a young German officer spat at him, shouted, "Dirty Jew!" and slapped him across the face. He never left the apartment again until the time came when he was forced to do so. Bank accounts were frozen, businesses confiscated, and they started to take everything else we had, ordering Jews to take their radios and furs to a warehouse. When I went there with our radio and the fur coat my father had given me and Bolek had forbidden me to wear, I had my first encounter with the Gestapo. They pushed us around with their rifles and shouted at us to hurry if we did not want to be shot. Then, soon after, they came pounding on our doors, bursting in and grabbing whatever was of value, whatever they fancied – jewellery, cameras, most of the furniture, my mother-in-law's large collection of crystal, which she had left in our flat – pushing us around, demanding that we help them carry our things downstairs to their trucks. But these were only our material belongings.

It was then that I found that I was marked, branded as part of a herd. Walking around with a sign on my arm. People, Polish people, looking at it and at me with disdain, a disdain sometimes mixed with pity, sometimes with triumph. "Jude Artz" is written on it in German – Jewish physician. Underneath that, the star of David, a symbol whose significance was new to me and which surely, on this arm band, could mean nothing but humiliation, even for those who identified themselves with it. For me it created a crisis of the spirit. It was more than a humiliation; it was abasement, mortification – my soul conquered by ugliness. I found myself compelled to confront the essence of that sense of inferiority which I had before refused to recognize and to name. I was no longer a Polish woman; they, the Poles, were looking at me with contempt. I was Jude, Zyd, a Jew. Never again could I feel that these were my people. The disdain in their eyes made me a lifelong refugee, forever a person without a country, without a place.

❧

It was December when the guide arrived again with a message from Bolek. Bolek had refused to pay him because he hadn't brought me. The letter said that this time I alone should go with the man, leaving Peter with my father, and that after I was with him on the Russian side, we would be permitted to reunite our family. Again I left the Marszałkowska Street apartment with the guide. This time we travelled by train until just before the border. Then we went into the forest, walking seventy kilometres by day and night through the snow in the bitter cold.

The guide was a young man, the type – if he lived long enough – who probably joined the partisans once they got going. He had worked for the Polish railways until they were taken over by the Germans. Now for a livelihood he was smuggling people over the border to the Soviet sector and making some extra money exchanging currencies. He was quick-witted. On the second day, when it was snowing heavily, we were stopped by a German patrol. He pretended to be glad to see them: "My wife and I have just escaped from the Russian paradise. We're trying to get to the German zone." They pointed us in the opposite direction, the guide thanked them, and we went on until we could circle back eastward. The last night, now in the Russian zone, we spent in a peasant's house. We were put into the same bed because we were supposed to be man and wife. I was nervous, but he was a perfect gentleman and didn't touch me.

The next day we got to a railway station and took a train to Lwów, but my reunion with Bolek was only fleetingly happy. I went immediately to the Soviet authorities to get permission to bring in Peter, my father, Lilka, and Janek. Particulars were taken, and I was told to come back. I kept on returning, queuing, waiting, giving particulars, and being told to return. I was distraught at the separation from Peter. Our money was gone; we froze in a rented room with a small wood stove for which we could afford fuel to boil a kettle only once a day. Bolek was earning a little money at a psychiatric hospital, and I could have finished my examinations at the medical school in the city, but it was always the same when I went to the authorities – "Take your place in the queue. Return next week. Return next week. Return next week."

I told Bolek I was going back. He argued and argued with me. "Who can know how long the war will go on? Who can know when we'll be together again?" Yes, I replied, and who could know when I would see my child again if I stayed? When he understood that I would not change my mind, that I was determined to leave him, he was very bitter. I did not look at him as I left the room.

You want me to tell you the truth, so I will: there was something else that had come between us, something that was destroying our marriage, undermining and subverting it. Professor H. was also in Lwów. He had started to pursue me before the war, when, pregnant with Peter, I was taken as a student to assist at an international medical congress. He had introduced himself and immediately began to wage a campaign of seduction, with constant declarations of love, putting into play his authority as a famous professor, all his charm, all his experience as a man. He used his wealth to inundate me with the most expensive flowers sent from wherever he was and to take me – usually by fiacre – to the smartest, most luxurious restaurants, where, in a private room, I could dine on anything I wished. He indulged me, pursued me, enticed me, overwhelmed me with his sophistication and persistence. He was forty-five when we met, and I, only twenty-three, was without any experience of this kind of courtship. However, it was not until Bolek left Warsaw that the affair had become "serious," and it was serious if only because it corrupted me and destroyed our marriage as surely as a hailstorm can flatten a field of healthy young wheat. Reconstructing it today in the stagnant, dulled perspective of my meaningless old age, I see it as having been based on a very strong sexual attraction on his part and an infatuation on mine. Perhaps I wanted from a lover the adoration I had from my father. Perhaps I was replaying the role of my mother with Karol. Anyway, he was there in Lwów, and he used to visit me in the freezing flat when Bolek, who knew nothing about it, had gone to the hospital.

⊰⊱

The marshes by the Bug River were now frozen. A guide was going to lead a group of us across the river back to the German sector. He counted us: we were fifty. (Why were the others going? One did not ask. Nobody asked questions in those days.) This time there was no mist, but it was inky dark. The guide himself became lost, and we circled, several times passing a familiar place, before he found the point from which we had to cross. He told us to spread out as we walked over the river's frozen surface. It was impossible to see the other people or what lay underfoot. There were cries as people fell through holes in the ice. Then the flash and stutter of gunfire – the Russians were shooting at us. I didn't know if I was going towards them or away. Nowhere to turn, nowhere to hide. Terrible screams. And then my feet on the west bank. By some mindless destiny, I had survived. The guide was there and he counted us: seventeen.

I made my way towards the lights of a small, unknown town. Curfew was at ten and the streets were empty. I didn't know where I was. I was afraid as a Jew, afraid of people I did not know, and in a small town it was dangerous if you were a stranger because you wouldn't know who was who. Finally, when I went into the yard behind a church, I found a door opening into a corridor, where I spent the night huddled on the floor. In the morning an altar boy found me there, half-frozen. He took me inside, made me some tea, and brought the priest. I told him I was trying to get home to Warsaw but had no money – I had given the guide my last few zlotys and had no idea how far it was. The priest gave me some food, told me there was a train from the town to Warsaw, and sent me to a woman nearby who would lend me the fare. With it I got on the train for the long journey back to the city and then spent the night on the station because it arrived after the curfew.

H. also came back to Warsaw. One day his wife came to the flat and asked me to end the affair with him. The poor woman – I ignored her. A letter came from their daughter, Krystyna, a beautiful girl not much younger than me, a promising poet who had already had some of her work published. She wrote to me, asking me for her mother's sake to end the affair. I ignored her. My father had found out about it when the wife came to the apartment, and he was upset. He thought that Bolek was the right husband for me. Perhaps he was also remembering the past.

My father had been pleased to have me near again when I arrived back in Warsaw, but he said I should have stayed in the Russian sector, which he thought was a safer place. "Piotr was fine with us. Children can grow up perfectly well without their mothers. You really didn't have to come back to be with him." He was such a good man, so incapable of cynicism, of seeing the evil that was around us. Later, in the ghetto, when the deportations started and I had my doubts about where people were being taken – where? to what? – he said to me, "You can believe the Germans. They are so well organized. If they're saying that you're going somewhere to work, then it must be the case. People are just spreading rumours." He wanted to believe. Even in the ghetto.

⋞≳⋟

A recurrent dream. It is night and I am lost in the thick black vapour swirling over the marshland, distorting shapes, swallowing sounds. The mud sucks my feet, leaden with the weight in my arms, pulling me down. I cry for help but nobody comes. Just silence and impenetrable darkness ...

The Ghetto

It is said that during the Inquisition, when the Jews of Spain were expelled from their country by King Ferdinand and Queen Isabella, they took with them the keys to their homes because, in their hearts, they held the hope that they would return. When the Nazis expelled us from our homes and sent us to the ghetto, we did not take the keys with us. It may be that we instinctively understood better than they. Perhaps we had premonitions of some nebulous awfulness; we simply knew we would never return.

The move into the ghetto was like some imagined biblical scene, with thousands of us walking in an exodus, but going not towards refuge, towards salvation or the hope of a better life. Most families were pushing some kind of crude handcart in which they transported their remaining possessions. As it was not large enough to take everything you needed and could move, you had to go and return across the city several times. Janek, my father's teenage stepson, was a good boy, and he and I did most of the moving, walking miles back and forth, pushing the cart. My father could not bear to go out on the street since the Nazi spat at him, so he made only the one journey – into the ghetto. People stood on the side of the road watching us, but I did not look at them. I kept my eyes on the cart, humiliated and unwilling to see their indifference or their pleasure. Exiled and marked with the Star of David, I was now part of a procession of Jews, sharing with them a Jewish destiny.

There was no choice in the place you were going to in a situation where one-third of Warsaw's population was crammed into a tiny fraction of its area.* We found ourselves in an airless, dark little slum flat. Lilka had gone in first, cleaning it up, and she and I made it as habitable as we could. The Polish woman with whom we had to exchange flats had told our neighbours what a great deal she had made, going from this slum to an attractive flat in a fashionable neighbourhood, and when the word got around that we were "Marszałkowska Street Jews," the attitude was "Ha, you thought you were so superior! You didn't want to mix with the rest of us, and now look where you are!" For a family of assimilated Jews, our position in the ghetto was peculiar and isolated. We were different, conspicuous by our manner and pure Polish speech, and here, unable to understand or to speak Yiddish, we were deaf-mutes. I knew people were despising us; they jeered at us, tried to humiliate us when we spoke. In the shops where we went to receive our rations,

---

* The ghetto represented 2.4 per cent of the city.

they would always serve us last and least. The irony was that we had been rejected from Polish society because we were Jews, and now, in the ghetto, we were in a no man's land, again rejected. But as the situation quickly worsened, all this became irrelevant, with every family closed into itself, desperately trying to survive.

The posters ordering us to go into the ghetto had gone up in July 1940. In the middle of November the gates were closed behind us. The Nazis had made Jewish work crews build eight-foot-high walls around the designated area, topped with glass shards and barbed wire, charging the cost to the Judenrat, the ghetto administration they had set up.

Except for my mother, camouflaged as the wife of Karol Adwentowicz, and Grandmother Schwartz, who lived with her (Babcia Sara had died some years earlier), all my family and Bolek's were there. My little Aunt Ola and her husband, their married daughter, her husband and their two children, and darling deaf Irka, who had grown into a beautiful girl, slender, with delicate features, white skin, pink cheeks, and short, curly auburn hair. She had been studying at art school. My father's brother, Uncle Franek, was there with his wife, Aunt Genia, and their son, as were many other relatives, including my cousin Roma, Aunt Bronia's daughter, and her husband – the most happily married couple I have ever known. Bolek's mother was there with his brother and his wife and their little boy, a year older than my Peter. Also Bolek's Uncle Herman, his wife, his son with his family, and Herman's daughter Lusia, who was a few years younger than me and a friend of mine. Lusia's husband, who had been a graphic designer, became a member of the corrupt and hated Jewish police set up by the Judenrat at the order of the Nazis. The men who joined the Judenrat police probably thought that this way they were going to be able to save their own necks. Also living with his Uncle Herman's family was a young woman called Alina. I scarcely knew her then, but later, after the war, she was to become my closest friend. We all tried to keep in contact, and I knew my colleagues in the hospital where I worked – some of them had been students with me at university – but the atmosphere, the situation, was such that we were in no frame of mind or physical condition for social life.

The German authorities had banned Jews from medical school before I had taken my final examinations, but they had given me a document permitting me to work as a doctor in a Jewish hospital in the ghetto. I was the only one in the family who could earn a little money, and I had five people dependent upon me because the Germans had taken everything. Yet even for those who had a small income, food was rationed to below subsistence level. We were alloted a small amount of fat, sugar, and bread, and at black market prices, we bought a few potatoes and horsemeat. My father would not touch the meat, so Lilka and I decided that the oldest and youngest – Peter and my father – would have the tiny amount of butter and sugar, and Lilka cooked the horsemeat for herself, Janek, and me, soaking it first in vinegar to make it palatable. After a while the rations were lowered to 400 calories a day, then less. The Nazis were creating the conditions for epidemics. And they were slowly starving us to death.

Our flat was in what was called the Little Ghetto, which was linked to the Big Ghetto by a specially built bridge. Under the bridge was a road which was part of the Aryan section of the city and which separated the two parts of the ghetto. Our flat was not far from the bridge, and at night you could hear shots as the Ukrainian and Latvian SS guards fired at the little children smuggling in potatoes over the walls to their starving families. Lying there, little crumpled bloodstained bodies. So small.

"Hat rachmunes, hat rachmunes ... stickele brot, stickele brot ..." "Have pity, have pity, a piece of bread, a piece of bread." I hear their chant, their wailing singsong chant, in their thin little voices. The doomed children of the ghetto, the living dead, their bellies swollen from hunger, wandering through the streets and courtyards of the ghetto, begging for life. We threw them a few bits of food from our window, but we were hungry ourselves and had so little to give.

"I am starving," says my beautifully dressed, indulged, and idolized little granddaughter, sitting in an expensive restaurant in this safe, kind Canadian city, permitted to order whatever she wishes from the menu. She toys with the food on her plate, then pushes it away, and I hear them, their thin despairing wail – "Hat rachmunes, hat rachmunes ... stickele brot, stickele brot ..."

The little corpses lay there on the streets, covered only with sheets of newspaper. All the orphans, all the children who had been separated from their families or abandoned by parents themselves sick or dying – the streets were full of them. Corpses of children, corpses of adults, corpses of old people. You couldn't tell their age. They were skeletons, bones covered by dark, spotty skin. There were too many to be buried immediately, so bodies would lie there while the living passed by, stepping over, walking around them. As though it were normal. But we could think only of our own survival. It was not possible to take care of others, even the children. I had my own to save from hunger, my own family to support, their lives my responsibility.

All those children with big eyes and adult, knowing expressions on their little faces follow me wherever I go, but nobody knows I have company, that there is an almost physical intensity to my memories. And I see them time and again, in Ethiopia, in Sudan, in Somalia. "I am starving," says my granddaughter – and pushes away her plate.

My friend, Professor H., got a loaf of white bread for me from the ghetto black market. It was very rare, very expensive, and I was so pleased to have a treat for the family. I had it under my arm, exposed because there was nothing to wrap it in to hide it. Out of nowhere, a frantic ragged boy jumped at me, grabbed the end of the bread, bit into it. He was filthy and must have been covered with lice, so instinctively I let go of it. In a second, he was gone round a corner pursued by other boys. Children, called catchers – usually lads of eleven, twelve, thirteen – were always outside the bakeries, waiting, watching.

It was difficult to get soap, but sometimes Professor H. got some for me, and he helped me with other things. One would dream about sweet things – a cake was something one longed for, fantasized about – and sometimes H. and I met in a little café, extremely expensive, where he would buy me something sweet. There were a few rich people for whom hunger was not a problem, and I even had a girlfriend who worked in a kind of nightclub, but I never went to those places. She didn't survive.

Sometimes they – the Nazis – came into the ghetto. They humiliated people, grabbing old, bearded men with those Jewish sidelocks, making them go down on all fours like a dog, and photographing them. Then they would disappear again for a while.

In the ghetto everything was grey; everything was grim, dirty. Spring never came to the ghetto. If the sky was blue, I never saw it. If a bird sang, I never heard it. There was no grass there; nothing was green, nothing grew. Everything was grey and shrivelled like the children dying on the streets. But at the hospital on Leszno Street, where I first worked, there was a courtyard, and in this courtyard the hospital staff who had small children decided to make a playground for them so that they could get some air and sunshine. We brought in some sand, provided them with simple things for their entertainment, and every day the mothers in turn would watch over them in this little oasis we had created. Perhaps it was summertime then because it was warm enough for them to be outside.

I do not know the date it happened. That day my father persuaded me not to take Peter with me because he had a runny nose. "Let him stay with me today," he said. It was one o'clock when we saw a big Gestapo car draw up outside. They came into the hospital and went through all the wards. They looked at the patients' charts at the end of their beds. If the patients were over fifty years of age, they shot them in their beds. Among the sick people were the elderly, frail parents of some of the physicians. They had brought them in thinking they could care for them better there. When some of the doctors threw themselves over their patients to protect them, they too were shot, while the rest of us, the nurses and doctors, waited for our turn to come next. The soldiers were young, well nourished, and very clean, their uniforms impeccable, their faces ruddy and well shaven, and they seemed to be in good spirits, loudly joking and laughing all the time they did their work. And then ... even to speak of this horrible thing ... and then, when they had finished this, they went outside to the playground. More shots, more laughter, and the car drove away. There had been perhaps twenty-five or more children there, and the woman who was watching over them. They killed all of them.

I can hear nothing. All I can see are the bloodied little bodies, and I am crazed with the horror in front of my eyes and at the same time with a strange joy because Peter is not here among them, and with guilt because he is not. And the other mothers are insane with the horror and the sense that they are guilty because they feel they have brought their children here to be slaughtered, and they are looking at me, and in their eyes I can see they are thinking I must have known what was going to happen because Peter is not here and I am an accomplice ...

I am running, running back home. I take Peter into my arms, and I kiss him and clasp him to my breast, and I am crying and crying ... I could not tell my father what had happened. For three days I was unable to speak.

❧

When the Nazis started to transport Jews from Germany and all over central and eastern Europe into the ghetto, an epidemic of dysentery and typhus came with them. They were put into the hospital for infectious diseases on Stawki Street, and medical staff were asked to volunteer to work there. I was young and physically healthy and said I would do it. Some anti-typhus vaccine had been smuggled into the ghetto, but only for one kind of typhus and only enough doses for the staff, so I brought my vaccine home and, because it was not suitable for children, gave it to my father. What I did for myself was to collect lice off infected people and put them into a matchbox and then onto my hand, where they could suck the blood. I did not get ill, and when I gave myself a test, I found I was immune. I worked with infected people day and night and was not afraid – why would I be when death was all around me?

We did not have enough room in the hospital. Patients were always two, sometimes three to a bed. Their bowels had turned to water and they were too weak to move. Those with dysentery were passing bloody stools up to two hundred times a day. They were skeletal, just bones and skin, their eyes sunk deep into their head. Their lips moved, but they could not talk. We had no medicine, no heat, no fresh linen for beds fouled with excrement. Nothing. In the winter, when the pipes were frozen, all we could do as they died was to moisten their lips with the little clean water we could get and comfort them as well as we could. I felt guilty that I could not help even one of them to recover. My duty was to help, my overwhelming desire was to help, but all of us were helpless. Starvation and sickness were everywhere. On the streets people were dying of disease and hunger, dying faster than the carts could carry them away, covered, like animals, by newspapers.

Because we had no medication, Professor H. invented a technique called "autohaemotherapy" – injecting patients' muscles with their own blood or doing a spinal puncture, taking off spinal fluid and similarly injecting it. It was supposed to do some good. Anyway, there was nothing to lose and nothing else to be done, and perhaps the patients would have the psychological advantage of thinking they were being treated. Professor H., who had a large private practice in the ghetto, taught me this technique. He passed some of his patients on to me, and at night, when I came off duty at the hospital, I used to earn some extra money for my family by treating them. My legs would get so swollen from fatigue that when I came home, my father would make me lie down and put a pillow under my legs.

My affair was still going on with H., even there in the ghetto, and when Bolek somehow made his way to Warsaw from Lwów and found me, I left the flat. He stayed with my father, Lilka, Janek, and our little Peter, while I had a room in another part of the ghetto that H. took for me. This was the crazy situation that I created within the nightmare madhouse of the ghetto.

Why did I do it? I ask myself now. Was it headstrong, narcissistic, thoughtless youthful folly? Infatuation? A desire for adventure or an illusory escape from the horror that surrounded me? Was it desperation? Premonition? Flattery? Or was it a warp in my psyche caused by my mother's behaviour to my father? Whatever it was, I have regretted it ever since. I know that my father did not like what I was doing, although he never reproached me. And I know that Bolek was humiliated. H. had been his professor at medical school and was twenty years older than him. Bolek went to him and asked, "What future are you offering my wife?" – a question I myself never asked, if only because I doubt that I myself knew what I wanted, and anyway, I had little belief that any of us had a future. "After the war I intend to get a divorce and marry Stasia," replied H. So Bolek told my father.

Then H. himself caught typhus. Although it was contrary to hospital policy – whatever policy could be enforced under the conditions in the ghetto – he stayed at home. In his hospital office he had a strongbox whose key he had left with one of his interns to give to me. The intern handed it to me with a smile that said my affair with the boss was common knowledge. I realized that H. wanted me to have it in case he should die, but I never opened it, so I never knew what it contained. (My mother, when I told her later – I had always told her about my affairs since my first, with Jan – said that I was a fool, that I should have profited from the situation. But it never crossed my mind.) Obviously I couldn't visit H. at his home, but he so much wanted to see me that he arranged for all his assistants to visit together. We did go one day, and everyone knew why we were all there. His wife didn't appear. His daughter, Krystyna, wasn't in the ghetto. She had been sent into the country.

H. was still unwell when Bolek was brought into the typhus ward. At that point the telephones were working and someone called H. to let him know. He gave instructions that Bolek be accommodated in his own office. Before Bolek was put in there, he needed to be bathed. I did it myself, first thoroughly disinfecting the bathtub. He didn't object, and I see myself sponging him gently, drying him like a child, and then looking after him, nursing him when I could, bringing him water and whatever food I could get, then books to read when the fever began to abate – he was young and otherwise healthy, unlike most of the patients. But we spoke of nothing personal.

It was later that Bolek and I stood by the third-floor window in the courthouse, looking down at the street below. The building had entrances on either side; one door led to the ghetto, the other to the Aryan side. The deportations had started, and we had got a message out to my mother asking whether she would take Peter if we could get him out to her. Yes, she had replied. The women who cleaned the courthouse were all from the Aryan side, and we bribed one of them to take him out. We dressed him in poor clothes and persuaded him to go with the woman, promising him a big treat when he got to Babcia. At the door onto the Aryan side a soldier stands with a rifle in his hands. My heart seems to stop beating. When she goes out, will he remember that she had no child when she went in? She comes out onto the street – beside her, his little hand in hers, our son, and they disappear from view. We went down the stairs out into the ghetto and walked away, each in a different direction. The next day the message arrived in my grandmother's handwriting: "The package has arrived safely."

Nobody can explain the impulse to commit suicide. And I am not speaking of the rational decisions I saw others make when it was a clear issue of avoiding a worse form of inevitable death. I had become increasingly depressed. I was working with patients for whom nothing could be done; I felt more and more isolated and alone; I had seen too much, and I was overwhelmed by a premonition of the total tragedy about to engulf everyone around me. I lost the will to live. One day I went into the ward's pharmacy and took enough barbiturates to kill a horse. But they did not kill me, and I was found – I don't know where or how. My stomach was pumped out, and then I was put into the chief nurse's room (she was very curious, salaciously so, wanting to know all the "whys," which she associated with my affair with H.). I spent days and nights not talking, looking at the ceiling, thinking of no one and of nothing. Now I wonder where my love was for my little son and whether he would have survived if I had died.

Bolek had inherited a house in the ghetto from his father. He sold it (though I cannot imagine what fool would have bought a house there in that situation), and he was paid in gold dollar coins. He told me that, one way or another, he was going to escape from the ghetto and join the partisans, and he gave me two of the gold ten-dollar pieces. I managed to send one of them to my mother for Peter; with the other I bought a work permit for my father from the German authorities. The permit said that the person named on it was to be given a place in one of the German-owned closed workshops in the ghetto and was not to be deported. I was delighted to get it because I thought I had bought him life.

My father and I met nearby the bridge between the Big and Little Ghettoes. In this dirty street, surrounded by ugliness, my father, in his grey suit with a blue tie, was, as always, immaculately dressed. The meeting must have been arranged because I had with me the work permit, the German certificate that said, "Unterliegt nicht der Umsiedlung" (Not subject to deportation). He, my dearest father, and I saw it as a life-saving device. Kissing and hugging me, he was so grateful when I gave it to him. Despite everything, he had such faith in the Germans. "I hope it will help," I said. "How can you have any doubts? You just don't know the Germans. You can count on their word. They are solid, reliable types. They always keep their promises. These Nazis are just an aberration." He would not believe the rumours we were beginning to hear, rumours that when people were deported for "resettlement," they were being taken away to places with names such as Treblinka, Bełżec, Auschwitz, Majdanek, killed by being gassed in their thousands, and their bodies incinerated.

As we were standing there, close to each other, looking into each other's eyes, my hands in his, he suddenly said, "I have something to say to you, my daughter. Or, rather, it's a request I want to make … Just in case we're not able to talk again – just in case we lose contact." "What is it?" I asked "I want you always, always to take care of your mother." I was so taken aback. There we were in that foul street surrounded by horrors that could obliterate us at any minute, while my mother was still living in her own home on the Aryan side, and yet my father was worrying about her. I promised him I would take care of her as long as she lived, as long as I lived.

He embraced me again, and we just stood there for a long time, not talking any more, only looking at each other. Then we parted.

—❦—

Sometimes it was the ss, sometimes it was the infamous Jewish police, who went from building to building, flushing out anyone they found hiding in an attempt to avoid the official decree to go to the Umschlagplatz, the gathering place, in order to be taken away for "resettlement." I am walking to work at the Stawki Street hospital when I hear German voices shouting inside an open fifth-floor window. They are pushing something out of the window. It is a chair, and onto the chair is tied an old man. It crashes to the street. The street is deserted, everyone has disappeared. There is just an empty space devoid of life like a macabre film and the broken body tied to the chair. I run.

How can I tell these things I have seen. It is only a small baby, perhaps a few weeks old. The ss officer grabs it from its mother's arms, takes the tiny bundle by the feet, and smashes and smashes its head against the wall. The brain and blood spatter against the wall, and the mother, as white as death, is screaming. She throws herself on the ground, begging that she too be killed, and he is beating her, and

I am afraid he will kill her. But perhaps it would have been better for her to have died then, rather to have looked at that terrible thing.

⊰⊱

A few minutes before she did it, she told me that she was going to kill her mother and her little daughter. I cannot remember her name, but I can still see her face. She was a friend of mine, a few years older than me, tall and slim with a dark complexion, dark hair, beautiful dark eyes. She was related to Professor H. and worked in the laboratory at the hospital. She told me that she had decided to kill them both with cyanide, to which she had access in the laboratory, rather than be shot here in the ghetto or get taken to the death that she was sure awaited them after deportation. She said that her decision was final and that she was going to do it right away. I did not try to influence her to change her mind, and I did not watch when she injected them both, nor, when the little one died in her arms, she administered a dose to herself.

The ghetto was being emptied of its starving, despairing, humiliated, hopeless human occupants. For a while, we medical workers, who wore the red, not the blue, arm band, were excluded. My cousin Roma, Aunt Bronia's daughter, and her husband disappeared. My other cousins disappeared; friends disappeared. They simply weren't there any more. Bolek's mother had died in the ghetto; all the rest of his family disappeared. One day I went to see Aunt Ola and her family. The door is open, nobody is there. Someone told me that when the rest of the family was taken by the Judenrat police, Irka, my beautiful, deaf young cousin was out, and that when she returned and understood what had happened, she went running down the street towards the Umschlagplatz, to her mother, her voice to the world. Did she ever find her? What horrors did she go through before final one?

Only my father remained in the ghetto, at the Schultz workshop. I decided to try to escape. At the hospital I'd heard that some people had got out with the groups of young Jews that were still being taken in and out of the ghetto every day on work details, but I wanted my father to come with me and was sure that the guards at the factory could be bribed. I went to the workshop gate and gave an armed guard a few zlotys to let me see him. The man nodded his head towards the wire fence that surrounded the compound. "All right," he said, "but you can only talk to him through the wire. You've got five minutes." My dearest father approached the fence. I can remember nothing of how he looked that day, how he was dressed, the condition he was in. I told him I was going to try to escape and pleaded with him to come with me. Shaking his head, he answered me slowly. "No, no, I don't want to go." I pleaded again, but "No," he said again. "No, I would only endanger you. I look too Jewish. But you go. Good luck and may God help you." As he said it, I had the feeling that he was giving me his final blessing. I went on trying to persuade him, but he would not change his mind. Then the guard came and separated us. My father tried to give me a smile. Then he turned and walked away. I knew I would never see him again, yet I wouldn't let myself believe what I knew.

The next day, taking nothing with me except my purse, not even any photographs, I joined a group of young people at the assembly point for the work party. The guards – Ukrainians and Latvians – looked through my purse and took a couple of little pieces of jewellery I still had, but they let me get on the cart. I'd heard that if they didn't like the look of somebody, they would just shoot them there on the spot, but this day they just took us outside the city to a forest, gave us cross saws, one between two people, and ordered us to cut down trees. When the guards moved out of sight for a minute, I ran. I was young and fast, and I ran – throwing my arm band into some bushes – running and running until I came to a tramway stop and got a ride into the city.

A few days later all the patients at the hospital were massacred, and the staff sent to the Umschlagplatz, to the trains.

It was 1946, a warm, late spring day in Warsaw, when she just materialized out of the blue, and we stood on the sidewalk talking, two young women in summer dresses. She was the first person I'd seen from the ghetto. We recognized each other from the Stawki Street hospital, where she had worked in the laboratory, and she had married one of my surgeon friends, Lolek S., a boyish-looking young man with light blonde hair and a round, pink-cheeked face. I'd known him since we were at medical school together.

She expressed no surprise at seeing me alive, and neither did I at the sight of her. What I felt was, it just so happens that she is here, and she must have felt the same.

"Did you know that Lolek died?" she asked in a matter-of-fact voice.

"No, I didn't. I'm sorry."

"Well, you know, almost everyone from the hospital is dead. Some tried to escape, but you're the first one I've seen."

"And so are you."

Then a strange look came into her eyes. "But I shouldn't be here, not really. I should have stayed behind, there in the sewers, where I left my baby, my little girl. I'm a murderer. You'd better not touch me," and she began to laugh hysterically.

"What do you mean? When did you have a baby? Why did you leave her?"

"Oh, she was only four weeks old, and she cried a lot. I probably didn't have enough milk. She was hungry; she must have been hungry. She cried and cried and cried. And we were down there in the sewers, and they told me … Well, they told me that I couldn't take her with me any farther because the crying was endangering the whole group. And so I had to make a choice. It was my own choice, it was me who had to decide. But I wanted to live, and so … and so I left her behind. Crying. I hear her crying ever since." She looked around at the street and then straight into my eyes. "You do condemn me. Say you do. Surely you do?"

I couldn't make myself answer or say anything. I could only keep staring at her. She was wearing lipstick; her hair looked as though she had just had it done; her blue eyes were accented with eyeshadow. She obviously still cared for her looks, for life. I couldn't find an answer; no words came to me. Did she read in my eyes a refusal to judge her? A condemnation, not of her, but of our murderers?

"Well, I must go now," she said. "I don't suppose we'll see each other again for a while. It was so nice to see you alive that I had to tell you. You're the first person I've told. I had to tell my story to someone who would understand." She looked at me a moment longer, then nodded, turned, and walked off. I never did see her again.

Cell 19

Among the scenes that return, bidden or unbidden. My cousin and I are standing at a window, looking into the distance at the flames and smoke that gush thickly into the sky from the ruins of the ghetto. The landlady comes and stands behind us. "I'll say this for Hitler," she shrills. "At least he's resolving the problem of the Jewish vermin once and for all. The only thing I regret is that I've got a house in there and it'll be burned together with all those Jewish bedbugs."

People used to say that it was by their eyes, by the fear in their eyes, that they could recognize Jews who were trying to survive by passing as ordinary Poles. I did not have those eyes. Wherever I kept my fear, at whatever subconscious level, it was not where it could be seen mirrored in my eyes. It was other emotions that propelled me, particularly after I heard that my father was dead. I had managed to establish contact with him, finding by some means a Polish policeman known to go into the ghetto and who, for a bribe, would deliver messages there. I know I had virtually no money or food for myself, but I got hold of some and paid him to take it to my father. The policeman returned with a letter from him which I later lost, but I remember every single word: "My beloved daughter. I am left all by myself, without family, without friends. Lilka and Janek were taken away from me, and I am here all alone. I have no one to talk to, and it is the first time in my life that I am so alone. I am also very weak because there is almost nothing here to eat. Take good care of yourself. I am happy that you are far away from me – how strange to say that. Love. Yours to the last breath. Father."

I sent money and food again, but I am sure it never reached him because I never saw the policeman again. I cannot remember how I knew that my father was dead. It may have been from Uncle Franek – he and Aunt Genia had escaped from the ghetto through the sewers. But I knew. In some way the news reached me, and I knew it was true. I put myself into deep mourning. For a year I wore only black. It was stupid because it made me conspicuous, and what was the use, but it seemed to me that I had to show my despair at having lost the person who was everything and everyone for me. My father was my whole world, and when I knew he was dead, something broke inside me, irreparable. It is as though since then I have been leading a second life.

From that moment, although I went through the motions of trying to survive, in some inward sense I really did not care. And paradoxically, the less I cared, the more luck I had because my eyes did not have that hunted expression that betrayed so many Jews trying to pass as Aryans. I heard Poles talking about it, them thinking that I was one of them. My manner was like theirs – indifferent. Perhaps in that way his death saved my life.

I went on wearing mourning until, for some reason – it may have been the time when we heard that Peter was ill – I met Bolek, who had also got out of the ghetto. He commented on my black veil, saying that I was being irresponsible, endangering my life unnecessarily by drawing attention to myself, and that Peter needed me alive not dead. He was having trouble making contact with the partisans – and staying alive. Once a big lout had come up to him on the street, accused him of being a Jew, forced him into a doorway, and made him take down his trousers to see whether he was circumcised. Bolek was very lucky because the man let him go after he gave him all the money he had on him.

By then I was living under the identity of Irena Ponikowska, a dead Polish Catholic girl. When I fled the ghetto work gang, I first went to my mother's and Karol's flat, but I couldn't stay there. Karol was in prison, suspected – correctly, though they couldn't get any proof – of being involved with the underground resistance, and their place was probably being watched. I had no identity papers, so my mother had to find a place for me to hide. She was working as a waitress in a coffee shop run by a group of actors who would not perform for German audiences, and not revealing that I was her daughter, she told one of the kitchen staff that I was in the resistance and needed temporary shelter. The woman agreed and took me home with her in a distant part of the city, where she gave me a sofa in her room to sleep on, with its back to her bed. I woke when I heard her coming into the room. A uniformed man was with her. I was terrified, thinking it was the police, but when he left, another visitor arrived and I realized that she was a prostitute. I lay there, not daring to move, my head under the covers. After that at night I hid in a storage place under the eaves, fearful of every knock at her door, sleeping in the daytime when she was at the restaurant. I would hear the men's voices, and some of them were Germans, but I was too scared to leave because I had no papers and my mother had told me not to go to the café or their flat in case I was seen.

I don't know how long I was there until I finally decided to go, and again I was out on the street, wandering all day, hungry, not knowing what to do, where to go. It might have been that day that I went looking for shelter to old Zawadzka, our housekeeper when I was a child, but she was too frightened to let me stay. Finding myself on Poznańska Street when it was nearly the curfew hour, I went into a building and sat in the stairwell, hoping to hide there for the night. Seemingly out of nowhere, an old lady appeared on the stairs. "What are you doing here my child?" she asked me in a gentle, friendly voice. "Nothing, nothing at all," I answered. "Do you need shelter?" I nodded. "You cannot sleep here on the stairs. Come with me, my dear. Come," she said, and took me into her small apartment, sat me down, and gave me some warm milk. Its warmth, her kindness, and the feeling of sanctuary overwhelmed me and I fell asleep.

I stayed with her for I don't know how long, maybe weeks. She had white hair, although I don't think she was very old, a sweet, delicate face with a small nose, thin lips, and blue eyes, in which there was never any laughter. She was always very serious and scarcely spoke. She asked me no questions and I never asked her about herself. Thus I never found out if she had any family or if she had lost it. She had little food, but whatever there was – some bread and artificial coffee or cabbage, soup, and potatoes – she shared with me.

There was a tiny kitchen and, separated by a corridor, two small rooms, in one of which I slept. One evening a Jewish couple arrived. I never saw them, but she asked me to share her bed so that they could sleep in mine. They were there for a few days. Then one night when I was so deeply asleep that I didn't hear footsteps coming up the stairs or anyone coming in, I was woken by a flashlight shining in my eyes: it was the police. I didn't react; my eyes showed nothing.

Stasia's identity card (*Kennkarte*) as Irena Ponikowska

"Who is this?" "Leave her," said the old lady beside me. "She is my niece." You will suppose that I was afraid, but I was not. Unless inside, deep inside. But I could show nothing because if you do, you are lost. They took the couple away.

There were posters up around the city warning that the punishment for helping or harbouring Jews was death. Soon after the couple were taken, I asked her why she took the risk. "Christ was persecuted too, was he not?" she replied. "And he too was innocent. Christ was born a Jew." "But aren't you afraid?" "No, not really. I am doing nothing wrong. Only those who do wrong to others should be afraid." That was the only conversation between us that I can recall.

I cannot remember her name, or how I left the flat on Poznańska, or why I never tried to find her again after the war. Could it be that I didn't want her to know whom she was hiding – that I was a Jew? I cannot answer this question. I can only suspect myself of the ambiguity that has never left me.

My *Kennkarte*, the wartime identity paper, has the old lady's address on it – Poznańska 23. When he was released from prison, Karol obtained for me the baptismal certificate of a dead girl, Irena Ponikowska, born not long after me, and with this, I went to the authorities. My photograph and fingerprints were taken and I was issued with the document that legitimized my existence. I bleached my brown hair, wore a cross around my neck, and carried a Catholic prayer book in my purse. I never wondered who she had been; I did not act the part. I was no longer Stanisława Ałapin, née Grynbaum. I was Irena Ponikowska.

The Nazis had what were called "catching days." They would surround a district, pick out able-bodied people, put them in a truck, and take them away for forced labour in factories and farms in Germany. Ironically, for a Jew who had a "genuine" Aryan ID like mine, it could be something you wanted because you were safer away, as a worker. Two of my relations survived that way – my Aunt Genia, Uncle Franek's wife, and their son.

※

I was on my way to the marketplace where you could buy second-hand clothes to get some boots for Professor H. – with money, nearly everything was possible, and H. had money. How, I cannot remember, but I had found a guide to get him and his wife out of the ghetto, and we were in contact. He had even visited me one night at the old lady's flat on Poznańska. His boots were worn out, and it seemed safer for me, a woman, to go shopping rather than him. I was standing at the tramway stop when I heard the boy shouting, "Jewess! Jewess! Hold the Jewess!" The boy, maybe nine or ten years old, was pointing at me. There was no use in trying to run; it would have been an admission of guilt. Anyway, I was Irena Ponikowska. The other people at the stop looked at me without interest, indifferently, and said nothing. No reaction – neither "Leave her alone" nor "Yes, fetch the police." It was just "Don't get involved." They themselves were frightened of the Germans and scared of being deported. The boy brought a policeman, who took me, protesting that I was not a Jew, to the police station. My manner was one of annoyance. "What am I here for?" I demanded of the chief. "What have I done?" "Ah, nothing," he said. "You just look like a woman who killed someone a few minutes ago." "But I didn't kill anyone," I said indignantly. He took my *Kennkarte* away to check that it was genuine, which of course it was, and soon returned it, telling me that I was free to go. But I am never free of the sight of that young Polish boy, brought up to hate another human being so much that he wanted to destroy her. It was worse than if he had been a German.

At some point, perhaps when I was staying with the old lady on Poznańska, I happened to meet my cousin Zenia on the street and we decided to get a room together. She was the daughter of my father's older sister, who had died young giving birth to Zenia, and she too had a "genuine" false *Kennkarte*. We found a place in the apartment of an old woman, a sour old bitch. She wouldn't let us use her kitchen, but when she went out, we used to sneak in and cook our potatoes and onion – that and a bit of bread was all we could afford. We would do it quickly, eat, wash up, and put everything away before she got back. We spoke to her as little as possible. One evening in April 1943, during the ghetto uprising, when a handful of practically unarmed young men and women were fighting thousands of Nazi troops to the end, she stood by us at the window watching the flames from the burning ghetto and was so happy that the "Jewish bedbugs" were burning – while regretting that she was also losing her house. I don't know why we didn't strangle the old bitch. No one would have seen us. What did we have to lose? But we just choked back our tears and said nothing, did nothing.

In order to survive, it helped if you had a "good" face – that is, if you could pass as a Pole. But it wasn't enough that no one recognized you on the street and denounced you as a Jew, or that the Gestapo did not stop you on the street and, if your papers weren't right, take you off or maybe just shoot you on the spot. It was also necessary to eat and to pay for the rent. Therefore I had to find work. What I needed was something that didn't require qualifications, so I started looking in the newspapers for jobs babysitting for working mothers, something in the outskirts of the city where I would run less risk of being recognized. I found a young couple in one of the suburbs who wanted someone to clean their apartment and cook their dinner as well as to care for their little girl, but they also wanted references, which of course I didn't have. I came up with a half-truth – I said I hadn't done this kind of work before because I was a student who was unable to study now for some unspecified political reasons. They accepted my story, maybe feeling that I looked trustworthy. Anyway, they took me on without any further questions, and I started to work for them the next day, arriving by 8 a.m. and staying until 5 p.m., when the mother came home. The cleaning was no problem, and looking after the little girl was a pleasure – she was only two years old, and after a while she did not want me to leave in the evening. But I had real trouble with the cooking because I didn't know how to cook! When I was living with Bolek, it was he who cooked because I was so useless at it and because I would often forget that something was on the stove and burn the saucepans. And here I was expected to cook a whole meal for people who were paying me for it. I tried to find cookbooks, but didn't dare to go to libraries. I consulted Zenia, but she wasn't much more informed than myself. So I just had to go by trial and error. The young couple had little money, so I mostly cooked vegetables and potatoes, or if there was a small amount of meat, I would make a soup. Sometimes it was passable, sometimes not too good, but they seemed satisfied, and being hungry, so was I. For two or three months everything went all right, until one afternoon, when the mother had come home early from work, a friend of hers dropped in for a few minutes. "Hello, Stasia," she said. I didn't know who she was, though obviously she knew me. But I was Irena, not Stasia. Nobody said anything, neither them nor me, but of course I never went back.

The next job I got was looking after a baby boy. All I had to do was to feed and change him and take him to the nearby park. It was a good job. There was little to do, the parents were well off and paid me a good salary, and the little fellow was easy to keep happy. I took him for long walks in the park, and when people made comments about "your baby," I didn't contradict them. Then one afternoon when we were in the park, a young man approached me. We had been at medical school together, and he started asking me questions about what I was doing. I told him that this was my child and that I had to get home to feed him. He suggested that we meet again the next day "to discuss some problems of common interest." I agreed to be there, though I had no intention of doing so – one could never know about people. I never went back to the job; it was too dangerous. Everything was.

Then Zenia and I got work from Triangle in the Ring, a store where German women ordered handmade sweaters, and we made the parts that were assembled to measure at the store. I could knit and crochet well because my Babcia had taught me when I was a child. It was exhausting and badly paid, but it had the great advantage that we had to go out only once a week to deliver the work and get more wool, so we could stay in our room most of the time without the risk of being seen and recognized on the street.

At one point, I heard that Peter was not well – perhaps from my mother, whom I telephoned fairly often. He was in an Ursuline sisters' orphanage at Milanówek, just outside the city. He'd been taken there after Bolek and I smuggled him out of the ghetto to my mother. It was too dangerous for him to stay with her, and Mira and Jerzy decided that the safest place would be with the nuns. To give him a legitimate Aryan identity for his protection, he had to be baptized, but this couldn't be done without his mother, so I also had to be baptized. Karol arranged everything. Peter was brought into Warsaw from the orphanage, and we were baptized together in a church. Peter was given the surname Pietraszkiewicz – the name of the man, an actor friend of my mother, who was standing as his godfather and because he wasn't circumcised, the nuns were taking virtually no risk by keeping him. My mother had given the ten-dollars gold piece that Bolek had given me for Peter to an actress friend of hers, and she was to give it to the convent to cover the cost of maintaining him.

When I heard that Peter was ill, I became frantic with worry, wanting to see him, although it was dangerous to go to Milanówek in case somebody followed me. But I just couldn't bear it and went. "No, he's not ill," said the nuns, and when I asked to see him, they brought him out to me in the courtyard. He was now four years old. My little boy just stood there, looking at me, moving from one foot to the other, his feet bare on the cold stone, clenching his little hands, tears welling out of his big eyes, and not saying a word. I asked if I could take him out for a short time, but the sisters said he had grown out of his shoes. "Then why not buy him a pair with the money you were given?" I asked. "Money? There's no money." Obviously the woman had not given it to them, but I couldn't say anything. However, one of the sisters had the idea that we could borrow shoes from another child, so the two of us went out into the snow. I took him into a little coffee house. He wanted some cakes, and I asked him what he would like as a gift. "I want a prayer book," he said. "All the other children have a prayer book." I gave him the one I carried with me. He did not call me "Mummy," so I

Five- or six-year-old Peter (shoeless, on the left) in the convent orphanage in Milanówek during the war

asked why. "I mustn't call you Mummy. If I do, my tongue will be cut out." I said nothing, but I found out later that someone had told him that to protect him.

When I got back to the city, I telephoned my mother's friend. I didn't tell her I had been to see him, but I said I had heard that he needed shoes. She told me that Peter was very ill. "I am sorry, but he has tuberculosis. He isn't expected to live, so they probably aren't buying a pair for him because he doesn't need them. I'm sorry to give you this bad news." I had to pretend to believe her because she held his life in her hands.

It was on one of the days that I had delivered Zenia's and my work to the store, when I was crossing the courtyard at the back entrance to the building where we lived, that I saw Stefa Kunowska. Our eyes met. It was definitely Stefa; she'd been at my school, and it was impossible to mistake the angelic-looking face, straight blonde hair, blue eyes – a nicely built woman typical of a "Rein Arisch," people considered by their appearance to be of German extraction. She had been in the class below mine and knew me, as everyone in the school had known me, because my Polish and French essays had often been read to the whole school at recreation time, and some of the girls had been resentful of my being held up as a model. Her moment of revenge had come.

She gave no sign that she had recognized me, but I knew that she had, and I also read her intentions on her angelic face. I went on walking into the building. Then I ran up the stairway and looked down from the window on the second floor. She was knocking on the door of the concierge's flat. The concierge came out, and Stefa, her white complexion on fire, was talking insistently to him, gesticulating, pointing at the door I had entered, making her point clear, wanting him to understand what she was after.

I ran up to the flat, grabbed a few things from our room, stuffed them into the bag I used for the wool, explaining to Zenia as fast as I could what was going on, and ran back to the stairs. Halfway down my way was blocked by a "blue" policeman, one of the Polish police who collaborated with the Germans. "Stop!" he said, grabbing my arm. "You are a Jew. Someone has identified you." I protested that I was not, that it was a case of mistaken identity, that I had my *Kennkarte* to prove it. "You are Ponikowska like I'm Schmidt," he sneered after looking at it. "What do you mean?" I asked in a tone of uncomprehending surprise. "Come on. You know what I mean – you're a Jew." "But I'm a Pole, the same as you. What do you need for me to prove it?" He gave a cynical smirk. "Well, I suppose you have some money you can prove it with?" But I had no money, only a few small coins, so he took me off to the local police station, continuing to insinuate that if I gave him a good bribe, he would let me go.

Still insisting upon my "innocence," I was put into a big cell with the drunks, petty thieves, and prostitutes who had been brought in that day. They were decent to me, and it seemed to me that they were by no means the worst elements in society. Nobody abused me or even spoke to me in an unfriendly manner, although it was obvious I didn't belong. Several times during the night I was taken out of the cell and questioned about my identity. The police tried to trick me, one of them saying that he knew my father and that my father had told him of my whereabouts. "He even showed me your photograph, so it's no use denying who you are. We know." I was as good as dead, but I was not going to give up until the last. At that moment I had a strong instinct to survive. I did not want to leave my little boy an orphan. I denied everything. "You are not telling the truth," I answered. "First of all, my father died when I was eight years old, so you couldn't have spoken to him. Secondly, I haven't had a photo taken for years – apart from the one on my *Kennkarte*. Look at it." He put me back in the cell for a while, then another one took me out and tried another story, but he couldn't catch me out.

The next morning I was taken out of the cell and told I was going to be transferred. To the Gestapo centre. Two policemen accompanied me, and we walked. It was then that the extraordinary happened: one of them, a young man about my own age, took my arm saying, "We'd better go like a couple, so people won't be looking at you as though you're a prisoner – that wouldn't be nice." Then he added quickly, "I've some advice for you," and he glanced over his shoulder at the other policeman, who was walking behind, keeping a distance. "You are an attractive girl and you don't look Jewish. Personally, I don't care if you are, but my advice to you is never, never admit to being Jewish. You're not a man, so they can't prove anything. Just keep denying it and don't budge." "But I really am not a Jew," I said, unsure if it wasn't another trick. "I've told you," he replied. "I don't care. Now look, I want you to phone someone close to you and tell them where you're going. They might be able to help you if they can prove you're not Jewish … Another thing, I want you to have something to eat because you won't get much in the Gestapo prison." As we passed a little coffee shop and bar, he gently pushed me in the door.

I decided to take the risk and call Mira – Mira Sawa, my classroom teacher when I was school, who had "adopted" me. I hadn't spoken to her or to her husband, Jerzy, for months because I hadn't wanted to expose them to danger. I dialled their number. It rang once, twice, three times. And then I heard my Mira's voice. Quickly I told her that Stefa Kunowska had denounced me as a Jew, that I was being taken to the Gestapo prison, and if my mother wanted to know where I was, Mira should warn her about what had happened. I didn't ask Mira to help me. She paused only for a second then spoke. "Don't say anything. Keep quiet. They will know that you are not a Jew, and we'll do everything we can to get you out as fast as possible. Don't worry, we'll be there. Courage, my dear. We will come. God be with you."

I refused to eat anything – I just couldn't – and only drank a glass of water. I didn't let myself think the obvious – that I would be shot that morning. All I thought about was Peter, that he still needed me, that I must live.

We went in through the heavy doors of the Gestapo building. Before he handed me over, the young policeman said to them, "This nice young woman has been accused of being a Jew, but she isn't." "That we'll see," the Gestapo officer cut him short – he was a Volksdeutsche (a German who had lived in Poland). "You can leave." My friend went, and I was alone in the jaws of the most bloodthirsty of brutes.

They took the few things I had with me – a silver powder compact, a gift from Professor H., my pen, and the small coins I had in my pocket. Then "To the Jewish cell!" one of them barked.

The cell was number 19, and there were nineteen of us women and a little child, in a space about four by five metres, not enough room for us to sit on the concrete floor at the same time. We took turns siting or lying. Twice a day we were taken to the toilet by a male guard, who stood there while we were using it. I had a corner under the only window, a small oval skylight. In another corner were a little boy and his mother, a young woman with a pleasant round face, deeply set, light brown eyes, and dark hair. The poor little boy, the same age as my Piotr, with his hair cut in a fringe, cried a lot and often wet the floor – what else could he do? – which so upset his mother that she'd apologize and try to wipe it up with her own clothes.

I never acknowledged that I was a Jew, but none of us spoke much, in some way sharing the suspicion that one of the women had been put in the cell as an informer. Dressed in ragged clothes, she had a shaven head and no shoes on her feet, although it was wintertime and cold in there.

Our food was a piece of bread a day and a bowl with a little potato and onion in water. I didn't mind the hunger, but I was a smoker and what I craved was cigarettes. One of the women must have managed to keep some, because although smoking was forbidden, one evening I had lit a cigarette, hoping that the smell would be carried up through the little window, when a guard came past and saw me. He pulled me outside the door and then he punched and hit me over and over again. He was young and tall, with heavy fists and boots. His rage was overwhelming, and it all flew against my small, thin body. When he shoved me back into the cell, my blouse torn, exposing my breasts, and with my nose bleeding, I was sure that my eyes were gone because I could see nothing. The woman with the little boy examined my face and tried to calm me. "No, it's all right, your eyes are there. It's just that your face is so swollen that you can't see." Amazingly, none of my bones were broken.

For two days my eyes were closed. Then, her soft voice almost in a whisper, the young woman asked me, "Before you were arrested, did you hear about Stalingrad?" "Hear what?" "You didn't know that the Germans were defeated there? That they didn't take the city, that they were forced to retreat? Could it be the beginning of the end?" A wonderful feeling came over me, flooded through me, and my eyes opened. There must have been some special shine in my expression because the woman with the shaved head started shouting at us. "Wishful thinking, you fools! The Germans can never be defeated! Never, never! They are victorious everywhere. They have conquered Europe, and they can conquer the world. You, you Jews, you disgusting maggots, you're already finished. You're done for, the lot of you!" The noise made the poor little boy cry again, but my excitement didn't subside. If the Russians could defeat them, so would I. Suddenly I believed that there was hope – the Russians will defeat the Nazis and they will rescue us from extinction. I was sure I would survive, that I would get out of the cell and see my little boy again. My friend quietly began to recite "Pan Tadeusz" – it's a nineteenth-century patriotic poem that all Polish schoolchildren learned – and we Jewish women all chanted it with her, while the informer kept silent. It seemed to soothe the little boy, and after that we often recited that or other old Polish poems, softly, when the guards were out of earshot.

I must have been there for two weeks when I received a package – one of the cleaners was bribed to bring it to me. In it was a towel, a bar of soap, a bottle of vitamins, and a note in Mira's handwriting. "We are here. There is another woman with us. Eat this." I ate the paper, and soon after, when a guard ordered me out, I gave the package to my friend to use in case I did not return. I was taken into a room; and there was Jerzy. He nodded and smiled at me. "Hello, Irena." Sitting behind a desk was a Gestapo officer who must have been Volksdeutsche because he spoke to me in Polish. He questioned me about myself and then said, "You tell me that you are not Jewish, that you are a Christian – so pray. Go on, pray ... a prayer to the Virgin Mary." I knew the catechism and prayers by heart because of my mother's insistence that I attend Christian religion classes at school. But I was Irena Ponikowska – why should I pray in front of this man? "No, I won't pray before you. If you want me to pray, bring me a priest." Then he questioned me about the Christian ritual, easy questions such as what one does during Holy Mass, when one kneels, and so on. I slipped only once. "Who confirmed you?" he asked. "The priest," I replied. Jerzy interrupted – "She means the priest-bishop" (a Polish expression). The interrogator let it pass.

When he finished his questions, he took my chin and turned my face from side to side, studying it from different angles. "Your mother must have sinned with some Yid because you have a Jewish nose." Finally, he said, "Well, three people have signed the guarantee that you are Aryan to the third generation, and your *Kennkarte* is in order, so I have to release you, as I have no grounds on which to keep you. You are proven to be not Jewish." Irena Ponikowska was now outraged at her false imprisonment. "So give me a document that shows that I have been proven not to be Jewish. I don't want this mistake to happen again." "You're not getting any document. You should just be glad you're being released. All those women in cell 19 are going to be ... deported."

Mira was waiting in an outer room with another woman whom I'd never seen before. She was middle-aged, brown hair tied back in a bun, wearing a dark coat. The four of us left the building together. I couldn't believe I was alive and free. I was drunk, walking on air. I wanted to dance. The other woman nodded at us and walked off in another direction. "Who is she?" I asked. "Don't ask," said Jerzy. "She has helped people before and she will help them again." I never saw her again, this good woman, willing to risk her life for a stranger. Mira took my arm, and the three of us walked away, out of the jaws of the beast.

❧

In 1952, at my own request, I would enter the headquarters of a different political police, also in Warsaw. My documents would be inspected, heavy gates close behind me, and I would be led up stairs and along corridors, until finally a door would be opened. Inside the room Jacek – Jacek Rożański – sitting behind a large desk. He greets me, asks me to take the seat opposite him, offers a cigarette, his manner calm and informal. "So, Stasia, what is your problem?" "It's about the case of Jerzy Sawa." "And why," Jacek would ask, "should this case concern you?"

The Forest

I often think about Jan Pikulski. Always riding his horse, afraid of nothing and of no one. I can see him as he rides up to Albinów – jumping off, leading the horse to the stable. I see him galloping off into the forest to look for the girl's body lying in the grass under the trees ...

If you met Pikulski, you wouldn't at first notice anything exceptional about him. Unprepossessing to look at, unassuming natural manners, easy to live with. I don't recall him ever going to church or observing any religious rituals; he was simply a true Christian. We owed our lives to his courage and intelligence, to his ability to think and behave coolly and quickly in emergency, and to his integrity.

After Jerzy and Mira rescued me from the Gestapo, they decided it was too dangerous for me to stay in Warsaw. They were discussing this and that possibility, until Jerzy suddenly slapped his head. "Jan, Jan Pikulski! Of course, why didn't I think of it before!" Pikulski was a cousin of Jerzy and lived far away in the country. They sent a message to him, and he came to Warsaw and took me with him on a train to Albinów.

Pikulski had a big house, a small farm under cultivation, and a stretch of the forest. The house was five or six kilometres from the village of Iwaniska, in the district of Sandomierz. He had inherited the land from his father, and after his marriage, he and his wife, Pani Zofia, decided to build a guest house on the property to accommodate the tourists who came to walk in the area. He was a land surveyor by profession, and so the local people called him "Pan Engineer Pikulski." ("Pan" and "Pani" were the formal, polite Polish terms of address for a man or a woman of good social standing). Pani Zofia was a bank clerk, and at first they both worked in Warsaw to finance the construction of the house. They were childless, and from 1935 he had been taking care of the property and the inn, while his wife kept her job to help pay for them, coming to visit once a fortnight and at holiday times, until the war, when she was rarely able to visit.

During the war the inn changed its character: now the guests were no longer holidaymakers, and their names were not their own. One of the women, Drzewiecka, was the wife of the famous Chopinist Zbigniew Drzewiecki. Somehow I knew who she was and that she was Jewish. Soon after I got there, my mother and grandmother also arrived. A list had gone out denouncing actors of Jewish origin, including my mother, so the ground was burning under her feet in Warsaw. There was a young woman with multiple sclerosis, who could scarcely walk, and her young son. I cannot remember the name she went by. I'll call her Anna. In a strange irony, she was the only one of us who looked Jewish, although I sensed that she was not; one did not officially "know" that anyone was Jewish. There was also a quiet, uncommunicative young woman called Wanda, friendly with Anna. She would be there for a week or so, much of the time keeping to her room, where Jan Pikulski would go to talk with her for hours. Then she would disappear for a while. The atmosphere was very friendly, but there was little talk among any of us except on day-to-day matters. We didn't ask questions. We weren't supposed to know each other's identity, and at Jan Pikulski's instructions, the others didn't know that my mother, my grandmother, and myself were related. We had to remember to call each other by our official names.

We all had our own rooms, Anna sharing hers with her little boy. Except for mine, they were upstairs, each one painted in and known by its different colour. Mine was tiny, tucked under the stairs, one of what had been two storerooms, with just enough space for a bed and a chair. It had a window looking out at the forest and a pleasant aroma of apples, a reminder of its previous contents.

We ate together in the dining room, around the big table, which could easily seat twelve people. Two peasant women who lived nearby came in to cook and clean, but they didn't know who we were. I too was an employee: my job was as a nurse for Pan Pikulski's father-in-law, an old gentleman who was semi-paralyzed, mostly confined to bed, and who occupied a large downstairs room. I wore a white uniform and spent much of my time looking after

Grandmother Franciszka Schwartz (undated)

him: I fed him, kept him clean, took him to the bathroom, read to him. This gave my presence additional legitimacy.

Albinów was virtually self-sustaining. The peasant women baked bread in the big kitchen ovens, and the farm produced vegetables; there were fruit trees, pigs, a milking cow, and of course Pan Pikulski's beloved horses. Nobody paid to stay there, absolutely not. He would not take any money. When he got our rations of sugar, ersatz coffee, and so on, he insisted on weighing it out in front of us so that everyone would know they were getting their share, and then everyone – except me, because I was an employee – repaid him for what it had cost.

Every Sunday I went to mass at the little church in Iwaniska village. Sometimes my mother came, and sometimes Wanda, when she wasn't away. We walked or we went in the horse and cart. My grandmother didn't bother. A reserved, rather cold woman to whom I was never close, she looked like an old Polish aristocrat with her blue eyes and white hair. At church I was never nervous or fearful when people chatted with me; everyone knew me as the nurse looking after Pan Engineer Pikulski's crippled father-in-law. I didn't consciously have to play a role. I knew how to conduct myself in church, the order of service, when to stand, when to kneel; I

Jan Pikulski with his horses, Albinów, 1943

knew the prayers and I took Holy Communion. The only thing I did not do was to go to confession. The priest never preached about issues relevant to the times, nothing on the wider moral questions that might confront people. He said nothing about doing no harm to others, about not persecuting other people; not a word about the occupation and the terrible times we were living through. He spoke only of trivial matters. Perhaps he was frightened.

Albinów was surrounded by trees, part of a forest extending for miles over gently undulating land. Tall trees with massive trunks – birch, beech, oak, and pine. It was only later that I could see how pleasant it was there, became aware of the sweet air, the birds, the sharp scent of the pine, of how the wildflowers pushed up through the fallen needles and the carpet of leaves. Stefan Żeromski, one of Poland's favourite poets, wrote, "We were not here, the forest was here; / We will not be here, the forest will be here."

Different kinds of people were hiding out there in the woods or using them for cover when it suited them. It was said that the Germans were afraid to enter the forest, knowing that it sheltered armed partisans. But the forest knew them all – different partisan groups from the extreme right to the extreme left, who sometimes fought each other. Most of them were a nationalist partisan group called Jędrusie, named from the initials of its leaders, two brothers who operated like independent warlords. From time to time they came to the house, usually for food, and Pan Pikulski always obliged them. It was not only the Germans that Pikulski had to protect us from: some of the partisans were supporters of the Endeks, the violently anti-Semitic fascist party who had persecuted us in university. He warned us about them and that they might come to the house.

The group of partisans arrived just before dinner time, and Pan Pikulski invited them to join us. There were six or seven of them, all young, the oldest no more than about twenty-three. It must have been summer because they were not wearing coats and there was no fire going. They were clean and well shaven for people living in the forest. So there we all were, sitting around the long dinner table. The important thing was not to slip up, to call my mother Pani Stefania, the name on her *Kennkarte*. The young men were at ease and talked about their life in the forest. Then the subject came up that we dreaded hearing. They began to boast and laugh about having chanced upon a Jew hiding in the forest. They joked about his ragged appearance, his fear, and his denial that he was a Jew, "though we immediately knew he was." "You should have seen how frightened he was," said one of them, smiling broadly. "We forced him to admit it. We made him pull down his trousers. We agree with the Germans on only one thing – killing Jews."

Writing this, I can still feel the sensation of panic, the clenching of my hands under the table, the effort not to react inappropriately. "They are real lice on the body of our people and one has to get rid of them whenever and where you can," says another. "You should have seen him begging for his life before we finished him off." They all laughed. None of us responded; none of us could let the expression on our face change. Was it not a moment of shame? Wouldn't it have been better if we Jewish women had expressed our disgust and then been killed like the innocent man they had just "finished off" out there in the forest? But none of us were heroes. I was young, I wanted to live. We all wanted to preserve our own skins, against the odds. The only cause we were fighting for was our own lives. Was it worth the trouble?

Death was all around, and it was no crime to kill a Jew. We were not considered to be human beings. We were hiding, running away like animals, like vermin with no right to life.

❦

Professor H.'s only child, his daughter, Krystyna, had been sent to a village to live under false identity with an old peasant woman, and she had been told never, never to tell anyone that she was a Jew. She was a lovely-looking girl, with long blonde hair, and she had bitterly resented our affaire. Before the war, although she was so young, she had already begun to establish a reputation as a promising poet. In the village, now aged nineteen, she fell in love with a local boy, and one day she confided in him that she was Jewish. The next day he asked her to go for a walk in the forest with him and some of his friends. When she failed to return, the old woman went looking for her. It is possible that the boys told her where to find Krystyna. What the old woman found was her body – she had been stoned to death.

❦

A short cut from Albinów to Iwaniska ran about a kilometre through the forest. There was little undergrowth, and the trees, although high, were not dense, so I wasn't afraid of walking through it on my own in the daytime. I went into the village infrequently, for fear of trouble or the chance, however faint, of recognition by someone from Warsaw. But that day I had a bad toothache, and I was in such pain that I had to go to the dentist to get the tooth removed. The weather was warm and humid. It happened on my way back through the trees.

She was lying there on her back by the path, black hair against the sodden leaves, her eyes closed, her chalk-white, sweet young face looking up at the canopy of trees, naked except for black stockings and black garter belt. Her killer – was he hidden, watching me from the deep shadows of the forest? Terrified, I ran, expecting footsteps and crashing branches behind me, hands grabbing at me, a blow on my head. I ran, thoughts flying through my mind. Who was she? Had she been raped? Who had killed her? Why? Running, knowing the folly of my thoughts, for this was a time when killing people was commonplace, when no reason was required and there was no punishment. But I was overwhelmed with horror, and my mind flew with my feet.

Pikulski was home when I ran into the yard, shaking and barely coherent. He saddled his horse and galloped back into the forest. But the girl's body had disappeared. So, yes, the murderer must have been hiding, watching me, when I came upon her.

To this day, every time I am alone in a wooded area, when the air touches my skin in a certain way, when the trees are of a certain height, the undergrowth and canopy in some way familiar, I see her, and I keep looking over my shoulder expecting a blow on the back of my head, and I fight the instinct to run away.

I saw them from the little window in my room. They were coming out of the forest in the dawn light – five ss soldiers with German shepherd dogs straining at their leashes. Drzewiecka, the pianist's wife, was with them, a bunch of lilies of the valley in her hand, a basket of wild mushrooms over her arm. They burst in the front door like madmen. I thought it was the end, my last minute. They went from room to room, obviously looking for one person in particular, apparently surprised to see so many people. In fact, the person they were after was Mrs Krause. She was an unusually beautiful, dark-haired young woman, obviously Jewish, who had arrived not long before. Then they looked at the rest of us, deciding who else to take with them. I had said I was the old gentleman's nurse, but they noticed that my brown hair was growing out at the roots – there had been nothing there I could bleach it with. They did not bother with Wanda or my grandmother, and when they came across Drzewiecka in the forest, she had said that she was Pani Pikulski, which they didn't question. They told Mrs Krause and Anna, who was so Jewish-looking, my mother, and me to come with them.

There was something almost inhumanly inflexible about German soldiers. You could almost smell the drill and discipline they'd been trained in. Their faces almost motionless, their eyes expressionless. Their steps were stiff, well measured. They were always in control. They seemed so devoid of any normal human feeling that it was difficult to imagine that these creatures most likely had their own families, children whom they missed.

They sent for two carts from Iwaniska and told us to get in, and we rode off towards the village. It must have been a warm day redolent with the aromas of the trees and fields around us, but I noticed nothing; my senses were numb. They had separated us from each other, sitting betwen us. My mother had followed me into the same cart. She was coolly playing her role as the sophisticated Polish lady, in complete control of herself, speaking to them when necessary in excellent German – which would be considered normal. A nurse, however, would not be expected to speak it, and I knew that I must show no knowledge of the language because the Nazis thought that all Jews could understand it, Yiddish being similar. Of course, I couldn't speak Yiddish, but I did understand German, having learned it as a child from Babcia Sara and then at boarding school. They kept on trying to trick me into reacting, but after a while one of them, an officer, said, "She's not lying. She probably doesn't understand." Sitting close beside me, he was deliberately knocking his leg against mine. "But anyway, why don't we have fun with her? She's a looker ... I wouldn't say she's diseased." "She might still be a virgin," said another. "Do you have any experience with virgins?" "No," laughed the officer. "Hey, I bet the captain will want her for himself." My mother's face was bloodless and I was near panic, but I did not react. Then my mother said casually, "It was good that you sent for the carts. Fraulein Irena is lame. She would have had difficulty walking all the way." I understood what she was trying to do. Nazis did not like physical imperfections.

Nothing happened by the time we arrived in the village. Anna and Mrs Krause were taken to another building, and my mother and I were put into a barn and given some potatoes to peel. On my way in, I put on a conspicuous limp. We were alone with two guards at the door. Under her breath my mother asked me if I had my diary on me, and I did – I had been keeping one, on and off, since I was with Zenia. "You've got to get rid of it. Ask if you can go to the toilet ... Flush it down." They let me go, one accompanying me. When I returned, two officers, one of whom had been on the cart, came in. The other one said to him, "Yes, I'd like her to do my bed for me." Then he took my arm. "Can you do my bed for me?" I stared at him blankly, pretending not to understand what he was saying. He went out and returned with a translator, who repeated the question. "I don't think I could," I replied. "I have never, never made it before." He translated back to the officer, who said, "Ach, she's probably a virgin. I don't like the idea." But through the translator, he said to me, "You must make a bed for me because I'm tired and want to have a rest." Rigid with terror, I went with him. But that was all I had to do – make the bed. He didn't touch me and I was allowed to return to the barn. Before I went, I'd caught a glimpse of my mother's face. I thought she was going to faint. She was sure that I was going to be killed, that he would use me, then shoot me, because it was *Rassenschande*, race shame, for a Nazi to have sex with a Jewish woman.

It was evening when we saw Jan Pikulski riding past the entrance to the barn. In a few minutes he returned with the officer. We were being allowed to go, Pikulski told us. Anna was already on the cart, but not Mrs Krause. The Germans hadn't given us back our documents, but he told us not to worry. "There's been a delay in checking them," said Pikulski. "The telephones are out of order. They've been sent to Opatów [the nearest town] for verification. They'll bring them back to us." We asked about Pani Krause. "She's all right." From his tone, we knew to ask him nothing further. The next morning, Anna and her little boy had disappeared. And Mrs Krause did not return.

A couple of days later Pikulski told us that the Germans were coming to Albinów with our documents and that he wanted me to keep out of the way while they were there. He said that I should immediately go to the loft above the stables of the old woman servant who worked for him. It was about half a kilometre from the house. Hours passed and night fell. Little animals rustled and scrabbled in the straw. Straining my ears for footsteps, suddenly I heard bursts of shooting in the distance. Too frightened to go back to the house and of what I would find there, I fell into utter despair, convinced that the Nazis had killed everyone. And then I heard a horse's hooves approaching. The rider dismounted and came into the barn. "It's me. It's Pikulski," called the voice.

What had happened was that when the Germans arrived, they asked where I was and were given the story that I'd gone to visit a friend in another village. Pikulski acted the host, offering them something to drink. They relaxed, asked my mother to play the piano for them, and stayed for a few hours. It was dark when they finally left, and they wanted Pikulski to accompany them back to Iwaniska – they were frightened of being attacked by the partisans – so he went with them, riding by the side of their car. As they drove, they fired off their revolvers into the forest in drunken high spirits or bravado. That was the shooting I'd heard.

It was only after the war that I learned a few other things. Beautiful Mrs Krause had been at Albinów under her own identity as the wife of a local Polish physician, and somebody must have betrayed her whereabouts to the Germans. The moment we were taken away in the carts to Iwaniska, Pikulski, buying time, rode off to tell the partisans to cut the telephones from Iwaniska to Opatów, where the Germans had their headquarters. He sent one of the neighbouring peasants to Iwaniska, where the man told the Germans that he knew the ladies were Christians because either he drove them to church on Sunday in a cart or they walked. In the meantime, Pikulski himself rode on to Opatów, where Dr Krause worked in a hospital, to warn him, and Dr Krause went to the Germans in Iwaniska and gave them a bribe big enough to free his wife. She was then taken elsewhere to be hidden and survived the war. Anna was the wife of one of the leaders of the Jędrusie partisans. Her identity card was forged, so when we returned to Albinów, she and the child were immediately removed to another place. Wanda was a Jędrusie courier, Albinów was one of their headquarters, and Pikulski its main supplier and organizer.

We were so isolated at Albinów, so cut off from the world, and there was no radio – or none that I knew of – so we had little idea of the progress of the war. We read only the occasional clandestine news bulletin, and we heard rumours that the Russians were pushing the Germans back through Poland. There had been no sound of gunfire or artillery when one day, towards the end of August 1944, suddenly, out of the blue, a Russian unit arrived at the house. My joy was indescribable. I kissed every one of them. I loved every one of them. They were my liberators, my saviours. With their songs and their music, they were different from any soldiers I had ever seen, and I will never forget them.

A group of officers and their orderlies were stationed with us, camping outside the house. We gave them a royal welcome, food and drink. Looking at them, talking with them, one couldn't imagine what ordeals they had been through. None of the officers who came into the house was dirty or unshaven; they were all neat and good-looking. Some of them had windup gramophones and records. They had them going constantly, and several of the men played the *garmoshka*, or harmonium. They sang about the war, about their homes and country, about their girlfriends, whom they begged to wait for them and whose love, if strong enough, would enable them to return home unharmed – nostalgic, beautiful songs that we learned to sing with them. They had their own cook, provisions, and vodka, and they invited us to share everything with them. Usually they just wanted to eat outside, under the trees, but sometimes the officers agreed to join us at the long table in the dining room, and we partied into the night, drinking, singing, dancing. They would never talk about the war with us; they only wanted to talk about love. And also to make love. One of them was so handsome – like a young Slavic god – that I wanted to make love with him, but the others got jealous and would never leave us alone. It was funny because, if we went for a walk in the forest, we always had company and even someone along with us playing the *garmoshka*. But I loved them all.

The Russian soldier is exactly the opposite of everything the German soldier seemed to stand for. He is friendly, not worried about the externals of discipline and drill. He is crazy about enjoying every minute of life. He is one of our own and could easily be one's own husband or son. I can understand why the Polish people see them differently, but it can never change my feelings. For me, the Russian soldiers were salvation. They liberated me from the crime punishable by death – of being a Jew. They freed me from the years of horror, shame, degradation, humiliation and, however I had supressed it, from the constant stress of fear. It really was a return to life, an awakening from an endless nightmare. I began to breathe and smell the sweet freshness of the air, feel its warmth on my skin, hear the birdsong, see the forest in its beauty.

The first group stayed only two or three days because the front was moving and they were still in the middle of fighting. A few days later another group arrived, and it was the same with them. By then I had decided that I wanted to go and help in the war. Although I had no papers, I had finished medical school and I had had experience. I wanted to give something, do something, contribute. I approached the commanding officer – a small Uzbek, who kept trying to get into my bed – and told him that I was a doctor, making up some story that I was hiding at Albinów because of my political activities, and that I wanted to join the army. But I did not tell him that I was a Jew. I had kept the cross, which I wore around my neck, and from their talk, I understood that some of them didn't like Jews too much. "Of course, you can help," he answered. "I have to send an orderly back to Lublin early tomorrow morning and you can go with him." Until the last moment I did not tell my mother or Pikulski what I was going to do. They were shocked, particularly my mother. "You can't possibly go. How can you go off with these men, all by yourself! Are you crazy?" But I was determined. "I'm going, so don't try to make me change my mind." I took virtually nothing with me because I had nothing to take. I just got into the Jeep and went into the unknown.

In the late 1980s a Polish television program was made about Albinów and the Pikulskis and what they had done during the war. An actress read out the words that I had written in the visitors' book on the 7th of February 1957, when I last saw them, a few days before I left Poland: "Thirteen years have passed since the horrible nightmare of the Hitler occupation, thirteen years since the time when there were people here in Albinów who had been rescued from death. Their human dignity was restored here, their right to life, to the sun and to simple human happiness. Dear friends, I will always remember your love. I do not have the words to express everything that fills my heart. Albinów and you – that is my Poland, my real homeland. Dr Stanisława Ałapin Rubiłowicz (Irena Ponikowska)."

The Liberators

In the night I sometimes wake feeling as though I am suffocating. A strong odour and taste like formaldehyde has invaded my nose, mouth, and throat. The camp is permeated with the smell. I start coughing and coughing, everybody looking at me ...

―❦―

The day after I left Albinów, I abandoned the identity of Irena Ponikowska, the dead Catholic girl who had been resurrected to give me life. It had been a long drive from Albinów to Lublin, another part of Poland behind the Soviet lines. We got there in the evening, and the driver warned me that he had business to do and wouldn't be able to wait. He had asked me where I wanted to go, but I didn't know because I'd never been to Lublin before and knew nobody. We drove to a main street, and I was standing by the jeep, wondering what to do, when a man passing by stopped and asked me what I was looking for. I explained that I had just come from a village to enlist in the army, that I was a doctor and had nowhere to stay, and I asked if he could suggest some place. He thought for a moment and then said, "Come with me, Pani Doctor. You can come to my home. It's small and my wife is pregnant, but we'll find room for you." So I said goodbye to my companions and went off with him. This man, a simple, poor Polish worker, took me, a stranger, to his home. He and his wife had only a kitchen and one room with their bed, a big table, and a sofa, on which I slept – nothing more. Although I told them that I had no money, they insisted that I stay with them until I was mobilized into the army. The next day I went to the induction centre and was immediately accepted. People were being recruited into the Polish army that had been formed under Russian command, and physicians were needed. I had no documents, but they took my word. It was at this moment that I went back to my real name. I was allocated to the job of examining

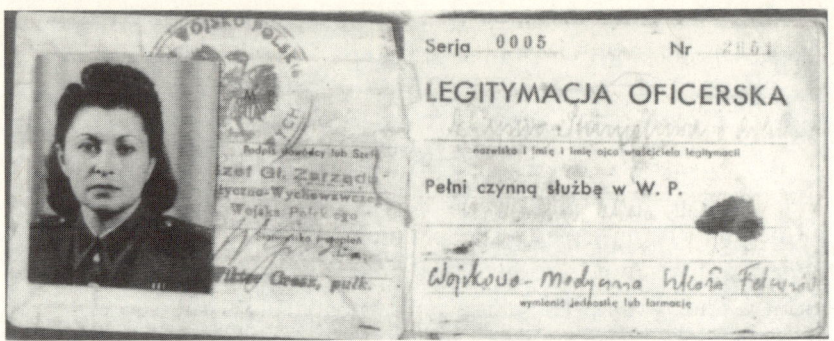

Stasia's identity document as an army officer

recruits, but this was not what I wanted. I insisted that I wanted to go to the front, arguing with them until the commanding officer finally said, "Please be quiet. First of all, you're a woman, and secondly, we need you here, now." They gave me a uniform, and when I went back to my friends, I was already First Lieutenant Stanisława Ałapin.

They were such a nice young couple. They asked no questions; their attitude was that here was a soldier-to-be and then a soldier, whom they had to help go through this period until she found her place. The strange thing is that later, when I went back to Lublin, I wanted to visit them to thank them, to compensate them for having maintained me, and I wanted to see the baby, but I forgot the name of the street. Or did I not really want to find them? Was it perhaps that, as with the old lady in Warsaw, I subconsciously did not want them to know that they had brought a Jew into their home?

For the next few weeks I examined recruits, and we dealt with minor ambulatory injuries. I used to laugh at the Russian nurse who worked with me because she had only one remedy, iodine, which she put on everyone. Every day I told my commanding officer that I didn't want to stay there, that I wanted to go to the front. "I want revenge," I'd say to him. "They've killed my family and I want to kill one of them. Even just one." And he'd say to me, "Stasia, Stasia. Please be quiet and get on with your work." Nevertheless, after a few weeks, they did send me to a fighting regiment, though it was always with a field hospital, far away from the front line. But I had problems dealing with wounded German soldiers. I was pulled in two directions – I wanted to poison them, and, at the same time, I

Stasia in the army in Lublin in late 1944 or 1945, with another physician and an "admirer"

wanted to help them. We – my boss, the other physicians, the orderlies – we used to discuss how we felt, but we all came to the same conclusion: we must help; it cannot be otherwise. In truth, never in my life did I betray my profession.

As an officer, I was required to carry a gun. This was quite funny because, although after a while I realized that I could never use it on anyone, I always had to carry it on me, and we were ordered to defend our guns if necessary. So, on the one hand, I knew that I wouldn't use it, and on the other, I knew that if I lost it, I would be court-martialled, so I was always worrying about how to defend it if I had to. There was a rightist opposition to the communists who were taking power as the Germans were being pushed back west, and these rightists wanted guns. I heard of several occasions on which they had disarmed officers, who then got into trouble. What I did was to hide it in my purse so that no one would know I had one and try to take it from me.

I had taken back my name, but nobody knew that I was Jewish, not until I was sent as a physician to the special unit for training political officers for the Polish People's Army. This was the army that was formed in the Soviet Union under General Berling, from Poles who had managed to flee east from the Nazis and who had not left the Soviet Union earlier for the Middle East with General Anders's army to fight under the western allies. Ours was the Polish army under communist control, the military arm of the new post-war government, the future establishment. The unit was called the Polish Army School of Political Education Officers. It was near Lublin and not far from Majdanek – yes, Majdanek.

I think that the months I spent with that unit were really the only time in my life when I have had no sense of alienation, of otherness. I felt completely at ease with the people I was with there and with the ideology. A communist army had been my liberator and had ended my ordeal; communist theory was opposed to racism, bigotry, and injustice. And now, here at the camp, I felt as though I were at last among my own. The talk and the approach was idealistic – of human rights and equality, of achieving a truly socialistic society – and everyone believed that this was the future they would create. They were mostly young men. Some of them had been with the communist partisans or the underground fighters; others had escaped to the Soviet Union. And one of the professors was a veteran of the Spanish Civil War. So they'd had these ideals and this ideology for years. They'd fought for them, and now the dream was about to come to reality, here in their own country. There was no sense of oppression, secretiveness, or fear. Were some of them spying on the others? If they were, I wasn't aware of it. Nor did I think about it. I shared the ideas and the ideology, and I was enthusiastic.

Jacek Rożański – the communist student I knew before the war – wasn't there. It was a few years later that I met him again.

⌘

On 17 January 1945 the Soviet army finally entered Warsaw. It had waited a long time on the opposite bank of the Vistuala – why, I did not speculate. We knew there had been an uprising and that the Germans had exacted ferocious reprisals before they retreated, destroying the city and driving out the surviving inhabitants, deporting them towards Germany.

That night there was a party in my room for my birthday. Everyone was jubilant, drinking and singing, and someone was playing a *garmoshka*. But I was tense and agitated. I couldn't join in the fun. That morning in the newspaper I'd read that some of the convents had been evacuated by the Germans, but it didn't say to where or to what. We'd also heard rumours that they were destroying all the convents and monasteries with everyone in them. Piotrovsky, my Russian general, was a kind, sensitive man. He was short and fair-haired, with small brown eyes and a little snub nose. He was infatuated with me, but for me he was just a nice man. "What's the matter, Stasia? Why are you looking so depressed?" he asked me. "It's my little boy, my Piotr. I don't know whether he's alive or dead." I told him where Peter had been left and the circumstances. He understood and asked no more questions. "You'll go tomorrow. In my jeep, with my orderly." He was a good man.

General Piotrovsky saw us off in the morning – the driver, the orderly, and myself. He gave me his own winter army hat, which covered all of my head except for the eyes, and I had my heavy military coat and *walonki*, the long felt army boots. It was two hundred kilometres to Warsaw and bitterly cold in the open vehicle, but though the poor men kept complaining, looking in vain along the road for a place to stop for a hot drink, I really didn't mind the cold because the only thing on my mind was whether I would find Peter. My trepidation grew when, just before twilight, we drove into the ghost city. It was only hours since the Germans had abandoned it. Most of the buildings were reduced to rubble or had gaping, open wounds exposing remnants of human presence – rooms with furniture hanging out at crazy angles, suspended in space; walls with a painting or a crucifix still attached. Nobody was on the streets – not a sign of life except for the occasional military patrol. How could Peter be alive? The men wanted to look around and take photographs, but I wouldn't let them delay.

Darkness was falling as we reached Milanówek, only about twenty-five kilometres from the city. My heart seemed to stand still. The street with the convent was standing. All looking quiet, undisturbed. I rang the bell. A nun came to the door, obviously frightened at the sight of men in Russian uniforms and me with my face obscured by a Russian hat. I told her who I was, and we waited in the covered entry while she went for the mother superior. "Peter is here," said the mother superior, in response to my urgent question. "And he is well." I don't know if they believed that I was his

Peter with a Russian soldier at the Polish Army School for Political Education Officers, Majdanek, 1945

mother or whether they were so afraid of the uniforms that they dared not protest. One of them went to get him. And now he is standing in front of me, my little boy, this skinny little fellow, his big dark eyes looking at me as though he has been waiting a long, long time for this to happen. "Mummy, it's you, it's you ... I recognize your voice. It's you." And he is in my arms. He had not seen me for at least two years and never in army uniform. "Please take me with you. I want to go with you. Please take me." I'll never forget this moment, the happiest in my life. I decided to take him with me and deal with the consequences later.

The good, dear nuns, concerned because he had no shoes, insisted on giving me a thick blanket to cover him, and all the long journey back, I held him in my arms, his feet tucked into my coat, kept warm against my body. The streets and highway were dark, and at one point the driver lost his way. The bitter cold intensified, but Peter never complained; he was getting the warmth of my heart. My joy was the only emotion in the world.

When we arrived in the dawn, General Piotrovsky came out, in his hands a bag of mandarin oranges for Peter. He had anticipated what I would do if I found my son and did not reprimand me at all. The oranges were the first that Peter had seen, and he ate them with fascinated delight – he still remembers them.

So Peter stayed with me in my unit. I was given my own orderly, Romek, and when I was working at the medical office, he looked after Peter, keeping the wood stove going and entertaining Peter with stories and fairy tales. But really he was looked after by everyone; they all spoilt him. He was given the best food, and the quartermaster had a miniature army uniform and a pair of boots made for him out of two odd soldiers' boots. I managed to buy him a little coat of white rabbit fur, and when he was running, he looked like a big snowball. Everyone knew him and everyone looked after him. He made friends with them all and had a great time, spending his days either with Romek in my room or playing with the soldiers when they were not busy. Some of them were Jewish, though that made no difference there. So few Jewish children had survived, so very few, that he must have been precious to them, merely for being alive. He was everybody's child.

The Majdanek death camp. This is as difficult for me to write about now as it was difficult for me to go there then. I had known about it as well as someone not there in the killing time could "know," but I did not want to see the evidence. I had heard that the camp was put into action at the end of 1940 for Soviet prisoners, most of whom were murdered. And I had heard that in the autumn of 1942 the gas chambers were constructed and that it became the second largest extermination camp after Auschwitz-Birkenau. The Nazis had started to close it down in April 1944 as the Soviet advance grew closer, but they did not have time to destroy the evidence, leaving it there for the world to see. After the Jews, the Poles were the second largest group to be killed there. No one knows how many Jews perished there, some sources estimate 200,000, others 1,500,000. They didn't keep lists of those brought to be murdered immediately.

It must have been the spring of 1945, soon after the end of the war, when I finally decided to go there. Some of the Jewish officers in the unit, especially Major Kermish, the historian (who later worked in Israel at Yad Vashem, the institute documenting Nazi crimes), persuaded me to go. But I resisted for a long time. Maybe the reason was connected with my awareness of my over-strong visual memory. I may have been unconsciously frightened that whatever I would see, together with my equally strong imagination, might leave its imprint on my mind and soul for the rest of my life. Which is exactly what happened.

I went there alone. It was a lovely cloudless day, and I was aware of the birdsong as I walked the mile or so along the road through the trees. Then on my left the general enclosure of a seemingly endless camp came into sight ...

I was in a huge, flat, treeless open space, with row after row of wooden barracks and, in the distance, a few other buildings. As I walked towards the first line of barracks, I could see some people and a man apparently explaining something to them. I joined the little group, and we entered one of the buildings.

A heavy, rank, windowless gloom lit by tiny skylights. Row after row of wide bunks rising from the dirt floor. "In here there are 250 bunks," the man is saying. "Sometimes as many as a thousand prisoners slept here ..." I hear no more of his words. I feel as though I am suffocating. Inside the building and outside, a strong odour and taste like formaldehyde invades my nose, mouth, and throat. The same smell that used to make me feel so sick in the dissecting room when I was a student. The camp is permeated with the smell. I start coughing and coughing. Everybody is looking at me.

He leads us to a gas chamber. There are seven of them, with thick metal doors. On some an inscription "Bad und Desinfektion" (bath and disinfection). "This one has the capacity of one thousand, the small ones over there only one hundred. The mass gassing reached its peak between May and July 1943." I am overwhelmed with nausea; it was here that they were brought or to Treblinka from the Warsaw ghetto to be disposed of. Are my family's ashes here, in those chimneys? Are their cries in the air that I am now breathing?

"Come!" he says and leads us to the "storehouses." "In this grinding machine, human bones were broken down for use as fertilizer." He points to discarded cans of Zyklon-B, the gas, and takes us over to a huge heap of something. It is human shoes, all sizes, all colours, every possible style. And then, with them but to the side, children's shoes. I see thousands and thousands of little Peters killed mercilessly, never to grow up, never to be seen again, the image so monstrous that I began to cry and to scream, completely losing control of myself.

Our guide – who was he? a former inmate? – puts his arm around my shoulder. He says – it seems, very calmly – "Come with me my child. I feel like showing you something else." For ten or perhaps twenty minutes we walk in silence until we reach a forest where fresh, young leaves whisper on the trees. "Before the gas chambers were built," he says, "the victims were shot down here by mass gunfire. The soil of this forest is soaked in human blood." I am in this forest of martyrdom and horror. Above my head and all around me, brushing against me, are leaves – leaves enriched and thriving on human blood. And I have survived. By what right do I live when they are dead? By what right do I live? By what right?

Grisha

This is what I wrote in 1988, a few days after returning to my home in this quiet Canadian city from my journey to the Soviet Union.

In the days that have passed since I came back, I have constantly had a strange sense of you being beside me, of you being very close to me. Russia has never been my home. Nor, Grisha, did you and I ever have a home together anywhere. Yet during those two weeks I have just spent there, I had the feeling that I had finally come home to you. Everything seemed beautiful, and all the difficulties I observed could not alter this. People were standing in long lines for food and for clothing, unable to buy vegetables or fruit, their children poorly dressed, with scarcely any toys, and they were still sharing their kitchens with their neighbours. Even in my tour group's huge Intourist hotel, there were shortages. Everyone else in our group complained, but for me the only discomfort was exhaustion, because I could not sleep. Everything was so lovely again after all these years. I felt that you were there and so close to me, so how could I sleep? It was too much for me, but I would not have missed it for all the world.

In Leningrad, when the tour group left the Hermitage, I stayed behind. I wanted to look at the Picassos, alone yet arm in arm with

Peter and Stasia in Łódź in 1945 or 1946

you. Nobody else but the two of us, as we used to be, reading the poetry of Mayakovsky or Ehrenburg's newspaper articles. As we used to be, only the two of us, when we went to the theatre, to concerts, the very first that we were able to go to after the war. So long ago. And yesterday.

Early that summer after the war ended, I had been ordered to leave the Political Education Officers' school and go to the School for Paramedical Officers in Łódź to teach physiology. Peter and I travelled there in a war-battered train, plywood covering its glassless windows. Under my army coat, Peter was pretending to sleep, but as soon as one of the officers travelling with me began trying to charm me, his eyes opened, and the little devil said with great seriousness, "Please don't try to seduce my mother. She's already thirty!"

Stasia in October 1946

During the war Łódź had been administratively absorbed into the Reich, and it was physically impossible for me to get one of the apartments abandoned by the Germans. One had literally to fight one's way into the doorway and then have someone stand guard while one fetched one's possessions and got a new lock for the door. The situation was imposssible, so until I could find a place, I put Peter into a convent outside the city. The Russian colonel in charge of the unit was a kind man, and when he heard about my situation, he called me in to see him. "Stasia, are you going to have your son brought up in a cloister? You have to get him out. Look, I'll arrange to find a flat for you." He said that he would station a soldier in front of it until I could move in, the only condition was that "you take your child from the nuns." Of course I agreed. "I'll get you the flat," he said, "but first I think you are badly in need of some rest. I see from your records that you haven't had any leave." He made out a special pass to an army rest house in Krynica, a resort in the Tatra Mountains, fashionable before the war. Giving me one of his

Peter in Łódź in 1946

fatherly smiles, which in this instance seemed to imply "This young woman needs some entertainment," he added, "By the way, a very close friend of mine is there on vacation right now – Grisha* Malinovsky. You'd do me a favour if you would track him down and greet him personally from me. He's an extremely nice man, and he's also a physician. Tell him I wish we were still working together. Don't forget ... Now go and enjoy yourself."

It was a lovely summer. The weather in the mountains was perfect, the air sweet and fresh, scented with pine needles. The army guest house was a requisitioned pre-war hotel, clean and simple. I shared a small room with a good-natured younger woman whose main purpose was to find herself a man, and when I mentioned that I'd promised my colonel to look for his friend, this Dr Malinovsky, she insisted that we act immediately. So off we went. And it was there in Krynica that I found him.

---

* Malinovsky's first name was actually Bolesław or Bolek, the same as Stasia's first husband. It has been changed to avoid confusion.

Stasia and "Grisha" Malinovsky in Krynica in 1946

You were standing by the swimming pool when someone pointed you out to me. You looked rather odd because you weren't wearing a proper swimsuit but some strange white pants. Rather hesitantly, I went up to you, and as I introduced myself and delivered the message, I looked at, in, your eyes. For me it happened at that moment, and from then on I was constantly watching you, waiting for some small sign of interest on your part. But you were a very reserved man, not casual, not the type easily to start a relationship with a woman. I managed to invite you and your friend to share our table in the dining room. "One step at a time," I'd say to myself. After a couple of days of this, your friend suggested that the four of us go for a walk in the mountains, and from then it was just the two of us, although it was not an easy conquest. It was the beginning of the love affair of my life – in fact, my only real love. I thought so then, and I still think so today, forty-three years after I last held you to me. My one true, bittersweet love.

I never asked you any personal questions. Whatever you told me seemed to be enough. Nothing else was needed. You told me that you had a wife and that you did not love her – of course, how could you, because you loved me? That she was Jewish, not in good

Stasia and "Grisha" Malinovsky in Krynica in 1946

health, and that she had a child, but it was not your child. You said you could not abandon her. Over the months to come, you slowly told me things, but I never asked any questions, and I never really learned anything about your background. The world had stopped and everything was now.

"I don't want to get too closely involved with you," you said that night in the hotel room in Kraków on your way back to rejoin your unit, "because I know the day will come when we'll have to part." I put my hand over your mouth. "Don't think about parting," I told you. "Forget about it. I don't want to know about tomorrow." "I can't forget," you replied. "I already love you so much I'm afraid of losing you, and I know we will have to." But I wouldn't let you talk about it any more.

We travelled to meet each other whenever we could, and maybe it was because we were not constantly together that it went so well. We read a lot of poetry together, Mayakovsky in particular. "Was Mayakovsky a communist?" I once asked you. "Yes, that's why he killed himself!" A strange comment I thought at the time, though you knew better. Once, when we'd been to a Rachmaninov recital, you asked me, "How is it that we both like the same things – the same poetry, the same paintings, the same music? We even like the same food." "Because we were made for each other," I answered. Do you remember the night we went to see my mother playing the leading role at the theatre in Łódź? I introduced you to her afterwards, and you took to each other. When we left her, you told me how amazingly similar we looked. "That's not true," I objected. "She once said that she didn't know how an ugly child like me could be her daughter." And you laughed and laughed, which was something you seldom did. You were usually serious, often lost in your thoughts.

Yes, it was a strong passion. You understood me well, and all the potential was there for our love to take root and last. I became more inextricably involved, and I think so did you. One day you told me that you wished you could stay and not return to "the abyss," but that you knew it was impossible. The idea came to me that we should escape together to the United States. The borders were still not tight, and many people were getting out of Poland. We were both doctors and still young enough to make a new life. When we next met – and this was months before they took you away from me – you asked, "What are we going to do?" And I suggested my plan to you. "But you have a child," you said, and I answered, "We'll take Peter and start a new life together." You pressed your knuckles against your forehead and after a pause replied, "You're living in a fantasy world. Do you think I'd go back to that godforsaken country if I had the choice?" Then you reached a hand over to me, clasped my wrist, and looked at me almost fiercely. "You have to understand – it can't be. It cannot be. I'm in the army and they know about every step I take. Stalin has long arms, and I would end in front of a firing squad."

You would not agree to try to escape, to go away, but I could see no limits. I would have done anything, gone anywhere with you, even to that "dump in the Urals" where you lived, if you had said, "Come with me. I'll divorce my wife, but we'll have to live there." We never talked about it again. There was so little time together, and all we really wanted was to close our eyes and forget the whole crazy world around us. Sometimes now I wonder whether you loved me or if you simply needed a woman. I cannot know, but from the way you made love to me, the way you spoke to me the way you used to look at me, and how you were every moment we were together, I always felt loved. Perhaps it was all make-believe.

When it happened, it was unexpected, a tremendous shock, an agonizing blow whose force I can sometimes still feel. One morning after you had been with me in Łódź, you were leaving in a rush to catch your train. We'd had a most wonderful night of love, but I had a cold and you didn't want me to go to the door with you for our last kiss. My last image of you was as you turned back from the door because you'd forgotten your revolver on the top of the closet. At that moment did you know that we would never see each other again? After a while, when I heard nothing from you, I started to telephone, but there was no answer. And then I called your friend, a Jewish doctor. "What do you mean, Stasia! Don't you know?" he asked. "Grisha's already back in Russia. They found out that he was having a very close relationship with a Polish woman, and they were afraid he'd defect. Anyway, they sent him back." I was crying and asking "Why didn't he tell me?" The friend told me to wait, that he would come and tell me all he knew. Later he told me that the night before you left, you paced up and down his room until dawn. "Grisha said that he could not bear to call you, that it was like cutting off his own hand. He felt terrible that he couldn't tell you, but he didn't know how to do it, how to say it. He felt as though he were being torn apart."

I never heard from you again, though I did get hold of your address and write. After the third letter there was an answer – from your wife. It was not pleasant. It said, "Forget him, because he never loved you at all. Like any man on his own, he just wanted to have a woman. It is me whom he loves, and I am pregnant with his child. It was merely a pastime for him, without any significance. He'll never write to you." That was the end of it.

If you are alive, you must be eighty by now and will have forgotten everything about me, long, long ago. Yet a few days ago, when I was in Novgorod, I felt you by my side. You came with me to see all the old churches, and in the airplane from Leningrad to Georgia you apologized for the conditions, for the missing seat belts, for the people standing as if they were in a bus. You apologized, but I did not care at all. You were with me in the ancient town of Tbilisi, where we sat in a café drinking sweet, strong Turkish coffee. The next day we went to see the old synagogue, you and I, and there was a man sitting outside with a big medal and his right arm missing, both mementoes of the war. In the plane from Tbilisi you looked at me, and the question was written there in your eyes: could you have spent your life here? could you have ever been happy here, with me, despite all the odds? I cannot know the answer, but all the same I was happy that you asked. Which means that the answer could most likely have been Yes. I did not want to leave as long as you were there beside me.

Back here in Canada I have been sleeping like an untroubled child. In fact, I have slept a whole week, a week that lasted forty-three years. And when I woke, I was a wrinkled old woman again. But this does not mean that I have changed. I will not, to the very end.

The Voice of the Hunter

Stefa Kunowska is walking down the street towards me. Our eyes meet and she looks away, pretending not to recognize me. I am, after all, supposed to be dead.

I had been trying to find out where Stefa was, and what I had learnt was that she was married and that she too was in Łódź. So I had been keeping a lookout, hoping for just such a meeting. And now here she was, a prosperous-looking woman with a self-assured, complacent manner, walking right into my hands. Hate, utter hate, was my first reaction. Then an overwhelming desire for revenge, and pleasure that it was within my grasp.

As she tried to walk past, I blocked her. "This time, Stefa Kunowska, you may not wish to recognize me, but I know you. You will come with me." Seeming to go almost into a trance, she turned to walk with me, making no attempt to run away. It probably helped that I was in army uniform. I stopped the first policeman that I saw, pointed to Stefa, and said, "This woman is a criminal, a Nazi collaborator. She denounced people during the occupation. Please take us to the nearest Security Police office. I want to make a statement about her." She started to protest, denying that she knew me or understood what I was talking about, but I insisted, and the policeman took her by the arm, and the three of us went to the Bezpieka, the Security Police, to the section that dealt with political crime.

The policeman left us in the building's waiting area, where several other people were sitting. Stefa was well dressed, her clothes casual but expensive. She began pleading with me: "I didn't denounce you. Whoever you are talking about, it wasn't me." I looked at her coldly. She was obviously very frightened, but I had no pity on her. Pity! Pity? She tried again: "I have a little child. Do you want to take away its mother ... and for no reason?" Oh God, that hardened me even more. Venom rose in my throat. "You have a child, do you? A child. I too had a child when you tried to send me to my death." For a minute that silenced her, but then with an edge of hysteria in her voice, she again insisted that I had made a mistake, that it was not her, that she was innocent. I ignored her. After a while, we were shown into the room of the officer on duty. He asked why I'd had her brought in. "I am accusing her of denouncing me as a Jew and getting me arrested by the Gestapo. This woman, Stefania Kunowska, nearly caused my death and would have orphaned my child. I want her tried and punished." While I told him the story, I could see how agitated she was – good, good, let her squirm, let her plead! – and she kept repeating that I had made a terrible mistake. After I finished speaking, the investigator told me to write a statement. I did so, specifying that I wanted to accuse her formally within the legal system, that I wanted her to have a fair trial, and that I could produce the testimony of witnesses to the events in question.

I also told him that I would go to my lawyer to reiterate that I wanted her brought to justice and given the due process of the law. At that time, soon after the end of the war and with fighting still going on with rightist groups who wouldn't accept the new government, I'd heard that legal formalities were sometimes being ignored. When I had signed the statement, he said that I could go, but that she should stay because he wished to talk to her alone.

A few days later, by coincidence, I again met Stefa on the street, but this time she was with her husband. They radiated prosperity – they were both practising dentists and apparently making a good living. I would have walked on past them, but her husband, looking furious, stopped me, clenching his fist in front of my face. "You lying bitch! My wife never did what you've denounced her for ... You'll pay dearly for what you're doing." His anger was so great that I'm sure he would have struck me if I hadn't been in uniform, which would have been a major offence. Anyway, I wasn't afraid of him. "I know what I'm doing, and I know what your dear wife did to me. My life was spared by a miracle, but I'm still alive and I want her brought to justice." And I walked off, with him still shouting after me.

But months passed and nothing happened. I told the story to a friend who was a state prosecutor. He let me appear before him to make a formal accusation against Stefa as a preliminary to proceedings against her. I listed three witnesses – my cousin Zenia, who had seen Stefa from the window, gesticulating to the janitor; the janitor himself; and Mira, to whom I had made the phone call on my way to the Gestapo prison, telling her that Stefa had denounced me. About a year after the day when I'd had her arrested, I received a letter from the court. It said that the case had been dropped for lack of evidence. Yet neither Mira nor Zenia had ever been called to give statements. I showed the letter to my friend the prosecutor – who was also a Jew – asking him how such an answer was possible, and he said that he would make some inquiries. Not long after, he telephoned to say that he'd been told that there were too many cases about denunciations and that "they couldn't arrest every man or woman who had been accused. That's how it is, Stasia."

So Stefa Kunowska was never brought to justice. It was one of many things which were to make it clear to me that although Poland was now supposed to be governed on socialist principles, in fact nothing had really changed. It simply was not important whether one more Jew might have been killed. And it hurt.

Years later, there was a fragment of revenge when a professor of dentistry whom I knew received an application from Stefa to be admitted to the Party. He'd heard rumours about the story and wrote asking whether it was just gossip, because if it was the truth, he would block her acceptance. So I wrote out the story again, and I took some small satisfaction from the fact that she was not permitted to join – though why she wanted to I don't know. Maybe she thought she would be safer if she were a member. Anyway, I never saw her again, and after the professor died, she was probably able to join without any objections being made against her.

❧

Peter had started school. One morning he refused to go, and after some persuasion, he told me what had happened: another little boy had attacked him with a sharpened piece of wire, calling him a "dirty Jew" because he was not attending religion classes. Peter had then taken a penknife – which I didn't know he had – from his pocket in order to defend himself. I went to see the principal. He told me that he could not have aggressive children using knives to threaten other children in his school. I was furious. We had not, I snapped at him, survived the slaughter so that my son could be called a dirty Jew, and this kind of filth was not compatible with a socialist society. I told him that I wanted the other boy to be reprimanded. After that, I registered Peter at a secular school where religion was not taught, and I never did find out whether the other boy had been punished. I doubt it.

❦

We recognized each other immediately when we met in a corridor of the hospital. She was the one who came up to me at the student ball, the one with the fascist green Endek pin on her blouse and the prim, thin-lipped, old maid's face, who had said to the boy I was dancing with, "You realize that you are dancing with a Jewish woman. If you do not stop, you will have to face the consequences and they could be unpleasant."

"Well, well! I heard that you were all killed," she said, the tone of a disappointed hunter who has lost her quarry in her voice. "But they must be mistaken, because you seem very much alive to me." She did not say the "Alas!" but it was there. "And," she sneered, "now you still want to be a doctor!" There was a silence. I wanted literally to strangle her. Then I asked slowly, "Did I ever know you?" and walked past her. She understood that my refusal to acknowledge her was the only way I could offend her. Not having had any inconvenient delays in her career, she was already qualified in her speciality, while I was only then sitting the final examinations, which I had been banned from taking when the Nazis invaded. It was for this purpose that I had been demobilized in June 1946. She never approached me again during the two weeks I was working in the pediatric clinic.

She and people like her were the extreme example, but this was still the reality of everyday life in Poland. Although we were born there and considered Poland our own country, we were never treated as fellow citizens, and no matter how Polish we felt, we were never Polish to them. People like Mira and Jerzy, like the unknown woman who helped them rescue me from the Gestapo prison, and like Pikulski, the true Christians, were the exceptions.

⁂

The poet said of them in distant times, "They waited one for the other many a long day, but when, in the heavens that know not sorrow, they met, they were strangers."

Not in paradise, but on this vast expanse of earth where every step brings sorrow, sorrow, sorrow, I waited for her as one waits only when one loves. I had known her as I had known myself; knowing her in blood, in mud, in grief. The hour struck; the war had ended. I turned my steps home. She came towards me; we were strangers.

If you can understand the feeling there in Ilya Ehrenburg's poem "Victory," then little more needs to be explained. He wrote it on May 8th, 1945. For us, victory meant defeat: we had lost the innocence of our beliefs in humanity, in the human heart. We lost our youthful illusions, but, above all, we lost hope. And if this was so, then what was left to us?

I am sure now that my life came to an end at some point during or just after the war. Perhaps it was the moment when I first heard of my father's death. Or when I left the shelter of Jan Pikulski's home and started a life of my own in the Polish army. Was it when I met Grisha Malinovsky and then suddenly had to understand that he was there no more? Or was it when I finally separated from my husband, Bolek Ałapin? Whatever happened after that particular moment was, and is, irrelevant because my life lost its sense and its substance and its meaning.

Bolek was alive. A man arrived in Łódź and told me he was in a Russian prison camp. I'm not sure how the man found me. Perhaps through the medical register, perhaps through my mother – she was famous now, her name on theatre billboards, and at that time she was working in Łódź. He said that Bolek had been in the forest with the AK (the Home Army) partisans as a physician; then, when the

Russians came, they had put out the order that partisans should go to this or that place and hand over their weapons. Many of them, particularly rightists, had not done so and had gone on fighting, refusing to accept a Soviet-imposed government, but Bolek's group had gone to one of the locations. It was at Majdanek, probably at the same time that I was nearby with the Political Education Officers' school. Then along with thousands of other ex-partisans, Bolek, by some accident, had been sent to a prison camp near Ryazan in the Soviet Union. And now, said the man, who had been there with him, he would be coming back in a few months. I do not remember what my emotions towards Bolek were at that time. It had been so many years since that moment when he left Peter and me alone in our flat on Marszałkowska Street, the last moment when we were a family, when it was Bolek and me beginning our life together. That life, that world, and the people in it had gone.

It was also over with Professor H. He too had survived and had tracked me down, wanting to resume our affair, but I told him it was finished. For me it was over when I heard of the horrible murder of their daughter, Krystyna, the young poet betrayed and stoned to death in the forest. His poor wife was out of her mind with grief, and I would not compound it. Anyway, I was in love with Grisha Malinovsky.

The man said that Bolek would need clothes. I was studying for my examinations in order to qualify as a doctor and had scarcely enough income to support Peter and myself, so I wrote to Bolek's cousin Lusia, the daughter of his Uncle Herman and the only one of his family to survive from the ghetto. Her husband, who had been a Judenrat policeman, had died there, and Lusia, after surviving a labour camp and a concentration camp in Germany, had got to England after the war and was now married to a wealthy man, much older than herself. So she was able to send clothing and shoes for me to have ready for Bolek.

I had a good friend in Łódź. I first met Alina in the ghetto when she was staying with Lusia's family, and she and Lusia had been together in the camps. Łódź was Alina's hometown, but all her family had been killed. Alina and I met again on the street. She was one of the first of the handful of people I ever saw again from the ghetto, and here she was, in front of my eyes, alive and walking towards me. We embraced and talked, and she immediately became one of my closest friends. It has remained this way, despite, in later years, our differences of opinion about politics. She was as she is today – someone who keeps her feelings to herself, very intelligent, honest, and interested in everything. We'd had a lot of similar experiences during the war, and she too had had a big love affair with a Russian officer.

Ida, my best friend from university, and her lovely warm family, who had lived in the Jewish quarter of Warsaw, were all dead, except for her older sister, Anka. It was at their home that I first met Jacek Rożański when Anka was his girlfriend. One night I had a dream about Lena, my old school friend. I'd not seen or heard of her since that night in the Adria when war was declared. The next day a letter arrived from her. She had married her boyfriend and gone with him to his family's home on a Yugoslav island in a stiflingly restrictive Orthodox Christian community. At the end of the war she'd fled to Rome, where she was now studying architecture, intending to move soon to England with her new boyfriend. It was probably the letter I wrote to her in reply that sickened her: I invited her to come to Poland to visit me. She answered that it was a joke in bad taste, that going to Poland was out of the question, forever. She said nothing about her family. All of them – her mother, her father, her sister, her little brother – had been killed.

Every survivor had his or her individual story – of hiding, of concentration camps, of ghettos, of living under false identity, of acts of kindness or betrayal. Most had seen things that no human can witness and remain entirely sane. Some had found refuge in the Soviet Union; others who had gone there had been sent to the Gulag. Of those in my family who had survived, Aunt Genia, Uncle Franek's wife, and their son had spent the last years of the war under Aryan identity in work camps in Germany. Uncle Franek had died during the last bombardment of Warsaw during the Uprising. My cousin Zenia, with whom I was sharing the room when Stefa Kunowska betrayed me, was alive.

My cousin Bob, the son of my mother's brother, Uncle Wicek, turned up one day in Łódź, filthy, covered with lice, and ill with severe malaria. I disinfected him and burnt his clothes, and as I slowly nursed him back to health, he told his story. At the beginning of the war, Uncle Wicek had fled to Czechoslovakia, but Bob had refused to go with him because he was in love. Then later he'd got into the Soviet sector and had been conscripted into the army. He had disobeyed an order, and since this was a major offence in wartime, he'd been court-martialled and sentenced to death. While he was awaiting execution he wrote a wonderful poem – "24 Hours in the Death Cell" – which he gave to me and which I later lost. At the last minute he was reprieved because he had a Dutch passport, and the Soviet president, Kalinin, had agreed to an amnesty for foreigners. So instead Bob was sent to a Siberian camp, from which he'd finally escaped, travelling back to Poland on the tops of trains and inside the freight cars.

We found out later that Uncle Wicek had died, and under the most bizarre circumstances. He had fled farther and farther east away from the Nazis, until he finally got to China. From Beijing he made contact with Theja, his and my mother's half-sister. Theja, who hid in Holland during the war, had now gone to the United States. She managed to get a permit for him to join her, but before he could leave, he broke his leg badly and was put into hospital. On the day he was to be released, he was in the hospital gardens when a bull in a nearby field pulled away from its tether, and unable to run from it, Uncle Wicek was gored to death. To imagine that happening after he had survived everything else!

When Bob recovered his health, he decided to get out of Poland and join Theja. She had obtained an entry permit to the United States for both of us, and Bob wanted us to go together, escaping from Poland by walking over the mountains into Czechoslovakia. But I was afraid that Peter, who was only eight, wouldn't be able to make the difficult journey. So Bob went alone, with no money or assistance. It was not only my fear for Peter that held me back. I felt that it was my duty to stay to help build a socialist society – the phoenix that would arise from the ashes, the society that would eradicate injustice and anti-Semitism. And I was waiting for Bolek.

I wanted to try again with him. I wanted Peter to have a father, someone to help me bring him up. I was all alone, and it was difficult to earn enough to live on, study for my exams, and look after him. To keep warm, Peter and I used to huddle around the gas cooker in the kitchen – I couldn't find coal for the fire or even afford it if I could – him doing his schoolwork and me studying after I'd worked all day at the hospital. If I was on duty at night, he'd usually stay there with me. I told him a lot about Bolek and that when Daddy came back, our life would improve. Everything would be better and more comfortable, and we would be together again, a family.

I had no idea when Bolek would return, what week, what month. I was having an affair, but it wasn't important. The man was a lawyer, a public prosecutor with the new government. Peter hated him, and Alina and my mother didn't like him either. He was a nothingness, but I just needed the attention and the company, a man to pay court to me. What Bolek intended before he came back, what he wanted or expected, I don't know. The evening he arrived, I was out with the man and Peter was alone, and to entertain his daddy, he showed him photographs that could not have pleased Bolek because mostly they were of me at the beach with this other man. Anyway, when I finally came home, it was not a warm reunion, not even a kiss or an embrace. I wanted him to share my bed, but he rejected me. He said he wouldn't start the relationship again because he didn't want to rebuild the marriage. He was not going to remain with me, therefore it would be dishonest for him to sleep with me. However, he had to stay in the flat because he had nowhere else to go for the time being. So I gave him my room – the kitchen – and I slept in the other room with Peter.

Look, he had been through a lot, and we had been separated for seven years. He had lived with a woman in the camp; that was normal when you are young. But neither he nor I was able to forgive – he wasn't able to forgive any more, and I wasn't able to forgive once.

Bolek had changed. He didn't like Jews – not that he loved Jews before; none of us loved ourselves. I gave a party for him, and many of my friends there were Jewish. And when he came in and looked around, what he said – in my home, in their presence – was "Oh, so many Jews still alive!" I remember it so clearly. Everyone was appalled because, you see, what he said and what was understood by it was so like the Polish anti-Semites who said, "Hitler did one good thing – he delivered us from the Jews." How could he say this, even as a joke, when his father, his brother, and virtually all his family had been sent to the gas chambers? Self-hatred. But so many of us suffered to some degree from this disease.

After a few weeks, when he'd found himself a woman and was staying with her at night, Bolek moved out of the flat. For a while I used to rumple his bed in the morning and tell Peter he had left early, but he soon realized that Bolek had not slept there. My boyfriend had disappeared when he heard about Bolek's return. Anyway, he wasn't the sort of man who wanted any obligation. Peter was very upset, so to cheer him up and because everything was getting too much for me, I took him to stay at Albinów with the Pikulskis, and I returned alone to Łódź.

I had lost Grisha Malinovsky, and now Bolek too had gone for ever. My marriage was finished. I became desperate with loneliness and self-disgust. My endless search had brought only emptiness, leaving me unloved and alone with the awful consciousness that I had abetted in the ruin of my life. It all came down on me, drowning me in despair – the hatred, the ghetto, all the horrors I had seen and been through, all the deaths, all the loss. The absolute understanding that I was the only one left, my unique, my perfect father gone for ever, and I was alone with the terrible feeling that I was saved for nothing, a thirty-one-year-old woman left with nothing, only responsibilities to be carried alone – alone after everything.

I was engulfed and overwhelmed with the horror of it all. The children's voices – "Stickele brot ... stickele brot ..." The young boy denouncing me in the market place. The little baby torn from its mother's arms, its brains ... The old man thrown from the window. Stefa Kunowska denouncing me, wanting me dead. The partisans laughing, boasting. All those babies slaughtered in front of my eyes. My patients murdered in their beds. H.'s daughter stoned to death in the forest. The girl's body on the path. The old woman saying, "It's good they are burning those Jewish bedbugs." Bedbugs, that's what we are for them, bedbugs that must be exterminated. The shot outside the door ... it opens and a man's body lies there, blood around his head. My mother screams. She pushes my father away ... I am alone.

I did not want to live any more. I don't know where I was, but I took a big dose of pills and fell asleep. I was very angry later when I found that I was still alive.

I am in a huge, flat, treeless open space with row after row of wooden barracks. The smell of formaldehyde is in my throat, my nostrils, the air. The ashes of Aunt Ola and Irka are in those chimneys; their cries hang in the air that I am breathing. The shoes of thousands of little Peters ... The soil of the forest is soaked in human blood, the leaves enriched with human blood, and I am a survivor. By living, I am guilty. By living, I am guilty. I am guilty. BY LIVING, I AM GUILTY.

Two

In which the memories of three people whose lives intertwined with Stasia's – her second husband, Mietek, her son, Peter, and her friend Alina – provide a story that is not only personal but one of place and of an era, of war and genocide, of a communist state that took shape behind the Iron Curtain, of how people were drawn into supporting it and how it betrayed and disillusioned them.

The figure of Jacek Rożański is also threaded through the narrative. His name first surfaced in talks with Peter, who knew Rożański, as did both Stasia and Alina. Mietek did not wish to discuss him. "Let sleeping dogs lie!" he said. Perhaps he was right, but Jacek Rożański is already in the historical record, and he played a part in Stasia's life as well as in the lives of her son and Alina.

Unrepressed Memories

It is a fact that the Jews fight against the Catholic Church; they are free-thinkers and constitute the vanguard of atheism, of the Bolshevik movement, and of revolutionary activity. It is a fact that Jewish influence upon morals is fatal and their publishers spread pornographic literature. It is true that the Jews commit frauds, practise usury, and deal in white slavery ... It is permissible to love one's own nation more; it is not permissible to hate anyone. Not even Jews.

From a pastoral letter of Cardinal August Hlond, primate of Poland, once considered a moderate in relation to Jewish affairs, written in February 1936

The exterior that Mietek presented to the world during his years in Canada was of a quiet, politely reserved, laconic man, rather withdrawn and distant. He was extremely clever and knowledgeable, and Stasia and Peter would often turn to him for factual information. Most of his comments were concrete, about events; very little was about his personal feelings. Stasia said that she saw Mietek in tears only once – when they left Poland.

She would frequently point out that Mietek's background was different from hers, which he reiterated. Born in 1920, he was brought up in Lida, a town that had just come within the newly defined borders of northeast Poland, near the frontiers with Lithuania and Byelorussia. This was the heartland of the rich culture of eastern European Jewry, whose complexity was reflected in its wide diversity of political opinions, movements, organizations, and factions, some religious, some secular – socialist, Zionist, Zionist-socialist, and communist. Half Lida's population was Jewish, and Mietek's first language was Yiddish. His father died when he was a child, and his mother supported him and his two older sisters on the proceeds of her small candy-making factory. His family was not religious and attended synagogue only on the anniversary of his father's death. He was sent to a Hebrew-language kindergarten and then to a Zionist primary school, where the children were taught through the medium of Hebrew, though he also learned Polish. Zionism, an important movement in the area, was tolerated by a government eager to promote emigration to Israel, which was seen as an answer to the "Jewish question."

Mietek was much aware of anti-Semitism when he was growing up. "As a child," he said, "I had no contact with the gentile world until I went to the gymnasium, the state secondary school, and there one was simply treated as something inferior. You would get frequent jokes about Jews, and they would mimic our pronunciation – this would come both from the other boys and from the teachers. I had a rather interesting – you could say "psychological" – battle with the Latin teacher, a plain woman with an enormous behind. She was the sister of a minor popular novelist, and it was obvious that she didn't like Jews, though she was what I would call a 'decent,' rather than a zoological, anti-Semite. Latin was her obsession, and she was a very demanding teacher, but it interested me and I could meet her demands because absorbing information was never a problem for me. Over the years, as I became quite good at it, she began to tolerate me and finally, in her way, even to like me. The fact that I was Jewish was somehow forgotten or overlooked because of our common interest. I had a similar battle with a history teacher who was more of a zoological anti-Semite, a bigot really. For some reason, he used to provoke me into political discussions in class – about the Soviet Union, socialism (I was already leaning this way), the Jewish situation in Poland, and so on. He thought I knew more than I did. Anyway, it started out hostile, but over the years it grew into a friendly fencing."

One of the ways, said Mietek, in which he was constantly aware of anti-Semitism was the feeling of exclusion. "For example, you weren't able to join the boy scouts or other extracurricular activities, whether ham radio or gliding, although there were no written rules saying that you couldn't. Also, the law was that when high school was finished, one had to go to the army, and the drafting commission used to come to the school in the last year to register us for military service. But all the Jewish boys were declared 'temporarily' unfit for military duty, although we were healthy. This wasn't the case everywhere, because my friend Max, who came from another town, was declared fit. But when we were at medical school, where military training was compulsory for all students who were 'fit,' and it was found out that he was Jewish, he was told to give back his uniform. This was particularly ludicrous because Max was very athletic and he used to be as strong as an ox."

Another manifestation of anti-Semitism was simply physical danger. "If you went out of a Jewish district, you were likely to be attacked. How did they know you were Jewish? They just knew. For example, once when I'd been visiting a girlfriend in the town where my married sister lived, I was cornered by two thugs. They were closing in, taunting me, when a group of people came out of a restaurant. Then they backed off. I remember a situation when I was a student. I had to go to a professor's room to get his signature. The room was at the end of a long corridor, and there was a line of students waiting on each side. On the way back, a student from a different faculty grabbed me. I was slightly built, and he was obviously going to beat me up, but another student said, 'Leave him alone. Let him go,' and he did, so I was lucky."

There was also the lack of prospects. "Young Jews would graduate from university, but however bright they were, they couldn't get jobs because Jews were not being hired, whether they were doctors or lawyers. The only parties to support equality before the law for all citizens were the socialists and the communists."

Mietek dearly wanted to be a mathematician, but knowing that he would be excluded from the faculty, he decided to apply to medical school because the profession was still marginally open to Jews. Despite the *numerus clausus* restriction, his exceptionally high marks in the entrance exams won him acceptance. It was when he was taking these exams in the city of Wilno (Vilnius), not far from Lida, that Mietek met his friend Max, with whose life his own would be in tandem for many years.

"Max and I took a room together. From our window we could see the student campus, but it was out of bounds for Jews. There were no signs spelling it out or regulations, but if we'd gone onto it, we would have been beaten up – at the least. Some Jewish students were killed at that time in Poland. Then in September 1939 the Russians occupied eastern Poland, and everything changed. We were immediately able to have a room on the campus, and this was just part of a whole attitude exemplifying that we were now part of the community, with equal rights and more trusted than Poles."

⁂

Both Stasia and Peter had said that Alina was a very private woman and would tell only what she wanted to. The meetings took place in the small, book-lined flat in Copenhagen where she had been living since her arrival in Denmark in 1972. Her manner reflected a self-contained, self-controlled independence, betrayed only by the constant presence of physical pain. Alina is not her real name: she had refused other people's requests to write about her and wanted anonymity and only minimal references to her personal life to be used in this book – only information that might be of general interest and had some bearing on Stasia.

She warned that there were selective blanks in her memory – blanks, she thought, to which she possibly owed her sanity. But she said that she would attempt to explain how people like Stasia and herself were drawn into the web of post-war communism and how their idealism was betrayed – though "this will be from my viewpoint, a viewpoint which, over the years, has increasingly conflicted with Stasia's."

Their first encounter had been brief, in the Warsaw ghetto, when Alina was staying with the family of Bolek Ałapin's Uncle Herman. "The impression Stasia made on me then was that she was beautiful, that she had a charming smile, and that she was well dressed for those times and the conditions we were living in. Her manner was rather aloof, and we didn't exchange a word, but when we met each other again on the street in Łódź in 1946, and though Stasia was in military uniform, we recognized each other immediately and fell into each other's arms. There were so few of us left that it was indescribably wonderful to see her again, and we immediately became very close."

Alina had been born in 1914 in Łódź, a textile-manufacturing city in the centre of Poland, with a skyline dominated by smokestacks. When she was a baby, her family moved to Moscow and then to Kharkov in the Ukraine. They remained there during the First World War, through revolution, the civil war, and famine, returning when she was eight to Łódź, where her father established a small factory. Her family were observant Jews, and as Alina says, she would not use the word "assimilated" because she did not think in those terms. She insisted that she had no recollection of anti-Semitism when she was growing up and stressed that her father had many Polish friends.

Alina became interested in politics because of her friendship with a group of young men in Łódź, with one of whom, Alexei Berdayev, she was particularly close. (She did not want references here to any romantic involvements, so these will be alluded to only where needed for the story to make sense.) At that time, she had recently returned from studying medicine in France at the University of Montpellier, where there were no restrictions on Jewish entrants, but because of family financial problems, she had to return home and took a degree in Łódź in bacteriology. Alexei and the other young men were communists, "but anti-Stalin, and they educated me in their way of thinking. They understood that the purges were one long and massive murder. Mainstream supporters of the party called them Trotskyites."

One of Alina's friends, a factory hand, wanted to be an engineer, another wanted to be a writer; a third Leon Gecow, was a doctor who could get no work because he was Jewish. His wife too was a physician; she had gone to the Spanish Civil War with the International Brigade's ambulance service. Leon was also supposed to go, but he had to stay in Poland because he'd been called up for military service. Alexei Berdayev's father, a communist, had left his family years before to take part in the Russian Revolution, and at one point there was a plan that Alexei and Alina would join him in the Soviet Union. "It was because of my friendship with Alexei and with Leon and the others, and because Jacek Rożański knew about it, that I got into trouble after the war."

Most Poles were strongly Catholic and also distrusted communism because of its association with Russia. The city of Łódź, however, with its large industrial working class, was known as a centre for communist activity. This was criminalized during the 1930s, but Alina used to hide pamphlets and books at home. "My father was a clever, though untalkative, man, and he used to worry about these fellows coming round to our home and talking politics. He made no comment about it until one day when he came into my room, sat down, and said, 'You know your ideas are all very fine in theory, but they're not realistic. We've got bad men in power now, but if the communists take over, things will be far worse.' 'So we should leave things as they are?' I asked him. 'Is that how we're going to make people happy?' He just sighed and shook his head. It took me years to learn that absolute power – of any kind – does corrupt absolutely."

Many Polish communists had already fled to the USSR before an order went out in 1937 for all leading members of the Polish party to go to Moscow. As this was during Stalin's great purge of the old

Bolsheviks, one must presume they were either ignorant of it or disbelieving, because they obeyed. Few ever returned; those not executed disappeared into the Gulag. This was the fate of the husband of a cousin of Stasia, as well as of the older brother of one Alina's friends, and Alexei Berdayev later found out that his father was "liquidated" in 1937. Stalin had a particular animus against Polish communists, especially those who were Jews, because of their tendency to independent thought, an internationalist outlook, and their long-held admiration for his old rival, Leon Trotsky. Trotsky, a dynamic, dominating personality and a great orator, Marxist theorician, and founder of the Red Army, had long been critical of the increasing bureaucratization of the Soviet state and of the monopolistic party structure. After Lenin's death, he was Stalin's main rival for leadership, but Stalin outmanoeuvred him. Trotsky fled from the Soviet Union but led the opposition to Stalin's rule until the Soviet leader had him assassinated in Mexico in 1940. An advocate of international revolution, Trotsky had strongly advocated the Red Army's sweep into Poland in 1920.

In 1938 a friend of Alexei's who was living in Paris helped him to emigrate to France, and there was a plan for Alina to join him there. When he left, her adored sister, wanting to cheer her up, organized and paid for her to go on a skiing holiday in Zakopane, in the mountains bordering on Czechoslovakia. It was there that she first met Jacek Rożański in February 1939.

"I'd arrived in the guest house after everyone had eaten their breakfast, so mine was served in the empty dining room. I was still there, reading a book, when the door onto the terrace suddenly opened and a tall, dark-haired, good-looking young man entered. He had a deep suntan and was wearing a sheepskin coat with a fur collar. He came over to me smiling and said, 'Who's the paleface?' Someone had told him I was there. He flirted with me – and probably others as well – although his girlfriend was around. She was a big, blonde, Aryan-looking Jewish girl. His name was different then … I'd rather you didn't use it. Jacek Rożański was his party name later. I heard afterwards that he was a lawyer and that his father was the publisher of a well-known Jewish daily newspaper. I also learned that Jacek was a real communist, an active one, and that before the war he had helped Polish communists escape to Czechoslovakia over the Tatra Mountains, though I don't know if that is what he was doing when I met him. Later that year, in the summer of '39, when I was home in Łódź, he telephoned me and asked me to meet him. We spent the day together, walking around, going from one café to another, and at one point he said that he wanted me to help him to buy flowers, the best and most beautiful available. Thinking they were for somebody else, I chose the loveliest and most expensive. Then he gave them to me. He was very clever, and when he wanted to be, he could be very charming. Anyway, I soon forgot about him because the war broke out shortly afterwards."

Alexei got out to the United States on the last boat to leave from Portugal. "He tried to keep contact, and managed to get some parcels to me, even in the Warsaw ghetto. The other friends went east to the Soviet Union when they saw the war coming, and one was later killed in the fighting. I was to go with them, but I had to delay leaving because my father was waiting for surgery. The idea was for me to join them afterwards. But by then it was too late."

⁂

Talking about his youth, Jacek Rożański would later describe himself as having been an introverted boy, rather untrusting and distant; disciplined and well organized but sometimes disobedient and impulsive.* He was to identify this impulsive streak in his personality as making him unsuitable for the particular task he was given to perform for several years.

Rożański was born Józef Goldberg in 1907, into a literary, intellectual, middle-class family. His father, who was strongly anticommunist, was the editor of a pro-Zionist newspaper, one of the two hundred or so Jewish-interest daily newspapers and periodicals published in pre-war Poland. Among the teachers at the Jewish gymnasium he attended in Warsaw, Rożański remembered there being Zionists, communists, and anarchists. He was interested in psychology, wanted to be a journalist, and also began his involvement with radicalism – activity that earned him a temporary expulsion. When he studied law at Warsaw University, he tried to convert

---

*Information about Jacek Rożański can be found in several of the sources listed in the bibliography.

Jacek Rożański (undated)

other students to Marxism, was involved in more than one fracas with fascist Endeks, and in 1930 was accepted into the Polish Communist Party.

Milovan Djilas, the leading Yugoslav communist dissident during the Tito era, wrote about the communist revolutionaries who dedicated their lives to the cause, "The accomplishment of such a grandiose task – the destruction of a social order and the building of a new society ... is a task able to attract only a minority, and at that, only those who believe fanatically in its possibilities."* During those years in Poland, whatever the motives of party activists such as Rożański, whether an intellectual or idealistic (or both) commitment to the ideology, they can scarcely have been opportunistic.

*Milovan Djilas, *The New Class: An Analysis of the Communist System* (New York: Praeger, 1957).

They were putting in jeopardy their liberty and even their lives; they might lose their jobs, be expelled from university, have to sacrifice relationships, or antagonize their families.

Years later, recalling his activities in the 1930s, Rożański talked about everything in the context of the Party as the focus of his life, everything measured in terms of party interest and how to carry out party orders. He spoke of being "delegated" to work on "the Jewish front" – of infiltrating Zionist organizations and the Bund (a large and legal Jewish non-Zionist socialist party), of infiltrating left-wing Jewish publications, of trying to nudge them towards communism. When the police infiltrated his party cell, he organized a new one. Another of his tasks was to identify Trotskyites and either get them out of the Party or persuade them to go to Moscow. If they went, "they never returned." He failed to convince one man, "so he survived." This primary loyalty to the Soviet party suggests that Rożański may have been working under the instructions of the NKVD, as the KGB was previously known. He used various first names, including Wictor – by which Alina first knew him – and, he said, was known as a "very camouflaged" person. In 1936 and 1937 he was sent to France and Palestine in some nebulous role to organize a Jewish congress. He later described a moment of revelation in Paris when he saw a Soviet poster in a shop window of a young girl athlete, "a new type of human being, healthy and strong, with a better future." Contrasting her with the sickly children in the Jewish slums of Warsaw, he knew what he was trying to achieve. He also received a proposal to go to the United States "to work with Jewish unions" but did not follow it up. This, he said long afterwards, was something that he always regretted, implying that had he done so, his life would have followed a different path.

Meanwhile, he had finished articling as a lawyer, making extra money as a journalist, passed his bar examinations, and then with "my university friend" Anka, opened a law practice in which he took briefs defending people accused of political offences. This work, he said, also enabled him to "infiltrate the courts" and "report on the judges" to the Party.

It was in the mid-thirties, when they were both visiting Anka's home, that Stasia first met the young man she described as "very good-looking, tall with black hair and dark velvety eyes, which looked at one as though they could see everything going on in one's mind," and, because he was involved with a clandestine organization, "an air of romantic mystery."

The young woman described by Alina as a "big, blonde, Aryan-looking girl" who was Jacek's girlfriend in Zakopane in 1939 was probably Izabela – Bela – Frenkiel. He had met her in the same mountain resort in southern Poland in 1936 or 1937, when he was recovering from tuberculosis and she was recuperating after her release from imprisonment. Bela, he said, was then twenty-five years old, beautiful, green-eyed, intelligent. She had a great sense of humour and was a fanatical communist. From a poor Jewish working-class family in Lwów, she had joined the Party in 1927; four years later she was sent to political school in Russia. After her return, she was denounced, tortured during police interrogation, and condemned to death. Her sentence had been commuted to four years, but her first husband was executed.

On 6 September 1939, a date that remained in his memory, five days after the German invasion, Jacek Rożański said goodbye for the last time to his family in Warsaw and with Bela, fled east towards the Soviet border.

⁂

Wilno, the city where Mietek and his friend Max started their medical studies, was in the area of Poland occupied by the Soviets after their invasion on 17 September. In June 1941, when the Germans turned their war machine against their erstwhile ally, the school authorities told a group of students, including Mietek and Max, to head into the Ukraine towards Kiev. The young men backpacked eastwards, on foot or on farm carts and by freight train. In Kiev they were given money and papers and advised to go farther east out of the way of the German advance, to the medical school in the city of Kharkov. Again they were welcomed and given a place to sleep and money to live on, and Mietek was tracked down there by his older sister and her husband, who had fled to the city. However, before term started, and with the Germans still advancing, the students were once again sent eastwards, this time thousands of miles away by train to Frunze, the capital of the Soviet republic of Kyrgyzstan on the Chinese border. There the authorities decided to condense their last two years of medical school into one because of the urgent wartime need for doctors.

Mietek: "Were we being indoctrinated with communist ideas? I didn't think about it at the time, but we were being manipulated. So was the rest of the population. We were being indoctrinated through the manner in which information was presented in the context of an ideology that cast its shadow over everything, whether the press and the cinema or student meetings. At the meetings – and this goes back to the beginning of the Soviet occupation of Poland – we had a very formalistic type of party study: 'Give the five characteristics of ... etcetera, etcetera' – like a catechism. You had to know things by numbers, and it was very rigid, but it didn't worry me. We were certainly under no duress, and being Jewish and knowing what the Germans were doing, we were in a psychological condition to accept it all willingly. It all coincided with what we wanted. And the important thing in a small community of students – our social position was so radically and fundamentally different from what we had known before the Russians came to eastern Poland in 1939 that we were blind. We saw little – only isolated incidents – that would cause us to doubt. Anyway, we were not trying to find anything that might contradict the ideology. It was a harsh government – we knew that – but it wasn't affecting us deleteriously. On the contrary, it was doing things that benefited us. I wasn't looking for its claws, and there was a sense of 'so long as it doesn't touch me.' My feeling was 'This government is on my side.' And I still think the same way."

Immediately after they had completed their final examinations, all the able-bodied students were drafted into the army, but although Mietek and Max wanted to join up, none of their group was accepted because they were born outside the Soviet Union. "There were also some others they didn't take because they had a political 'flaw' – like Bela Kun's son. Bela Kun was the leader of the communists who took power briefly in Hungary after the First World War. He'd been deposed. Then when he fled to Russia, Stalin imprisoned him. Anyway, his son, a strong, good-looking fellow, had come from Moscow to finish his medical studies in Frunze. But then the NKVD came to the school to draft any remaining Soviet citizens for their needs – probably to work in prison camps – and they wanted to take Kun's son. Even when he told them who his father was, they said, 'Okay with us.' He was very relieved when they came back after a couple of days and told him they wouldn't take him. The rest of us were given choices of places to work, so Max and I took jobs on the south shore of Lake Issyk-Kul in the Tien Shan mountains."

The two young men headed towards the town of Przheval'sk (named for a nineteenth-century Russian explorer) by train, truck, foot, and horse and cart and then by boat over Lake Issyk-Kul, fifteen hundred metres above sea level. There they parted ways, Mietek walking the next fifty kilometres to his isolated village in the dramatically beautiful and little travelled mountains. The indigenous inhabitants were Kyrgyz, a Mongol people. Russians were also living there; some were descended from settlers transplanted by Csar Nicholas II in the early 1900s after he'd exiled many of the Kyrgyz following an uprising; some had been deported there by Stalin. The mountains have a low rain and snow fall, but the people pastured goats, sheep, and horses. In the cultivable part of the valley around the village, they grew crops such as millet, oats, cabbages, and potatoes.

Mietek recalled: "The village had been stripped of men and produce for the needs of the army, so conditions were very austere. At first I had a bare room, no means of lighting a fire, and only unground grain and the occasional chicken to eat – although sometimes my medical orderly, a young local woman, would invite me home for borscht. And people would give me *bouza* – it's a nutritious, mildly alcoholic drink they made from fermented millet. The government had come up with a mutually convenient arrangement to deal with the absence of able-bodied men: they sent soldiers who'd been wounded at the front but could still give the women some assistance – and companionship. My orderly had taken up with Mischa, a Jewish boy from Galicia who'd been invalided out of the infantry with a spinal injury and could hardly walk. They lived together and he helped her. After a couple of months I went to another village and boarded with the orderly's mother. I slept on the oven there – it was cold as hell in the winter up in the mountains. Then I went back to the first village and lived with an old lady, a Volga German,* exiled there with her grandchild. That was a better

---

*Descendants of the German settlers brought to the Volga region in the eighteenth century during the reign of Catherine the Great.

situation for me because she was in charge of the village milk separator and the villagers had to give cream for the local *kolkhoz* (collective farm), so I had a milky diet. But as a doctor, I was able to do little for the people in the six months I was there, because I had virtually no equipment or medicine."

In April 1943 a message came for Mietek to go the draft office in Przheval'sk, where an officer told him that a Polish division was being formed and asked if he wanted to go. "'Of course,' I said. First of all, it was my duty, and secondly, the Germans were my personal enemies; it was my private war. I don't think I have to explain this. I didn't know then that they had killed my mother and nearly all my relatives, but what they were doing was common knowledge, so one could guess. Also, I felt useless in the villages, but I could do something useful in the army. So the officer told me to write a petition for permission to volunteer. Then I walked back to the village to get my few things and my pay. I exchanged my suit and boots with Mischa – his clothes were in rags, the knees out of the trousers, his boots ruined, not even any laces, and I knew that the army would give me a uniform. My orders came through after I'd been back in Przheval'sk for a week or so, and I travelled back to Russia with a group of other men of Polish descent or citizenship. How one of them joined up was really amusing. I'd heard a man shouting inside the draft office building, he was expostulating, demanding that he be allowed to join the Polish army. Apparently he was the manager of a *sovkoz*, a state farm, in the area and comfortably set up. He'd thought that if he made a big fuss about wanting to enlist, they would tell him he was too important to the national food production effort and wouldn't take him – but they did!"

The journey back east took weeks. Mietek recalled a scene when the train stopped near the Aral Sea, and passengers, including eminent members of the Soviet Academy of Sciences – he had no idea what they were doing on the train – got off in their dozens and ran over to a line of waiting peasants. "It turned out they were all buying buckets of the lake salt, so I also got some of it – it cost us 20 rubles a bucket – and later on at stops down the line we were selling it for a ruble a glass, making quite a profit." The group had to change trains at one town to connect with the Tashkent-Moscow train, but when it pulled in, it was crammed, and people were being put out of one of the cars because of a major mechanical problem.

"I was with the ex-*sovkoz* manager, and we didn't see where we could possibly get on. This was a real problem because we were told that it might literally be weeks before there was another train. Then a young officer standing on one of the carriage junctions gestured at me to get into the next car, so we jumped on, although the conductor tried to stop us, insisting that it was reserved for demobilized war invalids. Anyhow, we went into the compartment and joined the Russian boys. At first they were suspicious, but then we all became friends and spent the days playing cards together and sharing our food. They were just travelling up and down the line, back and forth, on their free passes. Later, down the line, my brother-in-law and sister came to see me at a station – the train passed through the city they'd been evacuated to, and I'd telegraphed ahead to let them know when it would arrive. I couldn't stop laughing at the shocked look on their faces when they saw me in Mischa's ragged old uniform."

After the German invasion in 1941, the London-based Polish Government-in-Exile, headed by General Władysław Sikorski and recognized by the western allies, had negotiated with Stalin for a Polish army to be put together in the USSR under Soviet control. It became known as the Anders Army, after its commander, General Władysław Anders. Enlistment to its ranks was from the 180,000 Polish soldiers taken prisoner by the Soviets when they invaded Poland in 1939[*] and from the estimated 1,500,000 civilians deported to Russia, where many had been sent to the Gulag. Anders himself had been held in prison in Moscow. The gates of the prison camps were pried open with difficulty, and so little food and shelter made available to the often half-starved men, women, and children who made their way to the recruitment centres that in August 1942 Anders pressured Sikorski into permitting him to evacuate them – about 115,000 – to Iran, where the British were in occupation. Sikorski had wanted the Anders Army to remain in the USSR so that in the event of an eventual Russian advance into Poland, the army would be a presence on its native soil, and thus the Government-in-

---

[*]Relatively few officers were found among the released soldiers. The answer lay in a forest clearing near the village of Katyn, in the Smolensk region, where mass graves containing the bodies of 4,300 executed Polish officers were discovered by the German army in early 1943. More than 10,000 have never been accounted for.

Exile would be in a better position to exercise the right to regain control over its own country. This major bargaining chip was now lost, and the Polish division being formed in 1943 was the basis of the Polish People's Army, under direct Soviet political, as well as military, control.

It took Mietek several weeks to get to its headquarters in a village near Ryazan, in Russia. When he arrived, Soviet army officers advised him to return to Kyrgyzstan, telling him that the Poles wouldn't take Jews. "But after I explained that I was a doctor, they said, 'Okay, maybe they'll take you. Go and try.'" The situation, Mietek said, was that most Polish doctors had already left Russia with General Anders; his interpretation of why Anders had taken his army out of the Soviet Union was that it was the result of political disagreements between Stalin and the Polish Government-in-Exile. "So when I got to the Polish HQ, I was told that of course they would take me. They needed every man, particularly if one had a speciality like medicine. And that's how I joined the first regiment of the Kościuszko division under General Zygmunt Berling."

At the outbreak of war, Alina was in Łódź. The city had been absorbed into the German Reich, and resident Jews forced into a ghetto. Some of her experiences in the years that followed were parallel to Stasia's, others quite different. As she herself admits, her memories are selective. "There is a lot about the war that my memory has repressed, things that are too painful and horrible to let myself think about. All of us had a story to tell that would fill a book."

Alina is anxious to emphasize that not all Poles are anti-Semitic. "All of us who survived did so because of the help of Poles – I was aided by at least six." In early 1941 she managed to get out of Łódź and, despite the ban on Jews travelling, went to the ghetto in Warsaw. She was escorted on the journey by a Polish policeman who had joined the Gestapo. A man of enormous courage and integrity, he had joined it as a cover for his resistance activities, although she did not learn this until after he died fighting with the partisans. He was a friend of her sister's husband and had already helped her family in the ghetto in Łódź. The plan was that after she arrived in

Warsaw, a Polish communist she knew would take her with him to the Soviet sector. But when the time came for the journey, Alina was too ill with influenza to travel.

Trapped now in the Warsaw ghetto, she stayed with Herman Ałapin and his family, with whom hers were connected. Dr Ałapin, an eminent dermatologist, was the uncle of Stasia's husband, Bolek Ałapin. The Ałapins had a daughter called Lusia, who was both Alina's and Stasia's friend.

Alina said that she could not describe the situation in the ghetto. Most of what she talked about was almost impersonal, though in a letter to Stasia, she wrote that she could still "hear the sound of the ghetto" – the wail of the starving children, begging for bread. She preferred to talk about things such as the marionette theatre that she and a group of other young people created in the early months. "One person would write the scripts; another wrote the music. Some played instruments, made the puppets, or made the sets. We had an excellent pianist and an artist who had worked at the Warsaw Children's Theatre, and I made the clothes. The ghetto administration let us use a large, dusty old meeting hall. We were always starving, but we'd rehearse and work for hours. We forgot where we were. When I got home, I'd invent funny stories to cheer them up."

Alina also talked about Janusz Korczak,* whom she met because of her involvement with the marionette theatre. Possibly the most original and revolutionary educationalist of the twentieth century, Korczak wrote many books about his ideas, laying great stress on children's rights and on treating children with respect. He was also widely known in Poland for his children's stories, which he used to tell on radio, and for the orphanages in which he put his theories of child rearing into practicale. A medical doctor and a veteran of the Russo-Japanese War, the First World War, and the Russian Civil War, Korczak was of Jewish origin. When the Germans ordered his orphanage into the ghetto, he went with the children, although he need not have gone. He was so well known and admired that even when he was there, some German Wermacht doctors offered to get him out, but he refused to leave the children. Alina and other mem-

---

*An excellent movie, *Korczak* has been made about him by the Polish director Agniezka Holland.

bers of the marionette theatre group went to him with the suggestion that they would put on a performance of Pinocchio for the children. He made an ineradicable impression on her.

"There were children everywhere, children all over you. They were thin, but clean and well. Dr Korczak told us that once a day 'they get a good soup.' Heaven knows how he did it. He said that many of them wet their beds at night. He thought it was because they were cold, so he made a warm drink, a sort of ersatz coffee, to give them if they woke up. The orphanage was run on democratic principles, and you could see that the children adored him. On Saturdays they had a 'journal' run by the children themselves to discuss orphanage matters. If a child had done something good, he or she was praised – that was their reward." The children never saw the marionettes: when the day came for her group to give a performance, the orphanage was empty. Janusz Korczak, his helpers, and all the children were murdered in the Treblinka gas chambers.

Alina caught typhus during the epidemic that swept the ghetto. She thinks that when she was going through the bread lines, she probably picked up the body lice that spread the disease. Herman Ałapin looked after her, not letting her go into hospital. When she recovered, she found that her fair hair had turned brown and that her flesh had become puffy, masking her malnourishment.

After the signs went up ordering people to go to the Umschlagplatz (the gathering place by the train station) for "resettlement," Alina managed to get herself into a licensed ghetto workshop making shaving cream and toothpaste for the Germans. Its owner was a profiteer who held court "like a sultan" for those who came seeking favours and making similar requests. Although the work was hard and virtually unpaid, for a while it offered a margin of relative safety. Different areas of the ghetto were being sectioned off and their inhabitants sent to the trains, so she had to stay there. Her friend Lusia escaped from the ghetto, but Lusia's father, Herman Ałapin, and the rest of the family disappeared. "This period is very confused. The Ukrainians and the Gestapo were emptying the houses, and they took the man who owned the factory."

The girls in the workshop had a protector of sorts, a Judenrat policeman called Szapsio Rothole, "a little blonde man with blue eyes and a broken boxer's nose – he'd won a gold medal, I think, for boxing in the 1936 Olympics. He'd make us laugh, and he tried to protect us. A few times when one of the girls at the workshop was picked up and taken to the Umschlagplatz, he'd dash off on his bicycle and sometimes get her back. I have to say that I don't condemn all the Judenrat policemen. Some of them were just trying to save their families. I can't condemn them any more than I condemn people who gave names under torture during the communist regime."

Alina has fragmentary memories of the occasion when, together with two or three of the other girls in the workshop, she was caught up in the "selections" – the process by which the inhabitants of the ghetto were rounded up and taken to the Umschlagplatz. "We spent two days and a night on the street, and then suddenly it ended. There was the order 'Left to the Umschlagplatz!' and those of us sent to the right could leave. Maybe the train was full ... I have probably blanked it out. We had heard about Treblinka and Auschwitz. We knew where they were going – and to what. I remember moving from one abandoned apartment to another, from room to room. Sometimes we'd find warm water on the stove, sometimes warm gruel – the people had just been taken away. We ate what we could find, and then, I don't know why, but each time we cleaned up after ourselves, although we knew that nobody was coming back."

Alina determined to try to escape from the ghetto. "By then there was no work for us to do, and all we had to eat were a few carrots. The building was by the ghetto wall, and on the other side I could hear the bell of the trams going down the road. It was the sound of liberty, and I became obsessed with the idea that I must go on a tram once again before I died." Sheltering next door to the workshop was a young smuggler whose sister had known Alina's family in Łódź, and he agreed to help her. When some Polish smugglers came to the other side of the wall to throw bread over the top, he arranged with them to take her out later that night. He put up a ladder, and with the Germans firing, she jumped over and ran.

In the morning, at the smugglers' home, her plan was to go to the flat where she knew that the woman who had been the Ałapins' housekeeper before the war was working and who, Alina hoped, would have Lusia's address. The smugglers gave her some food and other useful things, and then, preparing to leave, she put on a hat with a feather, an image that she retains: "For half an hour before I left, I stood in front of the mirror, getting the right expression on my face, smiling because it was said that Jews could be recognized by the fear in their eyes." She went out, holding her head up, trying to look confident, but within a few minutes, a tall, well-dressed young man walked up to her. " 'You're a Jew!' he said. 'No, I'm not. I'm French.' I showed him my passport with its pre-war French entry stamp. 'No, you're a Jew, and I'm going to take you to the Gestapo. They're just nearby.' 'If you want money, I don't have any.' He pointed at my hand – 'But you have a watch and a ring.' I gave him the ring – it was my grandmother's – but while I was taking off the watch, it fell to the ground and stopped. He made me go with him to a watchmaker and asked what it was worth. Looking at the young man with utter hate and contempt – you could see the watchmaker had guessed what was going on – he said, '150 zlotys.' A loaf of bread was then 24. Outside, the man took my hand, shook it, and said, 'Don't be angry.' 'How did you know I'm a Jew?' I asked him. 'I can smell them.'"

The Ałapins' former housekeeper was shocked and frightened when Alina came to the door, but she gave her Lusia's address. Having nowhere else to go, Alina returned to the smugglers, and one of them took her to hide in the flat where his wife was a live-in housekeeper with her own room off the kitchen. Alina was able to make contact with Lusia and also with another friend called Zofia, whom she had known before the war in Łódź and who had not gone into the ghetto. Zofia was a young woman with a strong personality and commanding presence, a striking, blue-eyed blonde, with a "good face" – that is, she didn't look Jewish and could easily pass as a Pole. She had contacts in the Polish resistance, and these people helped Alina to obtain a *Kennkarte*, the necessary identity papers, in the same manner that they were obtained for Stasia at approximately the same time – by using a baptismal certificate of a Polish girl of around the same age, a process in which some Polish priests cooperated. After six weeks, Alina left her hiding place when one of Zofia's contacts found a job for her as a live-in nanny with a well-to-do family. And there, the following Easter in 1943, during the uprising in the ghetto, she, like Stasia, was watching the flames and smoke spread into the sky over Warsaw.

"The people didn't suspect that I was Jewish, but their housekeeper, an old peasant woman with a rough voice and hands, must have known from the beginning. I was standing looking out of the window towards the ghetto, trying to hide my tears, when she came and stood behind me. I can still hear her voice – 'Pani Jadziu, dear Pani Jadziu' (that was from the name on my *Kennkarte*), 'If it is necessary, you will hide under my bed.' She never spoke to me about it again. I had an almost overwhelming desire to be in there with them, to die with them, fighting, but Zofia persuaded me not to try. 'You'd be dead before you could find them. Don't give the Nazis a life for free.'"

Alina received a message from a close friend still inside the ghetto. The friend wanted Alina to meet her at the ghetto gate and try to get her out. "'Help me,' it said. I went, but it was impossible. There were guards everywhere. There was nothing I could do. It has not been easy to live with something like that."

≈

Jacek Rożański was still Józef Goldberg, a.k.a. Wictor, when he and Bela fled to the Russian occupation zone in 1939. As he explained years later, they immediately came up against problems reflecting their position as Poles, communists, and Jews: they couldn't turn for help to the local people, and the Jews in the area, particularly if communists, didn't want to help them because they were frightened of being denounced to the Soviet authorities, and they also saw the Russians as occupiers. On the other hand, he said, the NKVD didn't trust Polish communists and was trying to isolate them – suspecting them of being Trotskyites or *panski* (Polish gentry), traitors, "provocateurs," "agents of imperialism." An extra ground for suspicion was that every Polish Jew was thought to have family in the West. (Rożański, for example, had an uncle in New York, a poet, Menachem Goldberg; Bela had close family in the United States, South America, and France.) The worst thing, he said, was that no one knew the rules of the game, "and the Russian authorities were satisfied with this uncertainty."

It is impossible to be certain about what Rożański was doing, and where, during the war (or indeed, before). There are inconsistencies and contradictions even in his and Bela's short official party biographies. Populations and frontiers were in flux; there were refugees and deportees, and armies on the move; facts often had to be adjusted and readjusted; secretiveness and camouflage had become habitual to him. Bela wrote that at first she was employed as a translator, and her husband was "delegated" to local newspapers. Both claimed to have worked at different times under the aegis of the NKVD and on a joint Russian-German commission dealing with deportees or refugees (those, he said, who wanted to go west, towards the German zone, he sent further east), and where Jacek had to identify people who would be "good candidates for underground work." Sometimes they were based in the city of Lwów, now in the Ukraine.

The atmosphere of suspicion, distrust, and fear of denunciation during the Stalin era affected party members even more than the general citizenry. If Rożański did not already know Luna (also known as Julia) Brystigier, another Polish communist, whose vindictive hostility was to dog him for decades, their mutual hatred may be dated to Lwów, when, according to a defector writing in the 1950s, "her feud" began with Rożański. "At that time she, Rożański and Borejsza [Rożański's older brother]* competed in denouncing people to the NKVD ... Eager to win, Brystigier wrote a report accusing him of being a member of a Zionist family. Rożański knew about that report, and I recall him complaining: 'Just think, comrade. That whore squealed on me! But Comrade Luna forgets that I have had a longer career in the NKVD than she.'"** Brystigier, wrote the defector, had organized a committee, one of whose roles was to help the NKVD locate party deviants, "and that was how Brystigier finished off some of the comrades."

"An ugly fat bitch," says Peter, Stasia's son, remembering her from the early 1950s. "Mietek was never a guy who went around hating people, but he detested her." One of her colleagues described her as being cultured and eloquent and as having "quite a nice face, but she was terribly ungainly, square and short with very fat legs. She was aggressive and headstrong, one of those women who announce who is to take her home today."*** Both he and the defector commented on her sexual aggressiveness. One may speculate that Rożański had rejected her advances, but there could have been many reasons for their mutual dislike.

---

* Borejsza, also a communist, was close to Rożański all his life and fled Warsaw with him with his own wife and child. He was a propogandist and writer.

** Quoted in Korbonski, *The Jews and the Poles in World War II*. See also *Behind the Scene of the Party and Bezpieka*.

*** Stefan Staszewski, quoted in Teresa Toranska's *Oni: Stalin's Polish Puppets*.

There are several references to Rożański in articles written in the 1950s by the defector, Józef Światło, a former Security forces colonel, for a publication called *Historical Notebooks*. In a piece entitled "Behind the Scenes of the Party and Bezpieka," he described Rożański as an old Soviet agent who before the war had worked for Soviet intelligence in the Near East, Palestine, and the Arab countries, among others. "When the Red Army marched into Poland, Rożański lived in Lwów where he quickly gained the reputation of being a master informer. He informed on everyone to the NKVD, and that included his own Party comrades. He is shrewd, very clever, but completely dishonest in his dealings with Party comrades and hence very unpopular." One informer – Światło – with his own motives, informing on another.

Among Bela and Jacek Rożański's problems was the fact that despite being communists and NKVD employees, they were given passports categorizing them as deportees, meaning they had no more rights than the 1,500,000 other Poles deported eastward from the occupation zone. At some point after the Germans attacked the USSR in June 1941, they went to Samarkand, in the Soviet republic of Uzbekistan in central Asia, to join friends. And that, Rożański was to say, was where they got into trouble: Luna Brystiger was also there. In circumstances of considerable difficulty, Bela had given birth to a daughter in November 1940 in Lwów. Now, in a situation where there was no medicine and little food for anyone, the little girl became seriously ill, partly from hunger. Desperate, her parents accepted help from a man Bela had known in Zakopane, and who had access to supplies left behind by the Anders Army relief administration, obtaining from him two kilos of rice, some grain, and a couple of boxes of condensed milk. After a while, food rations became available to the Polish communist organization set up in the city, with the distribution under the control of a committee headed by Luna Brystigier. In late 1943 the couple (they were never formally married) were brought before it, accused of being in contact with and taking aid from someone Bela admitted was the "the class enemy." And despite Bela's defence that her child's life was in danger, the decision was made that their behaviour was not that of good communists, and they were removed from the list of people being given food. Other accusations and interrogations followed. Everyone, Rożański said later, knew about their "error" or "crime," and their lives were very difficult. They were exonerated only after he was accepted into the army in 1944, and "someone" came to say the whole case had been exaggerated. His appointment was as a political commissar in the 3rd Division of the Polish People's Army.

※

In the spring of 1943 Mietek had travelled from Kyrgyzstan west across the Soviet Union to Russia to join the 1st Division – the Kościuszko – being formed under the leadership of General Berling, a pre-war Polish career soldier. Mietek explained that by calling the division after Kościuszko, a famous Polish patriotic military figure of the eighteenth century, the communist leadership was playing the patriotic card, attempting to appeal to Polish sentiment.* He was twenty-three at the time.

"I was given command of the regiment's medical company because when we were finishing our degrees in Frunze, we'd had some training in war medicine. It meant that I was responsible for equipment and supplies as well as doing medical work. The three other, older doctors in the company were more experienced, and it relieved them of that duty. Max also joined in June as the doctor of the anti-aircraft artillery battalion.

"The men who enlisted fell into several categories: there were Poles who hadn't been able to get out with the Anders Army and people of Polish ancestry who were more Russian than Polish, there were Russian officers and specialists, and there were a few Polish communists. And finally there were Jews who had escaped from Poland – in fact, most of the doctors were Jewish. Before the division was formed, some of the men had been drafted into building battalions, and they'd had a very hard time, treated as though they were expendable, doing very heavy work for long hours with little food. They'd had a high death rate, though in some places it wasn't as bad as others.

---

*Tadeusz Kościuszko was both a Polish patriotic hero and a military leader in the American War of Independence.

"Each regiment had a political commissar, and each company had a political deputy, and we were gradually sold the ideology and the idea that the new Poland we would create after victory would be a close ally of the Soviet Union. It was obvious that you had to be careful in what you said, but at that time I didn't have the urge to be critical. My company's political commissar was Aaron Grinstein, a real proletarian, who'd been involved in communist activity in Poland years before the war. He'd been arrested and told he could go either to prison or into exile, so he'd gone to relatives in Argentina. Then, when the Spanish Civil War started, he'd volunteered for the International Brigade. He'd been severely wounded in Spain and was interned by the French until the Soviets allied with the Germans, and then the pro-fascist Vichy government sent people like him to Russia. In spite of his being Jewish and a communist and not speaking good Polish, the soldiers liked Aaron because he was a good man, straightforward, and he had a natural authority."

The Soviets had defeated the Germans in January at the battle of Stalingrad, at horrendous cost of lives to both sides, and again in July at the great tank battle of Khursk. These battles constituted the real turning point in the war. So by the time the division was ready to move into action in September, Mietek said they had the feeling that the war was going their way. "Our first battle was on October 13th, in the area of the village of Lenino, near Smolensk – the city was completely empty and devastated when we went through it. I think our attack was for political, rather than military, reasons, to give us a chance to do something and to get battlefield exposure.* From a professional point of view, it was difficult at first because the unit had had little practice. But we learned fast. As a front-line unit, we did only first aid – immobilization, dressings, medication, prevention of traumatic shock, morphine for pain. We tried to get liquids and food into the wounded if possible, and we prepared them for transportation to the field hospital in the rear. I'd been immunized to the sight of battle wounds the month before when we had to deal with a lot of casualties from a mortar landing short during a regimental exercise.

---

*The battle of Lenino was a stalemate. Some historians maintain that the heavy casualties experiencd by the division were predictable, reflecting its inadequate training.

"After Lenino we regrouped, camping in open fields in dugouts covered with planks and earth. Then in late December we were billeted in villages with peasants for the rest of the winter. You never saw able-bodied men there. They'd either gone to the army or been taken by the Germans, and the remaining people were just surviving on a diet of potatoes. We had our own food, and I didn't talk much with them. In the spring of '44 we went by train to the Ukraine. We regrouped in the forest on the Polish border. Then on July 15th there was a big offensive, and we broke through. We pursued them, with some skirmishes along the way, until September, when we reached the Vistula River. At the Vistula there was a battle for Praga, the suburb of Warsaw on the east side of the river. And that, as you know, is where we made our controversial halt while the Warsaw Uprising was taking place. General Berling did send a regiment to try to cross the river on the only remaining bridge, but a whole battalion was annihilated. This was explained to us as a breach of the military doctrine that a city should never be attacked with a frontal assault, and Berling was dismissed and replaced. Sure, we knew about the Uprising – we could see it; we could hear it. But we had no sympathy with the AK, the Home Army. We were brainwashed."

It had taken the full weight of the German forces two months to extinguish the urban insurrection that broke out on 1 August 1944. The deadliest Europe had ever experienced, it took the lives of 225 thousand civilians and between 20 and 30 thousand of the mimimally armed partisans, mostly members of the Home Army. The insurrection was initially successful, but the Germans who had been retreating in the face of the Soviet advance, counterattacked, blocking the Red Army. With reinforcements, heavy artillery, and air power, they pummelled their way back into Warsaw, exacting terrible revenge on the population. The Soviets had initially called for the rising to take place, but even after the Red Army was able to advance again towards the city, the AK, on Stalin's orders, was denied any assistance, and Soviet troops went no further than the banks of the Vistula. The exceptions were the disastrous forays over the river by Polish units – such as the regiment referred to by Mietek – who were probably cynically sacrificed by the Soviet command to assuage Polish soldiers' outrage and frustration at what they could see happening to their capital city.

The AK leaders had been anxious to establish a de facto presence in Warsaw before the Soviets arrived, in the hope of reinforcing, in the eyes of the western allies, the Government-in-Exile's rights to a role in post-war Poland. This hope had been fading as the Soviets advanced across Poland, harshly making clear their intention to impose their authority to the exclusion of any other. The western allie allies, at the Teheran Conference in late 1943, had also failed to extract a promise from Stalin to respect Poland's pre-war borders when the war ended. During the Uprising, both Churchill and Roosevelt demanded that Stalin let them aid the insurgents through airdrops, but unwilling to antagonize him, they were able to do little to help when he would not cooperate. The Polish people have never forgiven the Russians – and the communists who took power on their coattails – for this betrayal.

After Alina's escape from the ghetto, she had been in Warsaw for nearly a year in relative safety with her "genuine" false *Kennkarte* and working as a nanny, when she got a phone call from her friend Lusia, Bolek Ałapin's cousin. Lusia had also escaped the ghetto and was living in the city under a false identity. In a panic, Lusia told Alina that her landlady's son-in-law had started to blackmail her, and she asked Alina to go with her to find work in Vienna. It was considered a safer place for Jews, where they were less likely to be identified. Lusia had bought herself a travel permit and rail ticket with the help of a friend of hers, the manager of the Adria nightclub – the same place where in 1939 Bolek Ałapin had been arrested for causing a disturbance when Mussolini's foreign minister was visiting Warsaw. Documents were also obtained for Alina, and the two young women boarded the train, only to find that they were sharing their compartment with some SS officers. They got as far as the Austrian border, but there, together with others suspected of being Jews, they were taken off the train by the Gestapo and put in a gaol. They were interrogated, and Alina stuck to her story, but Lusia, whose *Kennkarte* had been forged, admitted she was Jewish. The group was then taken to another gaol, in the ghetto of the town of Sosnowiec. (Sealed ghettoes had been created in every city or town, where the Jewish population of the area was being concentrated.)

Alina heard that every week a trainload of people was being taken from the town to Auschwitz. Like Stasia in the Gestapo gaol in Warsaw, she had not disclosed that she was Jewish, even to her fellow prisoners, but then she found that one of them was from Łódź and knew her family. He told her that her father and sister had been taken in one of the deportations from the ghetto. (Her mother was already dead.)

She remembers a young Judenrat policeman who used to play cards with a group of the younger people in the gaol. "We'd laugh and joke – the older people thought we were mad ... Maybe we were defying death. One night the Judenrat policeman came in, woke me, and said, 'I've got to tell you something – your case is going well.' But the next day he and all the town's Judenrat were shot, and all the remaining people in the ghetto were sent to the Umschlagplatz. We in the gaol were the last to be taken. One of the women tried to hang herself, but her husband cut her down. When they took us out, I was supporting her. She was so thin I could hardly feel her weight."

As they were being herded into the packed area designated as the Umschlagplatz, Lusia and Alina were among several young people called out by a Gestapo officer. Alina thought they were going to be shot, but they were ordered to join a work group. They were put on a cattle train and sent to a Luftwaffe factory in Lower Silesia. This they all survived, but the group was then transferred to a concentration camp attached to a chemical factory, part of the industrial base supplying Nazi Germany's war machine, which used millions of expendable slave labourers under conditions of dreadful hardship and near starvation. But it was not an extermination camp. They had to get up at 3:30 a.m. and walk several miles to the factory site, where that they worked for twelve hours in awful conditions. Alina said that they all tried to help each other, and with access to caustic soda, they made every effort to keep themselves and the hut clean. Three of the twenty-four young women in her hut died, two from illness, one crushed by a truck.

It was difficult to imagine that the war would ever end, but at some point Alina began to feel that she might possibly survive. A German foreman, an old anti-Nazi, helped the women as much as possible. He found an old jacket for Alina to wear when she was transferred to outdoor work with a transport group and smuggled newspapers into the camp for her. From the location of the battles being reported, he would demonstrate that the war was going against the Germans, and eventually, as the front approached, he assured her that it would not be long before it was over. By the spring of 1945, although their food ration had diminished even further, they were no longer being taken to work and could sit outside in the sun, waiting. And then the moment came when they could hear distant artillery fire. Finally the women realized that the guards had gone.

"We all stayed in the barracks, not sure what to do. Early one morning, a few days later, I was lying on my bunk looking through the window, when I saw a man wheel a woman's bicycle up to the gates, break the lock, and come into the camp. He stopped someone and then came straight into our hut, calling out, 'Good morning in freedom!' He was the husband of one of the women. It was only then that I began to cry because I knew inside me that my family were dead. I had not let myself think about it before. But then he lent me his bike, and while the men started to organize things, I cycled out. Just beyond the gates, I came across a line of Germans, old people, women and children, walking down the road, carrying bags and cases. I got off the bike and stood looking at them. An elderly woman asked me to help her, so I put her case on the bike and went some distance pushing it until suddenly I said to myself, 'What on earth are you doing?' And I put it down and cycled away. I felt almost intoxicated with an incredible sense of liberation. I went cycling along, just cycling through the countryside. It was May; it was springtime. There wasn't a soul around until I came across a Russian soldier, kneeling by his broken-down motorbike. He wanted to know if there was anyone around who could fix it. I told him I knew nothing because I'd been in a camp."

After a while, Alina came across a friend of hers from the barracks, who was also biking around the empty streets. They found a bakery and went in, the fresh, yeasty aroma making Alina feel dizzy. Somehow she was in possession of a few marks, sufficient for a loaf of bread, but the baker refused to sell anything to them until Alina thumped her fist on the counter. When they returned to the camp, they found an eating orgy in progress. People had gone to farms, taken pigs, chickens, and geese, slaughtered and cooked them, and were stuffing themselves. She and her friend did not join them and thus were among the few who avoided violent diarrhea.

A couple of days later some Russian officers arrived at the camp to have a look around. Alina, who was fluent in Russian and German, was asked to help them communicate with the women, and before they left, she had agreed to join their unit as an interpreter. The next day they returned with some clothes to replace the camp-issue rags, and Alina went off with them in their staff car – not unlike Stasia, who, months earlier, had gone off into the unknown with the Red Army.

"Years later," Alina said, "I was asked to inspect the laboratories at a prison, and when I was standing in the guardhouse, I looked out of a window and saw a row of barracks. I became paralyzed. I couldn't move."

※

When the Red Army and the Polish People's Army finally entered Warsaw, its remaining citizens had been deported westwards and the city virtually destroyed, house by house, by the retreating German army. It was then that Stasia found Peter, now six years old, in the convent on the outskirts of the ruined city and took him away with her. He remembers a few things from his years in the care of the nuns. "In fact, my first conscious memory of my father is from that time. I must have been ill because I was told that the doctor was coming, and this man who I felt was my daddy came and brought me a box of candies. And I remember my mother visiting me once and my asking her for a prayer book. The atmosphere at the convent was quite free, and we could go in and out onto the street. I've a strong image of a scene when the German soldiers came into the convent grounds to grab the pigs that were kept there, and the pigs running around squealing with the soldiers running after them. Another time, when I was in the convent courtyard where flowers were growing, a lady came up and asked me my name. When I said it was 'Piotr Pietraszkiewicz, but that's not my real name,' she told me that I mustn't say that, otherwise my tongue would be cut out. Obviously she was trying to protect me. I found out later that she was the mother of the other Jewish child there – a girl who became Miss Israel. I came across her again years later.

When the Germans were retreating, I remember looking out of a window at the tanks and jeeps and cars going past, the soldiers hurrying, horses running wild, and I asked, 'Why can't we get the horses?' Somehow I knew that my parents were fighting the Schwabs – the Germans. I remember my mother coming to get me and my saying, 'I know you from your voice, although your hair is dark,' and then being put in the open Willys jeep, with a pink quilt around me, and their having *walonki* – the thick felt boots – for me in the jeep. The hours it took to get out of Warsaw because of the rubble everywhere and the streets having been mined. The incredible cold. Then suddenly I was in paradise at the military camp. Mandarin oranges, chocolates, running around playing with the soldiers."

—⋘—

Mietek's division, pursuing the retreating enemy over the German border, advanced continuously until it reached the Baltic near Szczecin (or Stettin, as it is called in German). They stayed in nearby villages abandoned by their inhabitants, who had fled, probably in anticipation of the terrible reprisals visited upon German civilians in some places. Then in mid-April the division moved south, crossing the Oder on pontoons, inexorably closing in upon Berlin.

Mietek said that there was a difference between Jews who experienced Nazi occupation and people like Max and himself. "We don't remember the Germans as terrifying, all-powerful conquerors because we only knew them on the defensive, always in retreat, always running from us. From the beginning of the campaign we were on the offensive. There would be a half-hour to an hour of artillery and then an attack, and we would deal with about fifty to a hundred casualties. No, I didn't have any pity for the Germans. If I had to treat them, I did my duty by them medically, and that was it. Of course, some of my friends were killed, and I also lost several of my stretcher-bearers. One of my good friends was the commander of the stretcher-bearers' detail, Henryk Tislowic … Henryk had escaped from Kraków, his hometown, when the Germans invaded. He got to the Soviet zone and was then deported to Russia. He was a few years younger than me, a good-humoured boy, very lively, able, and energetic. Anyway, he had joined Berling's army, and when we were waiting in a village near Szczecin for the order to move on, he received a message from his sister – she'd somehow survived, the only one left from his family, and she'd found out where he was. You can imagine how he felt when he got her letter.

Mietek as a decorated officer with the Kościuszko division about 1945

So we went to the divisional command post, and naturally we got permission for him to go on leave to see her. This, let us say, was Thursday, and he was to leave on Sunday, but the next day we got an order that all leave was cancelled because we were going to move south to Frankfort on the Oder. So during the battle to cross the river, I had my post set up on the eastern shore, and Henryk and the other bearers went with the advance. They brought back some wounded, and then he went back for more. After a while, I heard that he'd been wounded on the river bank. A mortar shell. Then I had to cross the river to set up a new post, and on the way I came across the stretcher-bearers carrying him. I looked, and he was dead. Yes, it was tragic, very tragic. But of course I had to go on.

"Anyway, there were more skirmishes and pursuit until at the end of April, on a nice spring day when we were at Oranienburg and I'd been to see Max, the order came to leave all the heavy equipment, just get onto trucks. We went to Berlin. It fell on May the 2nd, and we went in pursuit to the Elbe, because what was left of the German army was fleeing to the western allies. You asked me whether there was a particular moment in my life that I remember as having given me satisfaction. Well, it was then, seeing the thousands of German prisoners. That gave me satisfaction – definitely."

After the capitulation, Mietek's division was sent back to Poland to fight partisan groups who were opposing "our" government and who, the men were told, were bandits. They went by train to Warsaw and then marched northeast towards the city of Białystok, where Mietek barely escaped court martial because most of the medical unit's horses – for which he was reponsible, along with the cows they kept for milk – died as a result of eating chemically treated seed grain unwittingly taken by his men from a German farm. The exception was a big, cream-coloured horse which Mietek was fond of and which the unit's two veterinarians had brought back to health after it was found wounded and abandoned.

The unit, at the tail end of the division, was particularly vulnerable to attack. "For two years it was something like a civil war, but we knew we had the upper hand. First of all, we had the army, and we had the support of the giant, the Soviet Union. But we suffered a lot of casualities. Ukrainian nationalists even killed the leader of the 2nd Polish Army, the man who had become famous in the Spanish Civil War under the *nomme du guerre* of General Walter. Jews were in the worst position: if the insurgents captured one of our soldiers, they would disarm him and let him go, unless he were a Jew; then they would kill him. This happened to our unit: a detachment sent to the forest to cut firewood was surprised by partisans and disarmed. The soldiers were sent back, but their commanding officer, a Jewish boy, was killed. On occasion, even the communist partisans were known to have killed Jews during the war. Some of the AK partisan units had joined us as we liberated Poland – in fact, the deputy commander of my regiment was from the AK – but during the civil war, quite a few of them deserted. However, many of the AK and the other partisan groups were arrested as we were advancing during the war. Imprisoning them was obviously part of a plan to impose the power of the new communist government and to undermine the Government-in-Exile in London."

The AK had been the largest partisan army in occupied Europe, with at least 250,000 members. As the Soviets advanced across Poland, their policy became clear: they were not going to hand back the territory they had invaded and occupied in 1939, and the post-war Polish state was going to be under their control. The AK, with its allegiance to the Government-in-Exile, had to be quashed. Thousands of its members were conscripted voluntarily or otherwise; many were tricked into surrendering with false promises; an estimated 50,000 were transported to prison and labour camps in the USSR, thousands of others were imprisoned in Poland; hundreds of its officers were executed. The new Soviet-controlled government-in-waiting decreed that not only was the AK illegal, but that it was an organization of fascist collaborators.

Bolek Ałapin had been a doctor with the AK in eastern Poland. In July 1944 his unit came out of the forest to enlist in Berling's Army. The officers were directed to a camp in part of the Majdanek complex – the Nazi death camp had been in another section. (Stasia was nearby at the same time, at the political officers' camp, though neither of them realized this.) Peter says that while Bolek was there he met an old friend of his who was already with the Berling army. "This man had been designated to be the first minister of health in the post-war government, and he was already trying to get things organized. Knowing that Dad was a leftist, he chose him to set up the administration for the Wrocław district after its liberation. As I heard it, Bolek was waiting for Wrocław – that's Breslau in German – to fall so that he could go there, but he never made it because one night when the Russians were loading a transport with partisan officers from another section of the camp to take them to a prison in Russia, they found that they were seven people short of their quota. So they came into his section and just grabbed the first seven from the list of names of the men who were there. And as it was in alphabetical order, Dad was at the top. Anyway, instead of setting up a health service in Wrocław, he went to a Soviet prison camp. In fact, he was in a couple of them. He did what he could as a doctor, but the conditions in them were terrible. There was semi-starvation, and many of the prisoners didn't survive."

Jacek Rożański (undated)

In April 1944, when Jacek Rożański was at the front with the Polish People's Army as a political officer, he got a concussion injury and was sent to get an x-ray in the city of Lublin, where the new government was being organized. The chief of the personnel department of its security apparatus, an NKVD officer, met him and offered him work. Rożański said later that it was not an order but a proposal "because I was a lawyer, had a good background, and was known as a disciplined communist." It was at the officer's suggestion that he then took the name Rożański, his mother's maiden name, "because it sounded more Polish." In 1945, after some training, he was sent to the Department of Investigation of the new Ministry of Internal Security, which soon became known as the Bezpieka, or UB. Nine years later he wrote about the experiences that influenced his being prepared to adopt the "methods" he was accused of having used in the department. In 1944, for example, he had gone with Red Army officers into a prison cell in Lublin, where communists had been murdered by the NSZ (another partisan group, associated with the fascist wing of the Endeks); he had seen "hundreds of murdered comrades, including people close to me"; and he was at the scene after General Walter had been murdered and where thirty-one border patrol soldiers had been killed (by a Ukrainian nationalist and anti-communist partisan group). "When we saw in what a bestial fashion they were cut into pieces, the way in which they had been murdered, even veteran Russian officers were weeping and saying they hadn't seen anything like that during the war. I am telling you this because the sight of the bloodied victims of counter-revolution had to leave a mark on me ... These images, together with images from the war, and the fact that people close to me had been murdered – this all put hatred in me of the class enemy ... Those things left a big imprint on me."

Bela was in Samarkand until the summer of 1945. "Someone" had started to spread gossip there that she had collaborated with the enemy and taken bribes, but before anything could happen, her new party documents arrived, signed by Poland's future minister of Security. The next day, without permission from the party, she and their daughter were on the train heading west to join Rożański in Warsaw, where he had taken up his new position with the Ministry of Internal Security.

༄

When the most intense part of the civil war was over, Mietek joined his older sister and her husband in Szczecin, part of the area of prewar eastern Germany now handed over to Poland. "My younger sister, who was a midwife, had been killed by the German bombing in Minsk, Byelorussia, and apart from a distant cousin who'd been in the Russian army, nobody else was left from my family. Nobody. It wasn't unusual. So I went to Szczecin, still with the regiment, and started to work in a hospital, training for my speciality in ophthalmology. Then after a while I was transferred to the Internal Security Forces. They were setting up their own medical services to look after their employees, and they had the best medical facilities in the country. That didn't bother me at the time, because, according to communist doctrine, the Security was in the front line of the class struggle, therefore they had to get the best medical care. Max also joined the Security as a doctor at about the same time. And it was in Szczecin that I met my wife.

"I had a vision of a new Poland, a Poland where there would be social justice, a Poland where there was no obscurantism, no chauvinism. A lot of us had those ideals. Now I think I should have left earlier than I did. I should have gone at the end of the war. Then I wouldn't have wasted my life."

❦

When Alina left the slave labour camp with the Russian soldiers to act as an interpreter, they went to their headquarters in a requisitioned spa. They were part of an intelligence unit. "I'd forgotten that people could talk and laugh and sing and tell crazy jokes – and these were bright fellows." Her duties included interpreting during interrogations of Germans suspected of having being in the SS, and she was to remain obsessively concerned that translations be precise.

For the rest of her life, Alina retained good memories of the months she spent with the unit, feelings of "just enjoying being alive." She had, in fact, formed a close attachment with the major, "a delightful man, a teacher of Russian literature, very clever and extremely decent." They both knew the relationship could not last, and in January 1946 she returned to her home city of Łódź, accompanied on the train journey by the major's driver-batman because they wanted to make sure she would get there safely.

After the war ended, millions of uprooted peoples and refugees, each individual with her or his own story, were criss-crossing central Europe, some evicted from their homes and lands, some trying to return to them, some fleeing, some determined never to return to places empty of all they had known except memories. Stalin had moved Poland's western border to where it lay in the eighteenth century, and Alina saw the German population of Silesia being forcibly deported, one more stream adding to the flood.

She already knew that her father and sister were dead. The only relative she expected to find in Łódź was her sister's husband's brother, with whom she had already chanced to make contact. He and his wife had survived in Slovakia working as farm labourers under "Aryan" identities. But when she arrived at the flat, the door was opened by her brother-in-law. He had survived the Matthausen concentration camp and Auschwitz. But he had to break the news to her that it was there, in the gas chambers, that her father and her sister had been murdered.

Alina's old friend, Zofia, had also returned to Łódź. Zofia had been picked up by the Gestapo in Warsaw for resistance activities and sent, as an Aryan, to Auschwitz. She later wrote a book about it.* She was now married to a colonel in the Security forces, and by chance they were living in the same apartment house as Alina's brother-in-law. The non-Jewish friend who obtained the *Kennkarte* for Alina had not survived.

Alina stayed in Łódź for the next three years, working and studying for her MSC in bacteriology and then her PHD. It was in that city that she met Stasia again, and the two young women, alive against all the odds, became close friends. When they met, Stasia was still involved with Grisha Malinovsky. They talked about everything. "With Stasia it was always men, and Peter. Her situation was more difficult than mine. I was alone, but she had the responsibility of looking after a child. She adored him, and it saddened me that she couldn't make a warm home for him. But there is nothing strange in that – she was psychologically broken, she was a single mother with a disorganized personal life, and she had financial difficulties. After Stasia found out that Bolek was in a prison camp, she asked me to intervene with Zofia's husband to free him. Of course, I agreed to, although I don't know whether it worked or not. Anyway, when Bolek was finally freed and she heard that he was on his way, she told me, 'I don't want him back with me.' I argued that she had to try again for Peter's sake.

"I've always loved Peter. He was always good-hearted, but he was not an easy child. He ran away from home once, I don't know why – maybe he didn't like one of her boyfriends. She called me in a panic one evening, saying that Peter had disappeared and that she'd informed the police. Around 11 p.m. there was a knock on my door, and there was Peter, about nine years old at the time, cold, hungry, dirty. He'd been at the railway station for hours. I think he'd been looking for his father. He pleaded with me not to tell Stasia where he was, so I fed him, put him in the bath, and

---

*Translated from the original Polish as *I Came Back* and published under the name Krystyna Zywulska.

tucked him into bed, and then I phoned her to stop her worrying and told her to leave him there for the night. I didn't ask him why he had run away."

Peter still remembers that incident. "I had a row with my mother, and I went to the train station and waited as the trains steamed in, wanting my Daddy to come, sure that I would recognize him, and thinking to myself that I would live with him. A trainload of men came in, Poles returning from Russian prison camps – you could tell because they were skinny and were wearing a sort of ragged military uniform without insignia. When he didn't arrive, I went to Alina's flat. Not long after that, one evening when my mother was on duty and I was alone, there was a ring at the door. I opened it and he was there. It was very emotional. I felt that I had to feed him and said I would telephone my mummy, but he told me to wait a while. I remember him putting his hand into a pocket of his long military coat and pulling out poems he said he'd written for me in prison, and he had a photograph of me that my mother had sent to him in a letter. He'd received it a year after it had been sent, and he'd been given it by the prison camp commandant only because he'd been called to give the man's daughter some medical care. He also asked me something about men, and I told him about a boyfriend my mother had at the time, a man I hated – not the Russian guy, Malinovsky, whom I'd liked. By the way, she tried to get a job in Russia so that she could make contact with him. She wanted to follow him there. Anyway, in the morning I telephoned my mum and told her that Dad had arrived. 'How do you know it's him?' she asked. 'How wouldn't I know it's my father?' I replied. I don't really know why they didn't stay together. Perhaps because they had ideological differences. And Bolek never had my mother's attitude towards Poles. His experiences in the war had been quite different."

Stasia retains no clear memory of the circumstances around Peter being taken from Łódź to stay with the Pikulskis in Albinów at about this time, probably just before or after her suicide attempt. Peter thought that he had been sent there because she didn't know what to do with him when she was moving to Szczecin. "I stayed with Jan Pikulski and his wife, Madam Zofia, for months. It was lovely there, and I had a great time going around with Mr Pikulski – he had me riding a horse after a few days. I had a lot of freedom. I

Bolek Ałapin with Peter in 1946 or 1947

used to play on the edge of the forest and explore the places where the partisans had had their hideouts. Mr Pikulski was grey-haired and balding, not very tall, and he loved his horses. At that time he was running a village school, and Madam Zofia also had a school in the Albinów dining room – they wanted to bring literacy to the peasants. And because I was a smart kid, my job was to help the other children. The Pikulskis had very little money, but they grew their own vegetables and had chickens and two cows. The parents paid a small fee for their children, and sometimes Mr Pikulsi would earn fees for doing land surveying. He was a completely self-sufficient person. He knew how to do everything, and he was friendly with everyone. You could see that the peasants had a lot of respect for him because they always raised their caps to him, and if problems arose in the neighbourhood, they would come for his advice – we knew everything that was going on there. I had a wonderful time. Once a week we would go by horse and cart to Iwaniska to get the mail, do the shopping, and go to church. Average Poles are religious in that they go to church, they pray and go to confession. But they don't really understand religion, unlike people like the Pikulskis and like Jerzy and Mira Sawa, who made the effort to understand its real meaning and the teaching of God and who believed that the way to serve God was by helping people who were in need or being persecuted. Men and women like them were never anti-Semitic, and it was they who tried to help Jews during the war."

Stasia also has no memory of another incident from this time or of where she was when she tried to take her life. Alina, however, remembered clearly. "Stasia spoke several times of her wish to commit suicide. Then one day she told me that she was going to do it. I followed her, and she went to the railway station and bought a ticket to Warsaw. I did the same, and when she got on the train, so did I, sitting down opposite her. She ignored me and was silent for the whole journey. When the train arrived in the city, she got off and so did I. She walked, and I followed her, through the streets and into the ruins of what had been the ghetto. We were there for hours, wandering through the rubble without a word exchanged between us. At some point she must have said something to me, because when dusk fell, she agreed that we leave and find a place to eat. I clearly remember we both ate veal and beets. In silence. Then we went back to Łódź. But soon after she returned to Warsaw and went to her Aunt Genia's flat, and that is where she did it."

It was while Alina was still in Łódź that she began to get letters from the United States. They were from Alexei Berdayev her girlhood love, the so-called Trotskyite. And it was there Jacek Rożański again crossed her path.

False Phoenix

On 5 July, 1946 forty-five Jews were murdered and forty-five seriously wounded during a pogrom in the town of Kielce. Most of them were waiting to emigrate from Poland. Kielce's pre-war Jewish population had been 50,000; in 1946 it was 850. Władysław Gomułka, the leader of the Polish Workers' Party, said, "The crime committed in Kielce has brought shame upon all Poland." Cardinal Hlond made a statement that while the pogrom was "highly regrettable ... it had occurred for religious, not for racial reasons ... The condition [of Polish Jews] is deteriorating because the Jews who

Polish Politburo at May First Celebration, 1953 (Archive of Audiovisual Records, Warsaw)

now occupy leading positions in Poland's government are working to introduce a structure that the majority of the people do not desire." The bishop of Lublin, referring to this incident and the murders of hundreds of other returning Jews, commented that the causes were "rooted in the general hatred of Jews as a result of their active participation in the present political life of the country ... . The Germans wanted to exterminate the Jewish nation because Jews spread communism."

As Stefan Staszewski, a leading propogandist in the post-war government, who had survived eight years in the Soviet Gulag, said, "the Party is simply the Party: it is a word which replaces all known concepts and expressions; it is an absolute, an abstraction. It is always right; it is our honour, our happiness, our life's goal. And if you ask any communist about its infallibility ... he will say to you: the Party didn't commit mistakes; people committed mistakes."*

Alina met Jacek Rożański again one evening in the late 1940s at the theatre in Łódź. Her friend Zofia, now married to Leon Andrzejewski, a colonel in the Security, was visiting Warsaw, so there was a spare theatre ticket, which Alina was using. "Before we took our

*Quoted in Toranska's *Oni: Stalin's Polish Puppets*

seats, Leon said, 'Wait a moment. A couple of friends are going to meet us.' Shortly after, I saw two men in officers' uniforms coming down the stairs into the foyer. 'Good God, it's Wictor!' I said. That was the name I had known him by. Leon looked startled and obviously worried. 'You know him?' I quickly collected myself. 'No,' I replied. 'No, I made a mistake.' He was introduced to me as Jacek Rożański, and he reacted as though he didn't know me. After the opera, we all went to a restaurant, and Jacek sat beside me, being his old charming self. We were all chatting, and after a while, he turned to me and, with a smile, quietly said, 'Well, Alina, it seems that we have a secret in common.' 'A secret?' I said. 'How's that? We never had a child together.' He just laughed."

Jacek Rożański was now chief of the Investigation Department of the Ministry of Internal Security, also known from its acronym as the UB or the Bezpieka. It had been created and trained under the Soviet NKVD, and its role was to neutralize all actual or potential resistance to the government and its policies and to ensure civil obedience. During the civil war the department's primary targets were the remaining partisan splinter groups, including Ukrainian nationalists and extremist Endeks, as well as those remnants of the AK who had refused to accept orders from the Government-in-Exile to lay down their arms rather than sacrifice more lives in a hopeless struggle. People suspected of supporting them were also targeted. There was a deep well of bitterness among the population generated by marauding Soviet troops looting and raping and by the terror tactics of the NKVD and Polish Security forces. Both sides had bloody hands.

Talking and writing later about the civil war years, Rożański said that the people in his department were developing their techniques at a time when they had enemies "who murdered 30,000 and more people on the left – peasants, democrats, communists ... We were repeatedly told that the concept is 'Answer terror with terror.'" At the beginning of his work as an interrogation officer, he said there were hundreds of arrested people in custody but little proof of their "crimes," and "I witnessed beatings by older comrades." He recalled a particular incident when the ministry "liquidated a band of terrorists who were preparing an assassination. Our agent had infiltrated into the band and was able to find out that they had infiltrated an informer right into the Security as secretary to the minister. I remember that Romkowski [Rożański's superior] beat the chief of the band to get more information from him. I concluded that that the moral reservations that I had from my upbringing had to be overcome." On more than one occasion, he was to refer to the department's role as being that of "the garbagemen of the revolution" – that is, he and his colleagues did the necessary dirty work. "We look after things that can't be made public."

Although sporadic incidents of violence took place into the early 1950s, the civil war was losing its intensity in 1947. By then the NKVD and the Security forces had overwhelmed most of the resistance to the new order. The regime had been imposed by force against the wishes of the vast majority of a people who had already suffered greatly during the war, and although the western allies made a few protests and futile attempts to demand some kind of representative government, there was nothing that they could or would do about a situation in which they had acquiesced since the conferences in Tehran at the end of 1943 and Yalta in February 1945. Władisław Gomułka, now the party leader, had escaped Stalin's deadly purge in 1937 for the simple reason that he was in a Polish jail at the time. He had taken over the leadership under the Nazi occupation but remained suspicious of Stalin and the NKVD; he wanted both communism and independence for Poland. These would always be incompatible – without Soviet power backing it up, the regime would crumble. This remained true during the forty-five years of communist rule that followed.

Before the war Ramon Dmowski and his fascist-style Endeks, along with religious leaders such as Cardinal Hlond, had made blanket accusations of Jewish support for communism when it was palpably untrue. But what was false before the war in a population of three and a half million was less so afterwards in a Jewish population estimated at no more than a hundred thousand by the end of 1947, when the majority of survivors had left the country. With clever cynicism, Stalin and the NKVD saw to it that Jews were visible, in disproportionate numbers, in the top ranks of the new and hated Security service, the enforcers of the new regime. It would be a while before they realized that they had been set up for future use as scapegoats.

In the early post-war days, even highly intelligent people such as Mietek, Stasia, and Alina, as well as many of their friends, did not want to think through the potential contradiction in their situation – how their association with a system in which anti-Semitism was theoretically unacceptable could be used by the regime itself to whip up anti-Semitism. "Stasia and I both supported the new government," said Alina. "Many Jewish survivors did. We thought that communism would bring justice and equality between people and that it would end anti-Semitism. We all knew that most Poles didn't want communism or the Bezpieka. Although it was mostly staffed by Poles and Russians, there were many Jews in it. We wanted to believe that the new idea, the new system would work. We'd been through so much, and we couldn't bear to think it had all been for nothing."

⁂

Mietek and Stasia met in 1947 in the city of Szczecin, shortly after he joined the Security forces as a doctor. "She was a party member," said Mietek, "and after I was elected secretary of the party organization at the school, this very handsome young lady came to me asking if I could help her get an extra job. She was an assistant at the medical school's obstetrics and gynecological clinic, but the pay was so low then that every doctor had to have one and a half or even two jobs, and she also had a child to support. After two months I asked her to marry me. I was twenty-eight at the time; she was thirty-three." After their marriage, they remained in Szczecin until 1951, when Mietek was sent to the central office of the Ministry of Internal Security in Warsaw as a medical administrator. By then the ministry had 50,000 employees. His friend Max was also posted to the city to work with the ministry's health services.

Mietek explained that there were several reasons for the disproportionately high percentage of Jews among the supporters of communism after the war. "First of all, at the beginning the Polish intelligentsia did not want to participate in the building of socialism. Secondly, the new Polish state had to carry out a struggle against fascism, and fascists were our particular enemy. And thirdly, the truly capitalistic part of the Jewish population had either been annihilated along with most of Poland's Jews or they had left with the majority of survivors when the borders were still open between '45 and '48. The few who remained were mostly middle class. We were not gentry, and we were not officers from the pre-war army. Nor had we been in the police or in government. Because of this we could accept the new order with less difficulty than the Poles themselves, and we were more easily trusted. We were more naturally the allies of the communists. Also, of course, we weren't under the influence of the Catholic Church. The Polish peasants and workers themselves had no alternative but to accept the new order, and few of them were sufficiently educated to see the positive aspects of socialism."

Mietek said that he knew the regime was harsh, "but at first I accepted this because the iron fist was being used against those we believed were the enemies of the Polish people, and if we saw excesses, these were the excesses of individuals or bureaucrats. No, I wasn't surprised when Jacek Rożański was accused of maltreating prisoners. I met him only a few times, but I immediately sensed that however intelligent and socially pleasant he might be, he was an egocentric opportunist, a cynical careerist. I had some contact with him when my wife and I were staying in a government rest house, and that was enough for me. I knew the sort he was." ("I'm not sure about that," commented Peter later. "Jacek was there with another guy from his department, and Mietek didn't say anything about him. The difference is that the other guy wasn't good-looking, and Jacek was. Plus he and my ma were both flirts.")

"At the beginning," said Mietek, "a lot of us in the ministry had ideals. We wanted to help rebuild the country. But idealism and loyalty can be exploited and manipulated and, finally, turned into cynicism. The closer one is to the top, the more easily one is corrupted. You start thinking it is your birthright. Gradually I found myself becoming cynical because I was benefiting from the regime and because I had become part of the system. One looked at it this way: everybody who could benefit from their situation was doing so. You didn't want to be seen as a fool – if you didn't benefit, you knew that others would continue to do so, and you knew that you would not achieve anything by not going to the special shops. Also, I thought I had some merit. It is all a complicated rationalization of one's behaviour. In this respect we are not clean, absolutely not.

"I can't say that I used to lie awake at night worrying about the situation, and I don't think that Max did either, but every day I weighed the reality against the ideals. First of all, you begin to see that there is no such thing as equality under this government, that human rights are being suppressed, and that the rulers are looking out for their own well-being, for their own benefit, and not for the common good. And then one sees that official anti-Semitism is beginning to show itself again."

One of the first clear indications of the direction things would go was when Nikita Khrushchev went to Poland in 1956 in the middle of anti-government strikes and riots and told Gomułka and the new leadership that there were "too many Abramoviches" in the top positions.

⋘⋙

Alina also described the mental contortions required to deal with the disparities between wishful thinking and reality, between propoganda and observation, with which she was constantly confronted. "During the years immediately after the war, I couldn't think about what had happened. I suppose I tried to shut it out of my mind. And I was confused about what was happening now. I thought it was Stalin who had won the war, and it was years before I learned how much the United States and Britain had done. On one hand, I saw the Russians as heroes, but, on the other, we were hearing that the Soviet government was still killing people who were described as enemies of the state and that their men who had been prisoners of war were being sent to the Gulag. Also the Soviet iron fist was the ultimate power behind the scenes in Poland. I had to say to myself, 'You are living here. You cannot influence what is going on, and you agree with the principles of the status quo.' I wanted to do my bit to rebuild the country, and I thought that things would change, that real socialism would finally win. But it didn't. It all got worse.

"I remember a Christmas Eve at Irena and Karol's flat, somewhere around '47 or '48, when a lot of partisan groups who didn't accept the communist government were still putting up a struggle. Stasia and Mietek were also there with Peter. We were talking, and I said something on the lines of 'I still think that the Security are heroes because it is they who are out there, fighting the rightist bandits.' Karol, who was a very clever and clear-minded man, just looked at me and smiled. Suddenly I felt ashamed. I knew I'd said something really silly. I didn't believe all the lies. I didn't believe everything we were told. I was always suspicious. But I did believe it would change. It was intolerable to think that the horror of the war had been meaningless. And I was waiting – waiting for socialism."

But by 1947 the Cold War was spreading its paranoid chill over central Europe. Poland and the other new Soviet satellites, still sickly from years of war, destruction, deprivation, and the death of millions, were sequestered from the rest of the world and being moulded into reflections of the USSR, with arbitrary, despotic rulers mouthing the ideological rhetoric of Marxist-Leninism and attempting to control all aspects of their subjects' lives. The governments of the satellite regimes had been imposed through force, broken promises, and trickery, and fear was the instrument used to intimidate populations into accepting them. While Stalin lived, much of the energy of the communist police states was turned not only against opponents of the regime but also against old communists and socialists. Since its first days, the Soviet state, like the French revolution before it, had been devouring its children as well as its opponents. This process was at its most extreme in 1936 and 1937, when Stalin, obsessed with asserting his absolute authority, ordered the massive purge of old Bolsheviks, and hundreds of thousands of men and women – including the father of Alina's girlhood love – were executed, imprisoned, or sent to the Gulag. A similar scenario, though on a smaller scale, was now to be enacted in the Soviet satellite countries. This time it was precipitated by the Cold War itself, by the fact that the new state of Israel, which the Soviets had hoped would become their dependant, had turned instead to the United States, and by Yugoslavia's decision under its leader, Marshall Tito, to reject the Soviet umbrella and follow its own road to communism. Again there were purges, show trials, and executions. On Stalin's orders, party leaders and other powerful party members in the eastern bloc were put on trial with various trumped-up charges of subversion, treachery, bourgeois deviationism, spying for the west, Titoism, and Zionism. Władysław Gomułka, the Polish leader, was fortunate in being simply deposed and expelled from the Party in 1948. Others were shot or imprisoned. International attention was given to the 1952 trials and executions of Rudolf Slansky and other mostly Jewish leading members of the Czechoslovak party. The proceedings had hysterically anti-Semitic overtones under the guise of anti-Zionism and accusations of "cosmopolitanism." In the USSR itself, a group of eminent physicians, many of whom were also Jewish, were accused of plotting to poison Kremlin top officials who had been their patients.

Mietek said that it took a few years before the Polish government began to use the instrument of anti-Semitism to achieve its ends. "At the beginning we were too useful. It wasn't a matter of us suppressing in ourselves the knowledge that anti-Semitism continued to exist but, rather, that I felt that we had enough power not to be concerned about it. We also dismissed a lot of things as being done for the sake of tactics. For example, when the first Congress of Polish-Soviet Friendship was to be held, I was initially asked to go as a delegate, and then I was told that I couldn't go because I was Jewish. I was very offended, but people said, 'It is tactics' – that is, an attempt to appease the population, an attempt to hide the fact that there were Jews actively supporting the new system. I thought – and think – that this was wrong, that they should have been open, that they should have said that communist principles were opposed to racism and bigotry, and they should have educated people to accept all their fellow citizens of whatever nationality and religion. If they had done this openly and honestly, the situation in central and eastern Europe might have been different today.

"We dismissed a lot as 'tactics.' In the 1950s, when we were asked to 'Polonize' our names, I went along with it because others were doing it, and this too was part of the tactics of concealing Jews, and I think it was wrong. Also we were manipulated (by 'we' I mean those of us who started as idealists), although I didn't really begin to see this until the Twentieth Party Congress in '56, when Khrushchev revealed what had happened under Stalin – the party purges, the show trials, the killings, his murderous paranoia. In fact, we had heard rumours of the anti-Jewish purges in Russia in Stalin's last years and the so-called Kremlin Doctors' Plot, and that he had plans against all the Jews there. We didn't hear it on the street but from very high profile communists. How did I feel? Very badly. I tried to rationalize it, to tell myself it was a matter of tactics, that it would pass, that there was nothing I could do about it, and that we'd outlive this as we'd outlived so many enemies. Then in 1953 Stalin died, and for a while things turned around."

It was when Alina moved to Warsaw in 1950 that she had to face the fact that her idealistic hopes for a just society were being betrayed and that she was living under the tyranny of a police state which would use her girlhood romance with Alexei Berdayev and the friendships of her youth to wrap its tentacles around her. The person, she often reiterated, who knew about her background and would have passed on the information was Jacek Rożański.

"The telephone calls would come when I was at work. 'Comrade,' the voice would say, 'You will go to such-and-such address.' It would always be some small, two-room apartment. I can't describe what they looked like – I didn't notice the room itself. What I remember was the intolerable stress: not to say too much, to say what I must say and yet not be on the line and not harm anyone or myself. It became a routine; there was always the same interrogator, a rather pleasant-mannered, small-built young man. The questions were about what was referred to as 'the Trotskyite clique' – Alexei and our friends before the war."

Alexei had located Alina in 1946 via a letter sent to the Łódź community organization. She had not seen him since 1938. So much had happened, and he was no longer central to her thoughts. She wrote back to him in the United States, they corresponded, and he sent her parcels. He had anglicized his surname and was now a college professor of economics. He also seemed to have changed, to be different. Their correspondence went on until 1950, when the Security police came to her apartment and took his letters, though when the interrogations started, she had burnt those with references to the new regime. "One day I was asked if I wanted to go the United States. 'Why?' I asked. 'To kill Alexander Berdayev.' I wasn't surprised: this was the atmosphere we were living in. I was shocked and not shocked. I don't remember my precise words when I refused, but the suggestion was never repeated. I don't know why they were after him – possibly he was saying or writing things against the regime." Eventually, the letters were returned to her, and she always kept them with her. In one of the articles written later by Józef Światło, the former Security colonel who defected to the West, there was a reference to a scheme hatched up by "the special office" of the Bezpieka to assassinate various Poles then living in the West. "The plan consisted of getting to the suspected person and organizing agents around them." The article says that the proposals from the office concerned a woman in West Germany, a man in France, "and Alexander Berdayev in the USA."

Alina recalled: "One of our other friends from before the war was arrested in East Germany. They claimed he was trying to escape to the West. It wasn't true, but he was imprisoned for two years. The interrogator once asked me if I knew that my old friend the engineer had four mistresses – obviously implying that I must have had an affair with him and so would be jealous and testify against him. I began to laugh because it was ridiculous – one had to know him and his relationship with his wife. She was the daughter of a Ukrainian peasant who rescued and sheltered him after he was wounded fighting with partisans against the Germans. I recently checked through an article by Józef Światło in *Historical Notebooks*, and it says that the engineer and I were arrested in 1952. In fact, I wasn't arrested, but I suppose that what it means is that they had a warrant to do so if necessary. In the event, I was only interrogated. I suspect that I owe it to Jacek that I wasn't. It was he who gave the names of those were were to be arrested, and he knew that I did not represent any danger to 'People's Poland.'

"I can't remember the questions the interrogator used to ask, only the lines that they were on – how was it that we had all become friends, what we used to talk about, what they were doing, their opinions of Stalin and the Party, whom they met, what they wrote. What he wanted to get out of me was that they were enemies and traitors – presumably of socialism and Poland and the so-called first country of peasants and labourers – the only paradise on earth – and that they were agents of American and British counter-intelligence. What did I feel? Hate, revulsion, contempt, and fear. I was frightened I would say what they wanted me to say and frightened of being sent to prison. These feelings came to me constantly both at the time and after I'd left the flat."

The interrogations went on for a period of two years. Alina did not tell Stasia and Mietek about them. "I don't think I told anyone, and I certainly wouldn't have told Mietek, because at that time it was his opinion that if someone were arrested, then they must be guilty. But maybe I am wrong. What I remember very well was that it was difficult to go on living. And what I am sure of is that it was Jacek who put the Security onto me."

Alina described some incidents that were typical of the times, as, for example, when an old acquaintance from Łódź turned up at her flat in Warsaw. "I'd known him when he was a law student, soon after I graduated from high school, and at that time I'd been told that he was in love with me. Now he was an army prosecutor. At first the conversation was pleasant. Then questions started that turned my hands and feet cold, ice splinters in my heart. It is an indescribable feeling. But I quickly pulled myself together and answered in the acceptable format. There was a war panic on at the time – this was at the height of the Cold War – and before he left, he said to me sarcastically, 'And for this war, I suppose I must thank you.' My response was something on the lines of my having a clear conscience and that he could repeat whatever I had said. I know the poor fellow didn't come to me on his own initiative."

There was a similar incident involving a young man who was the son of her parents' maid. His father, a master chimney sweep, had been sent to prison before the war for three years for communist activity – it was he who was going to help Alina escape to the Soviet Union after the Germans invaded. The father came to visit her in Łódź not long after her brother-in-law had left Poland for France – he'd gone during the immediate post-war period, when people could still get out of the country. "The man asked me why my brother-in-law had left. 'Because,' I replied, 'he didn't want to be made constantly aware that he was a Jew.' The man was upset and shouted, 'In socialist Poland there will not be any anti-Semitism!' He was one of the old idealists. Anyway, when his son grew up, he went to the army officer cadet school, and he came to visit me when I was living in Warsaw. He told me that his father had been made the personnel officer of the Party's provincial committee and was now the director of a factory. He joked about the fact that his parents were looking for a wife for him from a 'good' home – it was funny because it was such a bourgeois attitude. Then on one visit he started to ask those questions that froze me. He never came again – an officer couldn't have such an acquaintance. I'm sure that he too had been put up to it, but you can see that the Security and the Party were forcing themselves through all the cracks in the walls of your own home, intruding themselves right into your private life."

"On one occasion, I was asked to go to Łódź to report on the family of one of my old friends there. I bluntly refused, but there were no consequences. Nor were there any when I was asked to allow the Security to use my flat when I wasn't there and I refused. I was also called to the regional party committee and requested to stop corresponding with my brother-in-law after he went to France. I refused again, and again there were no consequences."

The consequences she could not escape were those resulting from Jacek Rożański's knowledge of her pre-war friendship with the "Trotskyite clique." This was to involve her indirectly in the notorious Slansky show trial being prepared in Czechoslovakia. One of those arrested in Poland in 1950 in connection with the case was her old friend Leon Gecow. He had escaped to the USSR in 1939 and, like Mietek, had enlisted as a doctor in Berling's army in 1943. When the Second Polish army was formed, he organized its medical service, and after the war he became director of the military office in the Ministry of Health, where he was working when he was arrested in July 1950. He was also known for his essays, well written and relatively free of jargon, on communist political theory.

"At that time" said Alina, "I'd recently moved from Łódź to Warsaw, and until I got my own place, I stayed with my friend Zofia and her husband. They were living in one of the best apartment buildings, for top members of the Security – Stasia and Mietek also lived in the same flat for a while afterwards. It happened that Jacek's apartment was on the same floor as ours, and one evening we all went to a movie. On the way back he said, 'I'd like to go for a walk with Alina.' He and I walked until 1 a.m. While we went through the streets, he cross-questioned me about Leon, insisting that he was spying for the United States and England. All I can remember saying is 'You can talk until you run out of breath, but I'll never believe that Leon is a spy and a traitor,' and Jacek replying, 'And I, my dear Alina, will prove to you that he is a bastard.'"

Józef Światło wrote a classic definition of show trials, describing them as "one of the propoganda weapons used by the Moscow Politburo and the Satellite Party Politburos. These trials are used to build up the political line the Party establishes at any given moment to fulfill its needs. They have nothing in common with the administration of justice and genuine judicial procedures: the verdicts are known beforehand."* The energies of the Bezpieka were now being used not only against opponents of the regime but against those who were part of it.

Gecow's connection with the Slansky case was through his acquaintance with two American brothers, Noel and Herman Fields, both socialist in their sympathies, whose disappearance behind the Iron Curtain in 1949 was a *cause célèbre*. Gecow had had contact with them before the war when he was a medical student in Zurich, where Noel was with the League of Nations; during the war the brothers were in Switzerland, assisting refugees, particularly communists. Gecow and Noel Fields had met again after the war when Noel was working in a Unitarian Services hospital in Polish Silesia. At the show trial of Laszlo Rajk in Hungary in 1949 and again, three years later, at the Slansky trial, the brothers were referred to as spies for the United States. In Poland a woman who was being beaten to extract from her names with possible connections to the Slansky case told her tormentors that when Leon Gecow heard of the accusations against Noel Fields, he had commented wrily to her, "There is no hope for me." Shortly afterwards he was arrested.

The files of the Ministry of Security from those years are now open. In them, and in documents in Alina's possesion, details can be found of Leon Gecow's interrogation and of Jacek Rożański's involvement in his case. The collision of wills between the two men, both communists since before the war, has echoes of Arthur Koestler's famous book *Darkness at Noon*. First published in 1940 in England, it takes the reader into the mind of a long-time Bolshevik, imprisoned and interrogated before being executed during the 1930s Soviet purges and show trials. In the West the book planted the seeds of doubt in many minds previously uncritical of, or sympathetic towards, the Soviet state (intellectuals had always been more attracted and vulnerable to the ideology than the "proletarian masses" whom it was supposed to liberate.) Rożański had read the book, which was banned for ordinary Poles, and it was only when he learned from an informer that Gecow had also read it that he became directly involved in his case. Another, cruder interrogator had used torture to extract from Gecow the admission that he had known that Noel

---

*Quoted in *Behind the Scene of the Party and Bezpieka*.

Field was a Troskyite spy and also the names of other "conspirators," but each time Gecow would later retract his statements. Rożański, who prided himself on his use of psychological methods rather than what was known as "physical pressure" – making the point that people would make any allegation just to stop it – attempted through argument to engage Gecow in a parallel replay of one of the book's scenes,* in order to extract from him the confession that was needed to give the case some legitimacy. The plan was not successful: when Gecow, using the jargon of the times, offered to criticize himself in terms of "socialist objectivity," because "my formulations are being applauded by rightist and opportunistic elements," and to plead guilty to being "objectively counterrevolutionary," Rożański responded, "What you are saying is wrong, unclear, and dangerous. You are under the influence of the Koestler book, and you are quoting from it." Like the protaganist in *Darkness at Noon,* Gecow was returned to what was known as the interrogation "conveyor belt." A doctor who examined him at some point later described him as having a horribly crushed hand.

There was a day in 1952 that Alina could never forget. "I received a note on april the first telling me to go to court as a 'witness for the prosecution.' I wasn't told against whom. I went to the courthouse, and a woman clerk said to me, 'The accused is not in the court. You must go to the prison.' She would not say who it was that was on trial. A man was being told the same thing, and we went together in a taxi. We were both silent until suddenly it came to me. 'It's the case of Leon Gecow!' I said. 'I don't know him,' he replied. In the waiting room at the jail there was another woman friend of Leon's whom I knew. The man was called first, then me. He was walking down the stairs when I was sent up. His face was ashen, and he just shook his head.

"I was shown into a small room. Four people wearing judicial robes and uniforms were sitting behind a desk. I was frightened and looked around for a familiar face, but I couldn't see anyone I knew. They began to ask me questions about Leon. Then I saw someone sitting to the side, a man with a chalk-white face. At first glance I didn't recognize him, until I looked at his eyes. Then I realized it

---

*The scene presents a confrontation between Rubashov, the old Bolshevik accused of subversion and treachery, and one of his interrogators, Ivanov, another old Bolshevik.

was him, Leon. He smiled, but I couldn't. The judge was very formal, and I think he asked me what Leon had said or written about Stalin. When it was over, I didn't know what I had said – I couldn't remember and still don't. When they'd finished with me, I waited outside the building for the other woman – she had asked me to. We walked together, not talking. It was then that I got my first stomach ulcer pains. I can't forget his face. Leon died in custody."

Later, Alina's old friend the engineer, who had also been arrested, told her that both he and Leon Gecow had the same interrogator, known as the "boa constrictor." It was he, Alina says, who probably "strangled" Leon. "Leon's wife was also in prison for four years, and when he was 'rehabilitated' in 1956, after Gomułka took over the government, she was allowed to exhume his body and bury him properly and to read the proceedings of his trial. She telephoned me and said, 'I read your testimony. It was beautiful.' It is difficult to express how much it meant for me to hear that. I never wanted to read it myself, and I'm still not able to talk or think about it all very intelligently. But I have no doubt that it was Jacek who gave the order for me to be called as witness."

Another witness who gave testimony at Gecow's trial described him as "a very honest and honourable man. Some people wanted to build communism because they hated the world, but Gecow wanted to build communism because he loved it." Gecow, he said, was "a true communist." Speaking of his death, an old Stalinist[*] years later referred to it as "a sentencing error."

Mietek's old friend Max was the medical director of the prison hospital from 1952 to 1955. Of the experience, he wrote that he had been assigned to the position without any warning and without being asked for his consent. "I was not aware of what was going on inside the prison, and with an instinct for self-preservation, I wanted to know as little as possible. I used to work for approximately five hours in the afternoons as director and in my speciality as an otolaryngologist. The main goals I set for myself were to fight for appropriate supplies of medicine and equipment for the hospital, to ensure that specialist care was available, to have a high

---

[*] This was Julia Minc, wife of Hilary Minc, the economics minister during the Stalinist years. Quoted in *Behind the Scene of the Party and Bezpieka*.

professional level, and to ensure that the prisoners received their health and sanitation rights according to existing regulations."

One section of the prison, Max wrote, was for people convicted of criminal and political offences, and in the other were prisoners still under interrogation, all of whom were politicals, both from the right and the left – communists and socialists. "I had no access to this section. Whenever medical help was needed, they were looked after by two physicians 'trusted' by the Security. The prisoners under interrogation were not identified by their names, only by their initials and numbers, and during medical examination there was always a prison guard or the interrogation officer present. My only contact with them was if they were hospitalized. We physicians restricted ourselves to talks about health problems, and of course, even between us discussion about matters behind the scenes were very rare – you couldn't be sure whom you could trust. Furthermore, it was very well known that there were many informers among the prisoners themselves, and that was another reason for being careful. The years 1952 and 1953 were two of the worst in the Stalinist epoch after the war. Then, after his death, the regime loosened up, and they started to release prisoners." Max was not asked whether he ever saw Leon Gecow; now it is too late to do so.

Alina finally joined the Party in 1953, despite, she thought, or perhaps because of what was going on. At that time she was working in a hospital that was part of the separate health facilities serving the needs of Security employees. "I was in charge of one of the labs and quite enjoyed the work. The department head was a pleasant man, and not just he but Stasia and all my friends had joined. Finally I said to myself, 'Can everyone else be wrong? Perhaps it can be changed from the inside,' so I joined. But I was always critical, and one could see that there were very few real communists in the Party. Most people joined for convenience or self-serving opportunism.

"The war had made me tough. It had hardened me. In 1956 I was thrown out of my job at the laboratory after I'd been visited by an old friend of mine from before the war, a man who was now a journalist in France, a correspondent for *Le Monde*. He was surprised that I wasn't afraid to meet him, but I wouldn't let myself be intimidated, and although I'd loved my work, it didn't upset me when I was fired. Anyway, I got another good position, at the Institute of Hygiene. After I started there, I was twice called to the Commission of Party Control. The first time I was met by three Jewish women, the type that we used to call 'the aunts of the revolution,' and they tried to lecture me on party morality. I told them that I was an adult and that I didn't need them to instruct me on the issue of morality. That silenced them. The second time I was met by a very nice old, working-class man who spoke to me in a fatherly way. I hadn't joined the party organization at my new job and didn't intend to, but he asked me to do so in such a warm fatherly way that I, like an idiot, gave in. In fact, I was made secretary to the branch of the Party in my department at the institute. I had to make a speech on May Day, and usually people came out with the expected clichés about how wonderful the Party and the leaders were and what great things they were doing, but I decided to talk about its historical origins as a celebration. They were a bit surprised, but afterwards a few people came up and said that they had really enjoyed it. By then, of course, the worst years were in the past."

Alina had another experience during that time. Józef Światło's wife was placed in her lab, obviously to spy on her. A nice woman, she was completely unqualified for the work and seemed scared. One day Alina was told to go to see Lieutenant-Colonel Światło in the Security's tenth department, where one of his jobs was the tracing and liquidation of all Western influences. Taken into a large building through a maze of corridors, she was ushered into a room where a small, ugly man sat behind a desk. He pleasantly offered her chocolates and cigarettes and asked her about botulism and paratyphus, to which she responded that these were not her specialities. Two months later she was called there again. This time the atmosphere was different. "Is it about botulism again?" she asked. "Another kind," he replied and began to ask her about what Alexei Berdayev was doing. "Światło defected a few weeks later, "so afterwards I wondered whether he wanted to make contact with him."

The show trials ended after Stalin's death in March 1953. Later that year Światło and another officer from his department were in East Berlin on ministry business. They crossed into West Berlin to look around, went into a department store, and Światło disappeared. When he surfaced months later, it was on Radio Free

Europe, through whose airwaves he broadcast a series of bombshell revelations about Security policies and its practices, including the use of blackmail and torture, about its control by Soviet officials, about his former colleagues, including Jacek Rożański and Luna Brystigier. His defection, to the United States, was probably less out of ideological conversion than to save his own skin. He had been in charge of detailed, intimate material about all the leading personalities in the regime: he knew too much. (The Polish press agency, of which Bela Rożański was director at around that time, described him as an "*agent provocateur* in the high echelon of the security system.") The furor rattled the regime to its foundations and, combined with the changes taking place in the Kremlin after Stalin's death, was one of the reasons for a shakeup in the Warsaw power structure. This, among other things, was to result in the return of Władisław Gomułka as party leader in 1956 and in changes in the structure and practices of the Bezpieka.

In mid-1954 Rożański was "released" from the ministry. He was made director of one of the state publishing houses, but official records note that he was never seen there; other employees were told he was on holiday. On the other hand, according to Polish writer Michal Komar, Rożański signed a deal during this time to publish an anti-Stalinist poet. Chatting with the poet, Rożański said cryptically, "Don't have any illusions. I am a villain only in so far as I agreed to answer the alphabet backwards." On 8 November, on his way out of a meeting of the Party's Central Committee, where he had been called to explain his actions, he was arrested for abuses of power and for acting against the interests of the Polish nation. At the same time, a search was being made for incriminating evidence at his apartment. It was conducted in the presence of the state prosecutor and Luna Brystigier. At his two-day trial, held in camera in December 1955, Rożański was accused of having brutally broken people's revolutionary rights, of having acted against the principles of socialist morality, and of having used methods of interrogation not allowed by law.[*]
He admitted to all the charges, and was sentenced to five years in prison, reduced on appeal to four years and four months.

[*] Swialto gave details of these methods, such as knocking out teeth, pulling hair, and kicking people in the head, and the names of some of his victims in the testimony in Behind the Scene of the Party and Bezpieka.

It must have been before that trial that Max saw Rożański. "Towards the end of 1955," wrote Max, "he was in the prison hospital – I think he had a duodenal ulcer. He was in a room by himself, and although we did not know each other personally, I went in and asked him what he was accused of. I remember his answer clearly: 'I am like a doll, and they'll dress me in whatever clothes will please them. Maybe they will dress me as a French aristocrat, or maybe as a Polish peasant, or maybe something else.'"

Translating Max's letter, Stasia said, "You see! It meant that Jacek was aware they would attribute whatever they wanted to him. And that he would be treated as a scapegoat."

Alina chose not to leave Poland in the late 1950s when many of her friends, including Stasia and Mietek, were given permission to emigrate. "Things were easier at that time. This was after Khrushchev's speech to the Twentieth Party Congress, with all its revelations about the murder of the old Bolsheviks in the thirties purges. It had a ripple effect through the satellite states, and the Security police became less powerful. There were no more interrogations. There was less censorship and more freedom. I went on holiday to Paris, and I could have stayed. But I felt I had to go back to Poland. Why? Well, four party secretaries who were Jewish had gone to conferences in the West, and one after the other they had defected. I said to myself, 'I can't do it. I don't want people to be able to say that Jews are traitors.' I also thought I had a duty to the country.

"We – people like Mietek, Stasia, and me – we all loved the country, and we wanted to work for it. The culture, the language, the literature, was mine, really mine. I don't know when the feeling, the sense of belonging and commitment, went, but finally it did. Perhaps it was in 1968, in the big anti-Semitic official purge, when most of the remaining Jews with good jobs were pressured to leave the country. Although I didn't go then. When my old friend the engineer and his wife were leaving Poland at that time, I was going on a holiday to Russia, to Sochi on the Black Sea, and he said to me – remembering what happened during the war when they had all gone to the east, and before, when Alexei had gone to the United

States – 'Alina, you know something? You are always going in the wrong direction!' I stayed until 1972 and finally left after I'd been in hospital. I had a lot of pain and I couldn't sleep, so I just thought about everything. I confronted the fact that this was supposed to be my country, yet because I was a Jew, I was being treated as though I were a stranger. It was simply and profoundly that I was offended. And I decided that I would not take it any more."

There had been a lot to take. In 1959 General Mieczysław Moczar, a wartime communist partisan commander, became minister of the re-created and expanded Bezpieka and, backed up by his supporters, began to challenge Gomułka for the party leadership. The Moczarites, whose numbers included pre-war Endeks and fascists, were nationalistic, anti-intellectual, and anti-liberal, and they used a crude anti-Semitism, under the guise of anti-Zionism, to achieve their purpose. Preparing for a witch hunt – at a time when there were only 25 to 30 thousand Jews in Poland (one in a thousand of the population), the ministry built up a list of names of all known Jews, half-Jews, converted Jews, and younger people who had no idea of their Jewish origins. The moment to strike came after the Israeli victory in 1967 was greeted around the country with spontaneous expressions of delight that "our" Jews had beaten "their" (that is, the Russians') Arabs. Furious, Gomułka publicly accused Polish Jews of being a potentially treacherous fifth column, and attempting to upstage Moczar, he gave orders for "Zionists" to be rooted out of the Party, where they were simultaneously accused of responsibility for Stalinist excesses, of revisionism, and of capitalist sympathies. People were "exposed" as Jews and pressured out of their jobs in the civil administration, the military, medicine and nursing, film and journalism, scientific institutes. Nazi-style editorials and pamphlets appeared. When thousands of students, dissatisfied and disgusted with government policies, hypocrisy, and mismanagement, rioted in 1968, their leaders were accused of being Jewish. Unemployed and harassed into leaving their country, people were then faced with bureaucratic obstacles, bans on taking savings and valuable belongings – with every book having to be listed in triplicate – and demands for heavy fees, to the point that Jewish overseas agencies had to send funds. Citizenship had to be renounced and only Israel put down as their destination. It had all been a smokescreen in a political battle and to divert popular attention from the

General Mieczysław Moczar (Archive of Audio-visual Records, Warsaw)

country's economic malaise, but though Moczar never succeeded in his personal power play, by the mid-1970s the Endeks' pre-war policy had finally been achieved: Poland was in effect empty of Jews.

Alina had been one of the last to go. A woman of strong will and loyalties, she said it was not easy to leave all her friends. Showing a photograph of the people who came to see her off at the railway station, she said, "Look, you can see Stasia's old friends Jerzy and Mira Sawa among them. It was hard, but I think that coming here to Denmark was one of the few clever things I have done in my life. Apart from Israel, Denmark and Sweden were the only countries letting in the Jewish communists thrown out of Poland. I know many of their children here. Like Stasia's Peter, they are very anti-communist. I was in Israel once on a visit, but I didn't want to stay there. I couldn't take the climate, and like Stasia, I didn't like the chauvinistic attitudes. When I was in Haifa with Stasia and Mietek, we visited an old friend of ours. Her brother had been murdered in the Soviet purges, but she still hadn't turned against the communist

Władysław Gomułka (Archive of Audiovisual Records, Warsaw)

system. 'I am only angry and bitter at whoever shot him,' she said. Mietek and Stasia agreed with her, but they were wrong. The problem was the system itself, and that is why I didn't like Gorbachev. He is still a believer. As for Jacek, he was terrible. Did you know that when Peter visited him in prison, Jacek said to him, 'History will rehabilitate me.' What is tragic is that possibly, possibly, he started out as an idealist."

History is a text open to interpretation. Rożański knew his Marxist analysis of history, and we know that he had also read *Darkness at Noon*. In that book the prisoner says of another purged old Bolshevik that history would rehabilitate him.

⊰⊱

Mietek commented that there was "difference between him and Alina in that although he was also critical of what had happened under the regime, he did not feel or see himself as having been a victim of it, whereas she did. "In fact, she was not a victim of it. Alina was very much connected with the higher echelons. She did benefit from the system, and she too used the special shops when she was working at the ministry. If she was a victim, it was of what happened later, in 1968.

"When we left Poland in 1957, I had the rank of lieutenant-colonel as doctor in the medical administration of the Ministry of Security. My wife and I had a good flat in the centre of Warsaw. We had access to special stores – though not to the very special stores for the top echelon – and it was easier for us than the general population to get meat, clothes, everything. I also had a chauffeur-driven car for my use if I required it. It was not I who made the decision to leave Poland; it was my wife who insisted that we go. I would have stuck with it, although pressure was beginning to be put on Jews to leave the country."

When they were leaving Poland was the only time that Stasia saw Mietek in tears.

"When we left," said Mietek, "Gomułka was in power and he was allowing Jews to go to Israel. The state had not turned against me yet, but ten years later I would have been pushed out, along with most of the remaining Jews. My sister and brother-in-law left with us, so did Max and his wife – he and I had always made the same moves since we were students. The Jews like Alina who stayed after the 1957 wave of emigration stayed because they wanted to. They felt Polish and were committed to the communist system. Then in 1968, after the Arab-Israeli War, when the Soviet Union supported the Arabs, Polish Jews were called Zionists. They were made to leave their jobs; they were turned out of the Party; they were ostracized and told that they should leave the country. Finally, no one wanted to stay because all their friends had left. It was a terrible disillusionment when that happened, for sure. But I wasn't surprised. A lot of us in Israel, including Max and my wife, sent back our war medals at the time. It was a dreadful feeling when I did that. But it was a stupid gesture of no importance – an empty demonstration. Anyway, after I left Poland, I didn't attach any importance to them – none."

A good number of people whom Mietek knew turned up in Israel. "Some of them became anti-Russian and strong anti-communists, some – let us say their ideological voltage went down, and others still regard themselves as political exiles because they feel they are true communists and that the regime in Poland was taken over by

Mietek as a colonel in the Bezpieka in 1955

traitors to the cause. One of the arrivals in '68 had been the chief doctor in my regiment in the Kościuszko division, and we'd bivouacked together. After the war he'd gone on to have a good military career in Poland. He'd been made deputy chief of medical services for the army until they decided – because he was Jewish – to transfer him to a less-conspicuous position as commander of the military medical academy. He is Max's neighbour now. Aaron Grinstein, my company's political commissar in the army, also left in 1957. Aaron couldn't adapt to Israel. He decided to return, but the Poles wouldn't give him permission. He went to Yugoslavia, where he had friends from his Spanish Civil War days, and they arranged for him to get a visa to Kiev in the Ukraine. From Kiev he went to Warsaw and asked some friends to use their influence – he knew them also from the war in Spain, and they were now in high positions. But it was no use – they couldn't or wouldn't help. Aaron was deported back to Israel, and he died there. I don't know why

Rożański didn't leave in 1968. Maybe he was still in prison. Maybe they thought he knew too much.

"I myself found it easy to adapt to Israel. I could speak Hebrew, and I had come to a place where I felt I belonged. Before that there had always been the fear of rejection. I had to do a four years' residence in my speciality – in fact, almost everything I know about my profession I learned there. Before retiring, I was deputy chief of the ophthalmology department in the hospital.

"My politics in Israel? Well, initially I supported the communists. There was a Jewish-Arab party with a platform recognizing the Israeli state and Arab rights, but it split after the 1967 war, and some of its supporters are now members of a coalition, with Mapam. It's a middle-of-the-road left-wing party. I would vote for them if I were still in Israel.

"Why have I said that I wasted my life? Because I think I should have gone to Israel, or even to the United States, after the war, when I was still a young man. It was wasted because we worked for ideals that we thought were intended to do something good for the general population and for ourselves, but what happened was ultimately detrimental to it and to us. Sure, the government did some good things, in health and education and so on, but Poland did not become what people like Max and myself wanted – a society in which everyone is equal and free. Nor did it solve the problems I wanted to see solved. All in all, I have the feeling that I was conned, that I was taken in by a lie.

"The history of the 20th century is one of indoctrination and manipulation, especially in the Soviet Union. The working class in Russia took power and quickly abdicated to gangsters who corrupted honest party members. It all became a big fraud. The real crime was that our government in Poland did not do what has to be done – that is, to give the country to the people, not to the *nomenklatura*."*

When Alina left Poland, she had to leave behind not only many of her friends but most of her possessions and savings. She was also refused permission to take her personal documents, but the Danish

---

*A Russian term for the party establishment.

embassy in Warsaw had them brought out for her. In a small wooden trunk, she keeps letters and photographs from her life in Poland. Although the only work she could get in Denmark was as a laboratory technician, she says that it did not matter and that she never regretted her move. "Living here in a real democracy, I have seen what socialism should be, what we really wanted. Many of these books I have around me here are about politics and the communist period. Stasia says she only reads literature. I read to try to understand what happened to the Soviet Union, to Poland, to us. And to the idea."

Child of the Nomenklatura

Careerism, extravagance, and love of power are inevitable, and so is corruption ... It is a special type of corruption caused by the fact that the government is in the hands of a single political group and is the source of all privileges ... the Communist revolution, conducted in the name of doing away with classes, has resulted in the most complete authority of any single new class. Everything else is sham and illusion."

Milovan Djilas, The New Class (1957)

Our will was hard and pure, we should have been loved by the people. But they hate us. Why are we so odious and detested? We brought you truth and in our mouth it sounded a lie. We brought you freedom, and it looks in our hands like a whip.

Arthur Koestler, Darkness at Noon (1940)

I think the logic of this is that in a good system a bad person can be controlled, and in a bad system good people can be spoiled. We got spoiled in a bad system.

Jacek Rożański, December 1954

※

Stasia's son, Peter, is argumentative, opinionated, tense, voluble, volatile, and unbuyable. His mother, who objects to much of what he describes, says he "confabulates."

He remembers the night after Stalin died. "It was 1953, the 5th of March. There was a heated discussion going on in the apartment above my mother's and Mietek's. The couple who lived there were

Peter, age twenty-eight

good friends of theirs, long-time communists. They'd been political prisoners in Poland in the mid-thirties, they'd fought in Spain in the Red Army, and then, like Mietek, they'd been in Berling's army. She was now a doctor in the Security and he was working with the Central Planning Committee.

"They were arguing about the so-called Kremlin Doctors' Plot – a group of prominent Moscow doctors, all of them Jewish, had been accused of plotting to kill members of the Politburo, the ruling group around Stalin. My mother's argument was that it didn't ring true that a group of people whose profession was to help people would conspire to commit murder, and that even if one or two doctors might do something like that, she didn't believe there would be a group conspiracy. Mietek has never been a talkative person, and he didn't like arguing, but it was obvious to me that he half-agreed with my mother. At one point in the discussion, the woman whose apartment we were in turned to her husband and said, 'Do you remember when we were in that *kolkhoz* in the Ukraine during the Stalingrad offensive, and the old *kolkhoz* secretary said to us that "everything will get better when the old Georgian dies", and we both knew what he meant?' Her comment might not seem earth-shaking to you, but for me it was a real jolt, a major eye-opener.

"There we were in this apartment block in which only ranking Security officers lived, the men sitting there in their uniforms. Consider what had brought them together that day: everyone was supposed to be in mourning for the 'god,' the 'grandfather' of all us children. And these people – my mother, Mietek, and their friends – were strongly affected by Stalin's death, although ordinary people were too, even people who had hated him and everything he stood for. Why? Because it was the end of an era, and there was a sense of uncertainty, of 'What happens next?' So if you can understand, it was a real shock for me, brought up among the *nomenklatura*, to hear these kinds of comments from people like them. I think it was from that moment in 1953 that I consciously started to question things, to try to understand what was going on. And for a long time I felt that I was being pulled in two opposite directions."

Peter spent his adolescence in the privileged world of the communist elite, Poland's new establishment, part of what Milovan Djilas, the Yugoslav communist dissident and writer, described as "the new class." Though it was not the innermost circle, which had its own extra privileges, they had access to special stores, holiday resorts, cinemas, health and sports facilities, schools, and apartments – this at a time when most of Warsaw's population was living in very difficult conditions while the city was being rebuilt.

"We'd been living in these luxurious – luxurious for the time and place – Security apartment blocks since we came to Warsaw from Szczecin. That was after Mietek got his promotion in 1951. The first place I found myself in was a large, beautiful apartment near the centre of the city. There were always Bezpieka police at the entrance to the building, and to get into it, you had either to be known to them or be personally escorted to someone's door. That apartment had belonged to Alina's friend Zofia and her husband – she's the one who wrote the book about Auschwitz. My mother doesn't like her. They didn't get on. All the people living in the block were top officials in the Bezpieka, and on the same floor as us was Jacek Rożański, the director of a special section of the Bezpieka. He was very charming and always nice to me, though I didn't like his wife, a hard, tough woman. She was personnel director of the Central Committee of the Party and later chief of the Polish press agency. That was a very powerful position in a state where the regime had control over everything that was published. His brother was president of the Polish Writers' Union, and even his old girlfriend Anka was chief judge of the Warsaw Children's Court. So between them, they controlled quite a lot.

"Jacek's daughter was three years younger than me – she'd been born in Russia during the war – but for a while we went to school together. This was a school for the kids of the top echelon, the big shots, and politically the atmosphere was highly charged. What was interesting was that the children's behaviour reflected what their fathers were really like, rather than their actual positions, and some of them behaved very arrogantly. Quite a few were driven to school in big limousines, and you would even find chauffeurs waiting all day to take them home. The school's youth committee was a reflection of the Politburo, and in '56, when the revolt against the Stalinists was going on inside and outside the government, the turmoil at the school was incredible. The Warsaw committee of all the youth organizations was frightened of our school committtee because they were all the kids of powerful people. Once when I was a kid, I had a fight with the son of a Russian general and won. The general came to the school and complained that he'd fought for Poland and here's his son being beaten up by a Pole. So my ma was called to the school, but she didn't buy his argument, though it was awkward for her. Her attitude was 'What's that got to do with a couple of boys having a scrap?' You didn't know what the repercussions were going to be of anything. The terrain was a minefield. A kids' scrap could turn into a political issue with international ramifications. For example, Mietek learned at a party meeting that I'd had a fight with the son of another Russian 'adviser.'"

Peter and his closest friend, Ludwik, used to walk to school with and sit next to another boy whose father at that time was the minister of communication and transport. During the civil war he had been one of the commanding generals. Asked whether he felt it a burden to be a "miracle" survivor, Peter replied, "Although I was aware of it intellectually, I didn't feel it emotionally because I grew up surrounded by similar children in the Security milieu, and we were affluent in comparison to most Poles at the time. For me, Ludwik was the real miracle survivor. According to what he'd been told, he was hidden by several families in the war – he was given the name Ludwik and at the end of the war handed over to a Jewish orphanage – like the one described in Jerzy Kosiński's novel *The Painted Bird*. Jewish survivors were competing to adopt the children, and he was given to a professor who was one of the people who set up the Jewish Historical Museum in Warsaw after the war. He was a nice man, but his wife was a pig, a real hardline communist. When Ludwik misbehaved at home, she denounced him to the school! So although Ludwik was fond of his adoptive father, he wasn't happy at home. He used to come round to our place a lot, and my mother took him under her wing."

If, as a result of the incident in the apartment after Stalin died, Peter consciously began to question the circumscribed world of the *nomenklatura*, its values and given truths, he was already aware that things were going on under the surface. "I'd heard my mother and Mietek arguing about the 'Doctors' Plot,' and there were other strange incidents that I hadn't understood when they happened. Like the time in '48 or '49 when we were on holiday at a rest house at Kudowa. Jacek Rożański was also staying there, and one day I was taken with him to a coffee house for ice cream. As usual, a Security car followed behind him. Outside the coffee shop there was a woman selling bunches of flowers, and suddenly two big Security guys jumped at her, and a gun fell to the ground out of the flowers. She was going to assassinate him.

"Anyhow, at some point when I was growing up, I started to become skeptical, questioning everything, not believing what I was told in school or what was in the official newspapers. I listened to Radio Free Europe and the BBC, which made Mietek and my mother nervous in case someone in the block would hear it, and read everything anti-Communist that I could get my hands on. I wasn't easy to deal with when I was growing up, and I know I got Mietek into trouble with the Party more than once, but he was never angry. He always tried to reason with me. In fact, he was a very good stepfather, and I've always been able to turn to him. He's also incredibly knowledgeable, and I never had to consult reference books when I was studying. He used to read books on higher mathematics for entertainment.

"It was Alina who lent me the first copy I saw of Koestler's *Darkness at Noon*, the ultimate handbook, you could say, for understanding the psyche behind Stalinism and the old communists. It was a *samizdat* copy, written on a typewriter. That's how people passed around books that were forbidden by the government. My mother was annoyed because Alina didn't give it to her first. Alina was sympathetic to the communist cause, but she also had channels to the intelligentsia and the opposition. She was always open-minded and not doctrinaire, and her way of thinking also had some influence on me. I didn't know until later that she was being interrogated, but I did sense that she was under some kind of intense stress. I transferred my rebellion to school as well. I got into trouble, not just for smoking and stuff like that, but for doing things like putting Stalin moustaches on the pictures of Polish party dignitaries like Bierut, the first secretary.

"Anyway, I dropped out of school and I left home. I moved out of the high apparatchik life, and I took a room under my dad's apartment in a building that was still half-wrecked from the bombing. When you looked over the stairway, you could see the gaps where a lot of the flooring had been destroyed. He and Ewa, his third wife, lived in a shabby, totally unluxurious flat. Ewa was a singer, but she wasn't any good. The flat was in the centre of the city, a block and a half from Nowy Świat, the main street, one block from the theatre, half a block from the journalists' club, and it was always full of all kinds of people – painters, composers, journalists, singers, actors, philosophers, writers, musicians – the intellectual and artistic elite of Warsaw. My dad knew everybody, and Warsaw was his place. You can imagine what it was like for a young guy in his late teens to be in this milieu, with people like the filmmaker Andrzej Wajda, Leopold Tyrman, the journalist, writers like Jerzy Kośinski and Marek Hłasko. Roman Polanski was also around. He was at the beginning of his career, and I envied him his red sports car. It was completely different from the atmosphere at my mother's and Mietek's place, where the few people you'd meet were other Jewish doctors in the Security, like Mietek's friend Max. Jerzy and Mira Sawa, never came to our apartment. Nor did Irena, my grandmother, or Karol. We visited them."

In retrospect, Peter said, he realized that although he was brought up by his mother and he acknowledges that he has no recollection of receiving any affection from his father, it was Bolek and his milieu which had more influence on the way he thinks and what he has done with his life – "though I was never aware of Bolek deliberately trying to lead me in any direction. My dad was easygoing and a very

Jozef Cyrankiewicz (Archive of Audiovisual Records, Warsaw)

bright guy, interested in everyone and everything. He was a published poet, and some of his translations of Mayakovsky, the great Russian playwright and poet, are still used in Poland. Several well-known Polish writers talked about him in their books, and his second wife wrote a novel based on him, but it isn't good."

There were other influences on Peter. The family connection with Jerzy and Mira Sawa remained close. "I saw quite a lot of Mira and Jerzy even after I'd grown up and my mother had left Poland and was living in Israel. I knew I could always go to their home and that I could turn to them, or to Alina, for advice and suggestions about how to deal with problems, and I had the feeling that they were pleased when I came. Jerzy hated the communist government, not just because of the ideology but for religous reasons. They liked to hear the inside stories of what was going on, and they were delighted that I was anti the system. Of course, the Sawas were in touch with the Pikulskis because Jan Pikulski was Jerzy's cousin, and the Pikulskis knew Karol Adwentowicz as well as my grandmother because Karol also went to stay at Albinów when things got too hot for him towards the end of the war.

"Karol was the arbiter between my mother and Irena. He was a very impressive man, clever, kind, and principled. No one could 'buy' him. Like Irena, he was always elegantly dressed, and he was my model of how a real gentleman should behave. Going into a restaurant with him was a real experience, and even when he was old and sick, he would never walk through a door before a woman. Another aspect of Karol: he had been a member of the PPS – the Polish Socialist Party, Piłsudski's old party – since before the war, and the PPS leader, Józef Cyrankiewicz, was his friend, but Karol walked out when he united with the communists after they'd taken power."

Cyrankiewicz, a non-Jewish Auschwitz survivor, was a politically enigmatic figure who served as Poland's figurehead prime minister for twenty-two years after the war. Bolek's milieu, said Peter, overlapped somewhat with Karol's and Irena's, and he too had close connections with Cyrankiewicz. "Dad had become a guru of Polish psychiatry and was the authority on alcoholism. One of his patients was Cyrankiewicz's mother, and twice a month a government plane used to fly him to Kraków, where she lived. Cyrankiewicz was a colourful character. Although he was the prime minister, he liked to be in a bohemian milieu, and he loved good-looking women, fast cars, and the theatre. His wife was a well-known actress, and she and Irena were friends.

"Karol never stopped being a leftist, but he was a strong democrat. Nor did my father. Bolek did not look on what had happened under communism as being a total failure of the idea, of the theory. His analysis was that a situation had developed in which the intellectuals had rejected communism and that you now had uneducated shoemakers being ministers of state and top bureaucrats – I'm talking about the period in the late fifties after they'd already got rid of many of the Jews in the government and Bezpieka. My father argued that if the intelligentsia stood aside, then ignorant self-servers would take over all the power bases, and there would be no hope for an enlightened intelligent government – at that time nobody could even hope for democracy. Anyway, my dad became a member of the Party after Gomułka came back to power in '56. That was when we'd had our attempt at a revolution for 'socialism with a human face.' I was involved in that with other students, demonstrating and so on. 'Are you crazy?' I said when Dad told me he was going to join the Party, and I argued with him about it. But he insisted that people like himself now had a duty to get involved in order to change the system from the inside and make it human. This was at the time that many members of the intelligentsia and the

Karol Adwentowicz (undated)

creative elite were packing and taking off, and lots of Jews were emigrating to Israel. It was then that Mietek and my mother decided to leave. So again I was being pulled in two directions."

Peter eventually decided to go with them. His friend Ludwik had been having more trouble with his mother and arrived shortly after. Ludwik decided to visit the kibbutz set up by the people who had run the orphanage where he had lived after the war and which had later been transferred to Israel. A teacher who remembered him put a notice in the Israeli newspapers in the hope of finding whether, by any chance, his natural parents were alive. "Can you imagine," said Peter, "over one hundred families tried to claim he was their child! But finally an Orthodox Jew showed up and described a hernia operation that his child had had as a baby. Ludwik had a scar in exactly the right place, and he was also found to have the same blood group as the man. A miracle was pronounced, and it was a big story in the newspapers. But here was Ludwik, brought up in an intellectual communist background, suddenly finding himself with a religious, primitively Orthodox father – the mother hadn't survived –

and under enormous pressure to go to a yeshiva – religious school – and wear a yarmulke, the head covering. Ludwik tried to cope with it, but after a couple of months he said, 'You may be my natural father, but I already have a father in Poland,' and he withdrew from the situation. When he was in the Israeli army, he wasn't allowed to work on aircraft electronics – he'd studied that after I'd gone back to Poland. He found out that it was because he was still corresponding with his adoptive father, the professor, in communist Poland – though he too finally emigrated to Israel. I didn't like Israel, and neither at first did Ludwik, but he stayed there."

Unable to settle down in Israel, Peter, now aged twenty, returned to Poland, where he lived for a while with his grandmother. "I'd been away for less than two years, but she was very critical of the accent I'd picked up there. 'What's that awful singsong inflection? Stop it immediately! That's not Polish! Repeat what you said properly!' She put me in Karol's room, which she left unchanged after his death. All his things – his books, his pictures, medals, hairbrush, and clothes – were still there, untouched, and I had to be careful not to move anything.

"By the time I was grown up, Irena had become a grande dame of the Polish stage, committed body and soul to the theatre and Polish culture. She never, ever, allowed me to call her Babcia – grandmother. It was always "Irena". No one in the theatre was supposed to know she was a grandmother, but of course they did. When the fortieth anniversary of her entering the theatre was coming up, she wanted to direct and act in a play. She gave me five pieces to read, and I recommended one by Ugo Betti about a wounded partisan who walks into a house occupied by a grandmother, a mother, and a daughter, who all compete for him. I suggested that she play the grandmother, but she got huffy. 'No, I don't want to be old.' So I had to persuade her, saying that she would be playing a woman of her age, but with 'coquetry and charm.' Finally I convinced her, and in the event, it played six months to full houses. One night when I was there, I overheard an elderly man in the audience saying, 'Old Grwyinska still has better legs than those young chicks.' I repeated it to her afterwards, and she said, 'How dare he say old!' But she was obviously pleased.

"Irena was director of two Warsaw theatres. Many people in the theatre were intimidated by her. Behind her back they'd refer to her by a word that is the equivalent of 'bitch.' But they respected her. She had a great deal of worldly wisdom, and I learned a lot from her. It wasn't until she died that I realized how very attached to her I'd been, but we got on well together, though she would never kiss me or anything like that. She demanded and behaved with great formality. There was no casualness in anything Irena did. If you visited in the afternoon, the coffee was always served in porcelain. At dinner everything had to be impeccably presented. A maid did the basic preparation, but Irena always put on the final touches. Napkins, serving dishes, silver – everything had to be perfect. Even when my mother was in her thirties, if Irena thought a lipstick was wrong, she'd tell her to take it off with a comment like 'Only a whore wears lipstick that colour!' Or 'Trousers! – a lady doesn't wear trousers!' "

Of all the confusing contradictions between official information and observed reality, between the world of the *nomenklatura* in which he had grown up and the other milieux to which he had been exposed, Peter said that one thing above all put him into an emotional and mental turmoil. "It was when I learned about Jacek Rożański. I'd already heard rumours about what he was doing. In countries like Poland you always heard a lot on the gossip circuit that wouldn't get through the censorship into the media, and you have to choose what to believe and what to doubt. I had such different pictures of him that I didn't know what the truth was. On the one hand, since I was a kid I'd had personal contact with this intelligent fellow that my mother had known since before the war, someone who had always been pleasant to me and whose daughter was a friend of mine. And now he was accused of terrible things, and I was perturbed, not knowing what to believe.

"In the spring of 1959 I was at a party in my dad's flat when the subject of Jacek's prison sentence came up. He'd been given fifteen years – I think they called it for 'abuses of power.' My mum and dad had known Jacek since they were students – in those days all those politically minded young Jewish intellectuals at Warsaw university knew each other. They were part of the same scene, and they went to the same coffee shops in the university district. My dad was saying that Jacek was a very bright guy and that during the war he was one of the first people to be parachuted in from the Soviet

Union to make contact with Gomułka and the communist underground.* And I was saying I couldn't believe he would torture people. Then my dad, gesturing at a young woman visitor – he was the director of the city's main psychiatric hospital, and she was one of his junior staff – said that she should tell me about Jacek.

"And here was the thing that so shocked me: she was one of his victims. She'd been the girlfriend of a guy who'd assassinated one of the main party propogandists on Warsaw radio – the propoganda then was the crudest kind of Stalinism – and the man he'd assassinated was one of the worst. After a big hunt, he was captured, and because she was his lover, she was also arrested and imprisoned. She'd had nothing to do with any plot. All she'd done was to sleep with the guy. And now, that evening at my dad's place, this young woman started to sob and to describe how Jacek had interrogated her for hours under bright lights and that he'd stuck needles behind her nails and done other horrible things. It put me into one hell of a turmoil."

In 1956, after the Khrushchev government threatened to intervene to end a protracted spell of strikes, unrest, and demonstrations, Władysław Gomułka was reinstalled with considerable popular support, and the top people associated with Russia and Stalinism replaced. A fresh start was to be made, and it was necessary that the new regime – committed, said Gomułka, to "our Polish road to socialism" – be seen to disassociate itself from the abuses of the past. A cleansing process was required, and one of the most expedient ways this could be done was by bringing to trial individuals who, in the public mind, symbolized everything most hated and feared: the imposition of Soviet power, Stalin, and the Bezpieka's hated and feared Department of Investigation. It was probably not by chance that, despite the fact that many other people could have been held to account, the three men put on trial were Jews. Of these it was Jacek Rożański whose name became the most infamous, perhaps

---

*There is no evidence of this being the case, despite the fact that Peter later quotes Rożański making the same claim.

because he alone never denied his methods of interrogation or apologized for what he had done. He was brought to trial again on the grounds that not all the evidence against him had been heard the first time.

The fall of the regime has now made the trial records publicly available, and one can see Rożański putting the Leninist argument that the end may justify the means, as well as stating unambivalently that what he had done was the accepted policy regarding crimes of a political nature – that is, extracting information by use of torture, or what he described as "terror." It appears as though he was determined that the court would hear and face the reality of what had been done in the name of the Party.

First, however, he insisted on taking responsibility for what he described as the damage done to his subordinates by being involved in the process. "Many interrogations were damaging to the enemy, but many inside our apparatus were damaged." Of himself he said that it was a "strange and disturbing thought that someone like me, coming from an intellectual family that was well known in the literary sphere, and who had interest in law and legal problems," could have got involved in these activities. He thought that his impulsive personality and lack of calmness should have disqualified him for his work – work with which he said he had been obsessed. He described the routine of a normal day, working from 9 a.m. to 4 p.m., three hours off, then back to work until 2 a.m. or later, and never wearing his medals or uniform – "we weren't after effects." The law, he said, "was disregarded all through the ministry." He and his colleages would ask themselves "what was needed as a basis for the case against some who had been arrested," and they would create it. "We created false truths ... but it was we who were the false truths."

He spoke of the situation during the civil war, when he and his colleagues were repeatedly told to respond to terror with terror, of how he and the others had been instructed to use beatings. (Soon after his arrest in 1954, he had written that during the civil war "Gestapo methods had entered our system.") They were, he said, ordered to break "our own and other people's moral reservations ... I think that the logic of this is that in a good system, a bad person can be controlled, and in a bad system, good people can be spoiled. We got spoiled in a bad system."

The 115 witnesses against Rożański and the other two men included three who had previously been top members of the Politburo but had now been removed. One was the notoriously ruthless former minister of the Bezpieka, Stanisław Radkiewicz, a non-Jew, by then thrown out of the Party by Gomułka. One of Rożański's co-defendants, Roman Romkowski, had been his superior. Each pointed a finger at the other. After the Światło broadcasts on Radio Free Europe, Romkowski wrote in an internal memo that Rożański should have been removed in 1949. "People defended him on the basis of his professional status and political dedication, but really we were camouflaging his destructive activities. Now we have to clean the system." According to Rożański, however, Roman Romkowski had been one of his instructors.

Rożański raised the issue of a choice between greater and lesser evils by referring to situations where they had saved lives by using "terror" on prisoners who refused to testify about underground organizations and their stores of arms. "This is the tragic truth about how, on the one hand, we broke the law but, on the other hand, saved lives." As an example, he made an indirect reference to the young woman Peter listened to in Bolek's apartment. The same terrorist organization that had killed the radio announcer was, said Rożański, carrying out various kinds of sabotage, such as blowing up trains. In the spring of 1952, trying to track down the leader of the organization that had just derailed a locomotive and two carriages on the Berlin-Moscow mainline track, "our apparatus" interrogated three people, one of whom was the group's courier. "Here was our dilemma: should we stop the formal questioning when she says she doesn't know where the leader is? Do we permit trains to be blown up and people to get killed? Or do we force her to give information, despite the fact that the law prohibits us from doing that? ... Nobody is allowed to break the law, but the moral dilemma is different. I had to act ... I slapped her a few times on the face, and then she told us where he was hiding ... Legally it was a crime that I beat her, but in this instance I do not regret it."[*]

At the end of the trial Rożański made a final statement putting his case from the viewpoint of a loyal party comrade: since 1954, he said, when he had been called before the party leader and then to

---

[*]One may surmise that "slapped" was an understatement.

the Commission of Party Control, he had never hidden his faults or errors – hiding nothing, "certainly not from the Party, and without regard to my own interest ... We have been talking here about painful things" – and he had fought only "to have the case viewed in a wide context and not make one person a scapegoat." He said he had never lied to the Party, he had worked wherever it had directed him, and – his final words – he felt that "against my strongest wishes, I have done disservice to the Party."

In November Jacek Rożański and Ramon Romkowski were sentenced to fifteen years in prison, the other man to twelve years. It remained Rożański's stated belief to the end of his life that he had been a scapegoat, someone upon whom to lay the blame for Stalinism and Soviet control.

❧

When Peter, unable to settle down in Israel, returned on his own to Poland, he got a job with the State Export Company, a branch of the Ministry of External Trade. At the same time he studied political economics at the University of Warsaw. He made extra cash in a variety of ways peculiar to Iron Curtain countries, especially Poland – after 1956 it had become less socially restrictive and the economy less sealed off from the west. Peter was used to getting away with things: Ludwik says that when they were teenagers in Warsaw, Peter would get them into nightclubs barred to boys of their age by intimidating the management, telling them that his stepfather was a colonel with the Bezpieka. During the period after he returned from Israel and later, when he got a passport, he went in for what he describes as "Mickey Mouse" business – activities varying from arranging deals and speculating in currencies, to bringing in goods from foreign trips and selling them himself – as did many others in the State Export Company. In effect, he was operating on and over the edge of the law. However, when he came under pressure from the Security, it was not because of this.

"About a year after I got back from Israel, my father could see that I was under stress about something, and he asked me what was the matter, so I told him. It was the Bezpieka – they were trying to lure me into the service. It had started with a telephone call from one man asking me to meet him for coffee. There were other tele-

Peter in Canada in 1968 or 1969

phone calls and 'accidental' meetings with him and another guy. I kept saying that I wasn't interested, but they kept after me. Bolek asked me, 'Are you sure you don't want to work for them?' I told him that I was quite sure. 'Do you want me to help you?' I said yes, and after that they stopped bothering me. Dad knew Cyrankiewicz, the prime minister, so he was able to use his influence. The next time I had a problem with them, it was more to do with Jacek.

"A while after he was put in prison, I had a romance with his daughter, Stefka – we'd known each other since we were children. She was working in TV and was bewildered and upset that people hated her because of him. Jacek had heard from her that she was going out with me, and he asked her to bring me along to visit him because he wanted to get my impressions of Israel. To please Stefka, I agreed to go. Jacek was in a special prison, a small one opposite the Bezpieka headquarters in central Warsaw where they kept guys like him, and the only way in which I would have known that it was a jail was that there was a guard on the way in. He had a suite of two rooms, nicely furnished. He offered us coffee, chocolates, cognac. I knew that he had committed atrocities, and here he was, living in this style, with the guards addressing him respectfully as 'Pan Colonel.' Jacek's presence was as imposing and strong as ever. He was still good-looking and very bright and charming. He knew the best political in-stories and jokes that I'd ever heard, and he also asked me about Israel, about what I thought of the life there.

"Then the conversation became more ideological. I wanted to know how he could have done these terrible things. His justification was on these lines: he said that he believed in communism; that people like him had been given the task of implementing it, and that 'we had to carry out the mandate of communism ... It was us or them' (meaning the anti-communist groups who went on fighting before and after the war ended), 'and we were constantly exposed to the possibility of a bullet in the head from them.' As for his 'methods of interrogation of anti-social elements who were attempting to subvert the proletarian revolution ... We had Russian advisers, Piotr. Their advisers taught me.'

Intellectually I could relate to him, but I still couldn't understand – I was outraged. I had to narrow his generalizations to the particular, to the young woman crying in my father's apartment. Just before we left, he said, 'Piotr, history will rehabilitate me.' But the truth of the matter, whatever my mother says, is that he was a degenerate sadist. And that was the opinion of most Polish Jews who knew about it. And the Poles thought, 'Fucking Jewish bastard, serving his godless, tyrannical Russian masters.'"

The visit had repercussions: when Peter was working for the State Export Company, he needed a passport to travel abroad, but his application was turned down by the Bezpieka. He was tipped off to go to see a man at the ministry, one of the "Spaniards" who were now running it. "They were called that because they had fought in the Spanish Civil War, and they were now a group within what was called the 'partisan faction' – super-nationalistic and chauvinistic ... You know, even those communist countries always had opposition groups within the party, and there was even a sort of democracy in the way they operated within the system, one faction trying to get party support so that they could dominate in the government." The minister responsible for the Bezpieka was now the faction's leader, General Moczar, and the man Peter was told to see was his chief of staff. His office overlooked the Mokotów prison, where much of Rożański's activities had taken place. "Anyway, he agreed to see me, and when I asked him straight why I was being refused a passport, he told me that there were a few 'unanswered questions.' I said that he knew my background, he knew that my stepfather had been an officer in his organization and that I had grown up close to the apparatus. I said that I realized there were only two possible reasons for the refusal, one of them being my visit to Jacek, which I knew they would have on my record.

'So why did you go?'

'Because his daughter was my girlfriend. And I know you guys don't want him in prison.'

'It's political,' he said with a shrug. He wanted to know what I'd thought of Israel, so I said that my having returned to Poland signified something. He asked what Mietek was doing, and I told him that he knew that Mietek was a good man, that he'd signed a protest against the discrimination experienced by Arabs, and furthermore that Mietek never said a bad word against Poland or communism – 'And you know it.'

'How would I know?' he asked.

'You know because there are Bezpieka and KGB agents there.'

He smiled and said, 'I like you, but I have one more thing against you.'

'There's nothing I can do about that one – what you object to is that I don't want to work for you.'

'Why won't you? You grew up among us, you're educated and knowledgeable. So why don't you want to serve us?'

'It's because of that,' I said. 'Sure, I grew up with people like Rożański, and look at him today – in prison for what he did, and so are the others. Perhaps someone has to do your work, but I don't like it and don't want anything to do with it.' Then he smiled again and said, 'All right, we don't have to talk any more. Let's see what happens when you apply for a passport again.' So I applied again a couple of months later and got it."

Jacek Rożański did not serve all of his sentence in Warsaw. He was transferred – in what he would describe as "a provocation" – to another prison, in the city of Wrocław, where he spent years in isolation under threat of attack from other prisoners. In 1964 he requested an early release, and his case was reviewed. In its decision the court wrote that after it had talked with him and heard reports on his behaviour, it was clear that his sentence had effected no change in his understanding of the nature of his crimes or any self-criticism of his methods. In prison, the judges said, he had behaved in a manner reflecting a sense of superiority to the other prisoners, refusing to talk to them during outdoor exercise. These reasons were given for granting him only a conditional release. A member of the panel of judges hearing the appeal had been his old enemy Luna Brystigier*.

A criticism the court had made was that in prison Rożański had tried to create around him "an atmosphere of being specially privileged," of having "contacts with and protection from people in high positions in the state." In fact, later that year, through the intervention of the party leader, Władysław Gomułka, Rożański and the two men convicted with him were formally pardoned and freed.

⤝⤞

In 1967 Peter went on vacation and did not return. With a disastrous marriage behind him, he had both personal and political motives. The year before he left, he had felt disgusted and betrayed when a close friend of his joined the police arm of the Bezpieka after graduating from university. As a hard-up student, this man had often eaten at Peter's flat at the end of the month when his state student allowance was running short, "and now he was gloating over the enormous and immediate improvement in his financial status." Then in early 1967 Peter learned that this former friend had been a leading prosecution witness in the trials of three leading dissidents – Adam Michnik, Jacek Kuron, and Zygmunt Modzelewski – who were to become future leaders of Solidarity. "It was the last straw. I felt contaminated and wanted nothing more to do with the whole rotten system." In 1969 Peter emigrated to Canada, where he would work for nineteen years as an economic policy adviser for the provincial bureaucracy and where he would also own a couple of small retail businesses. The role of government in economic policy should, he believes, be minimal and market-oriented.

Peter remembers an experience in Montreal shortly after his arrival. "Through a contact who was an old school friend of Mi-

---

*Up to 1956 Brystigier was director of a Security department overseeing cultural affairs and infiltrating youth organizations and the church. After that she wrote novels under her maiden name, Preiss.

etek's, I was taken into the Jewish milieu. The idea was to find a wife for me, and one evening at a big dinner party at someone's house, the subject of Poland came up, and some of them were saying that the Poles were all anti-Semites and other things like that. I interrupted and told the story of the Pikulskis and Albinów during the Occupation, of Jerzy and Mira Sawa and the unknown woman who helped get my mother out of the Gestapo prison, people who saved our lives at the risk of their own. I said that because of them and others like them, one could not call the whole nation anti-Semitic. There was a silence because no one could answer me, but after that the story went around about me that here was this Jewish guy who had been brainwashed into becoming communist! It was ironic in two ways: because people like Pikulski and the Sawas hated communism and because after the war Stalin used a lot of Jews – as long as it was convenient – to implement communism in Poland. They were never the majority of the ministers in the government, but unfortunately, from the point of view of the general population, they could see many Jews in sensitive positions – in publishing houses, the press agency, in the Security. I used to argue with Mietek and Stasia about it, saying that it was foolish to have let a situation arise in which Poles could see Jews as the instruments of what they hated – Russia and Communism.

"Anyway, I'd wanted to get away from it all and lead a normal life in a country that had been built by immigrants. But you can't escape totally. Early on, I had a job with Marconi, and the second day there, when I walked into the cafeteria, who should I see but the grandson of Paweł Finder – he was parachuted in to lead the party during the war, but the Gestapo shot him. The funny thing was that Marconi was involved with classified electronics work for the U.S. Army, and both of us had been given CIA clearance. I was also offered work in the Polish-language section of Radio Free Europe, but I decided against it. I'd had enough of all that stuff. Once when I was visiting Alina in Denmark, she asked me if I wanted to see some of my old friends – people brought up in the same milieu as myself – and some of them were now involved with Solidarity. I said, 'Sorry, but I'm out of it.' It had been a horrible world where the revolution ate its own children."

Three

In which Stasia tells the story of her second or "no" life.

Many of my contemporaries who accepted the Revolution went through a severe psychological crisis. They were trapped between a reality which could only be condemned and the need for a principle by which to justify it ... many of them had awaited the Revolution all their lives, but at the sight of what it meant in terms of everyday life, they were horrified and looked away.

Nadezhda Mandelstam, Hope against Hope

A Member of the Party

How strange to say that although I have continued to exist all these years since the war and although I show all the usual external signs of life, yet there has not been any life. I have been dead. And with me all this time there has been company – the images and sounds of the war and of the ghetto – from which I am never free. Nobody knows that I have this company, that there is an almost physical intensity to my memories.

Sleepless nights when the past comes to me as fragments of a film seen long ago on an afternoon spent in one of my father's movie houses or as a passage from a book once read, then forgotten, and now remembered again. A bowl of cream of wheat is in front of me at the kitchen table. Babcia Sara and old Zawadzka nod and smile, promising never to leave me. My father brings me a pineapple at the Sara Höniger boarding school, asking me to have patience, promising to take me away as soon as he can. Bolek is swimming out of sight through the leaden Baltic waves. A nun brings Peter into the convent courtyard, and he runs into my arms. Grisha Malinovsky stands by the swimming pool in Krynica, and I walk towards him. Jacek Rożański picks up a fallen pine cone as he says to me, "Stasia, my friend, I must do whatever the Party asks me." Jerzy Sawa throws himself on my mother's grave, shouting "This is a pagan funeral."

I get up and take out her photographs. There are so many of them, stage photos, studio portraits. I look at this beautiful woman with her charming smile and captivating personality, her exceptional intelligence and iron will, amazed that all these things were to be found in one person.

She was there in the hospital in Łódź when I regained consciousness after my suicide attempt. For hours, day after day, she sat by my bedside. It was the first demonstration of my mother's affection of which I have any recollection, and it was then that I started to love her and to try to understand her, to forgive her for my father's heartbreak and my own ruined childhood. One question perplexed her: she asked me several times if I had not been concerned that I would leave Peter motherless. I had no answer. Sometimes we talked about politics. She was appalled that I had become a member of the Party; in her opinion, I was crazy to join because nobody liked the new regime. She said that most Poles saw no difference between the Germans and the Russians, that both were enemies and both exploited the country, but the Russians were also repressing the church. Furthermore, unlike the Germans, they were here to stay.

I had been persuaded to join the Party by a distant cousin related to me through my Babcia Sara. My cousin and her sisters had been communists before the war. They were from a well-to-do background and had been brought up in a beautiful house in a fashionable district of Warsaw, and my cousin had been my kindergarten teacher. It was she and her sister who used to annoy my little Aunt Ola because they were always getting money from my uncle for "the cause." My cousin ran off to Moscow in the 1930s with her husband – he had always been "underground," so I never met him. During Stalin's purge of party members in 1937, about whose extent I knew little until recently, her husband disappeared, together with most of the other Polish communists who had fled to the Soviet Union and were arrested at Stalin's order. When her only child was eleven years old, he was pushed off a crowded tram in Moscow and fell under it. He lost both his legs and then died from infection. After the war my cousin was among the first group of émigrés to return to Poland, and we recognized each other on the street in Łódź. The only thing that she had brought back was her son's cremated remains in an urn. Despite her terrible ordeal at the hands of the government that had murdered her husband, she didn't seem to be disillusioned. She was still an ardent communist, still believed in the Russian Revolution and the Soviet system, and was extremely idealistic. She told me that she had returned to Poland in order to help build "our new communist Poland," and she urged me to become a member of the Party. "You have an obligation. They liberated you from the Nazis."

At that time I had just received an affidavit that my Aunt Theja, my mother's half-sister, had managed to get for me and Peter to immigrate to the United States, and my Uncle Wicek's son Bob wanted me to escape with him to Czechoslovakia. Although Peter has never forgiven me, the decision was not very hard. Poland's liberation by the Red Army after the hell-on-earth of Nazism was to me a real miracle. I was still young; I was idealistic; I wanted to build a better future for my son, and I believed this better future belonged to socialism. My cousin sponsored my application to join the Party, and I was accepted.

Although my life, and my cousin's, was lonely, we met rarely because we both worked, I had Peter to take care of, and there were endless queues to get the bare necessities of life. I didn't see her for the few months after I joined the Party. Then one day I happened to come across a neighbour of hers in a line of people waiting outside a shop. In conversation, the woman referred to my cousin being dead. "Dead!" I exclaimed. She seemed surprised at my shock, and told me that my cousin had committed suicide; she had gassed herself. I asked if she had any idea why my cousin had done it. "Well, she left no word, no explanation," said the woman. "But one can imagine how depressed she was, how disappointed with what is happening, after everything she went through. And then to be disillusioned with her ideology." "Disillusioned?" I said, taken aback. The woman looked at me with raised eyebrows. The only answer I got was a faintly mocking smile.

My cousin's suicide did in fact prompt my first stirrings of doubt about the situation in my country, about the social justice that I had dreamed about, and about the Party. For a few nights I lay awake wondering if perhaps she had really been disappointed and disillusioned. At that time I had no privileges as a party member. If anything, there were disadvantages. Other members of the staff at the hospital where I was working were friendly to me until they discovered that I was in the Party; then they did their best to avoid my company. And the moment that I walked into the doctors' room, all conversation stopped, as though they were afraid to talk in my presence. Nor did I make any friends in my party cell. Suddenly there were a lot of people in the Party, but few of them seemed to have an idealistic commitment. If anything, I got the impression that their main concern was to defend their own interests, whether to do with their salary, their prestige, or resolving personal quarrels. There seemed to be little concern for the Party as a whole, about its standing, its honesty, or its good name among the people. If a speaker addressed one of the bigger meetings, his words sounded like empty propoganda, and I would go away with a bad taste in my mouth. I could also sense that many of these new members were anti-Semitic.

May Day parade with the Medical Academy in Szczecin in 1949; Stasia is second from the right in the front row

Yet I felt that communism would change this situation. I had no real cause yet for disillusionment, and I couldn't see that this would be the reason for my cousin taking her life when she had retained her beliefs in spite of everything she had been through. Finally I rationalized her suicide as the action of a desperately lonely woman who had lost her husband and her only child.

It was only later, after I met Mietek and joined the so-called communist elite, that I began to understand that my cousin's neighbour had probably been right – although even today I am still not entirely convinced.

⋆

Mietek was a "big fish," a lieutenant-colonel in the medical administration of the Ministry of Internal Security. We met in 1948 soon after I went to Szczecin, after I had recovered from my suicide attempt. I had been offered a good position there as an assistant at the new university's gynecology and obstetrics clinic, but the salary was low. I was renting a small room in an apartment, and I needed an extra job in order to make enough money to have Peter with me – he was still with the Pikulskis at Albinów. I'd sent him there from Łódź after Bolek moved out. My Aunt Genia's brother-in-law, himself a doctor in the Security's health system, sent me a letter of introduction to the chief of the UB's health units in the Szczecin district. I went to the home address where I was told I could find him and explained the purpose of my visit to the man who opened the door – it was Mietek's sister's husband. He left me in the hall, and I could hear his voice calling, "Mietek, wake up! There's a nice chick here to see you." A minute or so later, a good-looking and pleasant young man came into the hall. He obviously wanted to be helpful, and he told me that a part-time hospital job in my speciality would be coming up shortly, but for the time being there was a vacancy for me to do extra work as a general practitioner in the ministry clinic. I took the job, and Mietek began dropping in to the clinic "to see how you are doing," sometimes giving me a lift home after work in his chauffeur-driven car. He had beautiful eyes, whose colour changed from grey to green to brown depending upon the light, and beautiful hands with long fingers. My father also had lovely eyes and hands.

Mietek had been allocated the lower half of a house in the residential part of the city, one of the many houses evacuated by the previous German owners and now government property. He wasn't occupying it because he was living with his sister and her husband on the opposite side of the road. Giving me a drive back from work one day, he suggested that I might as well move into the house so that I could bring Peter back from Albinów. Mietek didn't want any rent because he wasn't paying any himself. The flat had three rooms, a kitchen, and a bathroom and a big garden with plum and cherry trees – an enormous amount of space for a bachelor when there was an acute shortage of space for "ordinary" people. I accepted the offer and found a live-in housekeeper to cook, clean, and look after Peter when I was at work.

I was too pleased with my luck and with being able to have Peter with me to worry much about the contradictions that any of this implied in a theoretically egalitarian society. Nor did I want to consider the implications for my ideals of the other benefits I was able to receive not long after that, when I got the transfer to the ministry's hospital. This position entitled me to a card that gave me access to its special stores. In these places one was able to buy all kinds of scarce commodities such as meat, butter, white bread, shoes, and clothing, without waiting in endless queues, and I could now use the special restaurants where one could eat well and cheaply. The cards also enabled their holders to use the separate health system, with its own clinics and hospitals, and UB employees had easier and faster access to better and bigger low-rent or rent-free apartments. I had suddenly, and almost without realizing it, taken my first steps towards becoming an active member of the privileged elite. It was a situation I had not anticipated, and although it eased or removed many of the difficulties with which I was trying to cope, what I felt at first was a sense of degradation. Communism, in my mind, was associated with idealism, and as I understood it, under communism we were all supposed to be equal. Our goal was to build a society in which all would work according to their abilities and get paid according to their needs. I was, however, usually able to suppress my doubts about a situation that had made my existence so much easier. After all, the war was scarcely over, and the new "reborn Poland" was in its early days. Surely it would all get sorted out.

Five years younger than myself, Mietek was rather shy and nicely innocent, almost naive in spite of his long experience with the army. We were attracted to each other, but our relationship did not become intimate until we were with a group of people spending an evening together at a nightclub, a situation set up for us by a couple of friends who had decided to act as matchmakers. (The nightclub was probably the first one I had been to since that evening eight years before, when Bolek and I were dancing at Under the Rooster in Warsaw as war was declared.) When Mietek's sister realized what was going on, she didn't like the idea of him marrying a divorced woman with a child, so she invited a good-looking girl who was the niece of a friend of hers to visit from Warsaw. Mietek was polite to her but distant. We had known each other only a few months when he asked me to marry him, but I had my doubts and hesitations. Although I felt secure and comfortable with him and I was beginning to love him, there was the age difference. Furthermore, I was unsure that I wanted to take on more obligations and commitments, and doubtful about the institution of marriage. I suggested that we let the situation stay as it was so long as it pleased us, but this response outraged Mietek, who was adamant that he was not prepared to be a casual boyfriend. We didn't see each other for a few weeks. Then somehow it started again, and the question of marriage resurfaced.

When I was lying in hospital recovering from my suicide attempt, my mother had made me promise to get her approval before I married again, so I asked her to visit. Mietek joined us for dinner nearly every evening, and her verdict was a definite yes. "He is a very decent and honest man. In fact, he reminds me of your father." With regard to his decency, his integrity, and his honesty, she was perfectly correct, as she also was in saying that he would be a good father to Peter. But unlike Bolek, with whom I had so much in common, Mietek's and my tastes and interests were different, and we came from two different worlds. The circumstances of our backgrounds and upbringing, our childhood, school years, family life, and adolescence, were totally different, unknown territories. And he had experienced the war as a soldier. He had not lived through the humiliation and horror of a ghetto, trapped behind walls and barbed wire, a sheep marked for slaughter. Nor had he gone through the experience of being pursued, of being hunted like an animal. Of course, he knew and understood, but knowing and understanding is not to have lived through it. What we did have in common was our ideology and idealism.

※

The rest house was a former German sanatorium for the wealthy, luxuriously and elegantly furnished and set in a lovely area of forest and parkland. Beautiful paintings in heavy gold frames on the walls, expanses of gleaming waxed wooden floors. It was the summer of 1948, before Mietek and I married, and we were having a four-week holiday at the UB's rest house for upper party officials at Kudowa, a pre-war health spa in the mountains of Silesia, annexed by Poland from Germany after the war. There was a huge dining room with big tables, exquisite food in endless supply, delicious desserts that Peter and I loved. We were given a suite so that Peter could have his own room.

"Stasia? Stasia Ałapin? My God, you're alive!" A tall, dark-haired man had come over to me in the entrance lobby. It was Jacek

Stasia and Peter in Kudowa in 1949

Rożański, as he was now called. I hadn't seen Jacek since before the war, when he was courting Anka, my friend Ida's sister. Jacek, as good-looking as he had been as a young man, was now the chief officer of the UB's Department of Investigation. He told me that he was married and had a lovely little daughter he adored. In the following weeks we often went walking together while Mietek, always an avid bridge player, took every opportunity to take part in a game. Jacek was entertaining. He made me laugh a lot, and I was at ease with him. He asked me about Mietek – was I happy with him? And was Peter happy? Sometimes I asked his opinion about the political situation, and I naively accepted every answer he gave me. The Ministry of Internal Security controlled all the police and prisons and security units, and Jacek's department was the most feared and hated. One day, with little forethought because we hadn't been

Stasia with Mietek in Kudowa in 1949

talking politics, I said, "May I ask you an important question?" "Sure, go ahead." We were walking through the woods, the air sparkling and pungent with the pine trees. "Jacek, you are a lawyer and it's a good profession. So why are you doing this work? Why should you put yourself in a position where the people hate you?" He did not seem to be suprised by my question or embarrassed. He responded immediately and simply, without evasion. "You see, Stasia. I do what the Party orders me to do. I have to obey. I have to accept the duties that are given to me. I must do whatever the Party asks of me."

Being a party member myself and still a believer, with no idea about Stalin's crimes, I had no answer. I accepted his explanation, ignorant of all the things that Jacek was actually doing. Or anyway, what he was later accused of having done.

Mietek and I were married in 1949 in a civil ceremony in Szczecin. We moved to Warsaw a couple of years later, when he was made a chief administrator at the headquarters of the Security health services. For a while we lived in one of the ministry's best buildings, in a lovely flat previously occupied by the Andrzejewskis – Alina's friend Zofia and her husband, who'd been posted away, out of the country. I didn't like Zofia, which made things difficult between me and Alina. She had made a literary reputation for herself by writing about her experiences at Auschwitz. She was a self-dramatizing, blonde woman who always had to be the centre of attention, surrounded by men. She used to brag in a vulgar manner about all her lovers. The flat opposite ours was occupied by Jacek and his wife and daughter, a beautiful, fair-haired girl three years younger than my Peter. His wife was also good-looking, but she was unapproachable and aloof. From time to time, when he'd sent away his black chauffeur-driven limousine, I came across Jacek in the street, and we would walk along together and chat. On one occasion, he started to talk about Anka, my friend Ida's sister, referring to her as his "first wife." Anka had emigrated to Israel. "I sometimes wonder what it's like there," he said. "Don't you?" But I wasn't interested in the subject then. I don't think he was testing me for my party loyalty. I never had that feeling with Jacek. I always felt perfectly at ease with him, and that is one of the reasons why I've found it difficult to imagine him in any other way – to imagine him doing these things they say he did.

In Warsaw I worked at first at a big Security hospital – Alina also had a job there, in charge of one of the laboratories. I stayed for only a year. One day I was told by the director that a patient of mine, a severely ill woman, would have to be moved from her room because the wife of one of the top people – probably one of the Politburo – needed the bed. "It's not possible. My patient is too ill," I answered. But he wasn't interested. "She can't stay here. I need that bed." I persisted in refusing to give my permission, and when I found that he'd ignored me, I resigned my position. But here's the irony – years later when I was visiting Peter in Montreal, I discovered that this man was the medical director of the Jewish General Hospital!

My next job was in the Department of Obstetrics and Gynecology at the Municipal Hospital on Leszno Street, which had been the old Jewish hospital where I worked before the war. I'd passed my examinations in my speciality and also taken a PHD in it before we left Szczecin. My chief, Karol Hanke, was a wonderful man, totally devoid of anti-Semitic sentiments. Over the years I learned a lot from him; he taught me the most complicated surgical procedures, encouraged me, and eventually chose me as his deputy, giving me responsibility for the most difficult work. Professionally, I was advancing well, but when my colleagues found out that Mietek was in the Security, it was the same as it had been in Szczecin. They were obviously afraid of me, avoiding my company, sitting apart from me in the doctors' room. The atmosphere was very discomfiting and unpleasant until they got to know me better and could trust me not to denounce them if they said anything against the government. The reason for the change of attitude was, I think, because Dr Hanke must have reassured them. The suspicion and hostility was part of the price I had to pay for being a party member, and for Mietek's position with the Bezpieka.

Now that I was the wife of one of the "bosses," enjoying all the privileges that accompanied the position, I could no longer hide from myself the main reason that the so-called elite were hated. We were the beneficiaries of a system that was supposed to be for the good of "the people," but while "the people" did not have enough to eat and had to stand for hours on end waiting to buy basic necessities, we had our own stores, which provided us with everything that we needed without any queueing. Although Mietek and I were still far away from the upper echelons, there was no limit to our privileges: chauffered cars, special resorts for our vacations, even special schools for our children. (We wanted to have a child together, but I was unable to conceive.)

Peter was a very difficult child, particularly as a teenager. He was always very much his own person, constantly criticizing us for belonging to the Party, embarrassing us by turning the sound up loud on Radio Free Europe, the anti-communist station. Party members were not supposed to listen to it, and we were living in a UB flat! He was thrown out of schools for his rebelliousness, including the special one for the children of people in our position, and at the other schools he always associated with the worst boys, smoking and drinking and making trouble. Once I was called in and told that Peter had to leave because the previous night he and some other boys had gatecrashed a teachers' party; he'd got drunk and made fun of one of the teachers. I said that it wasn't possible because he'd been home all evening, but when I asked Peter about it, he admitted he'd climbed out of the window and down some scaffolding and back up again later without us knowing. He was expelled time and again for his behaviour. One of the school principals, himself a Jew, told me that Peter was behaving this way to try to show that he was not one.

Peter would not listen to me or to Mietek, so on several occasions I wrote to Bolek for help, but he always refused. It was one of the things he did to try to punish me. We had been divorced, by mutual consent, when I still lived in Szczecin. He had wanted custody of Peter but was furious when he failed and said he would have nothing to do with him. And he didn't. Bolek gave me no child support, and I was too proud to ask for it or to go to the courts. He had remarried, to a writer – she wrote a novel about him, but it isn't any good, though I'm told that her poetry is passable. They broke up before the birth of their child, a girl, and this ex-wife brought up their daughter alone, refusing him any access to her. Bolek married again, to one of his patients – a third-rate actress, though she used to be quite good-looking. At some point during this marriage he converted to Christianity. I don't know why, because he was never religious. In the last letter I received from my mother, a couple of weeks before her death, she wrote that she had recently met his daughter from his second marriage, a nice-looking girl, she said, who could be Peter's twin, but that Bolek didn't care about her – which, my mother said, was all the fault of his wife. But Bolek never cared about Peter either.

After we moved from the Andrzejewskis' apartment, we were given our own lovely flat in a renovated building reserved for UB officers in a fashionable district in the centre of Warsaw, with a room near the kitchen for a live-in housekeeper, who cooked, cleaned, and shopped when I was too busy with my work, which often involved night duty. This was the time when Warsaw was being rebuilt, and most people were still sharing apartments and using a common bathroom and kitchen. How easily and how fast I became accustomed to and accepted my new status! How fast I took everything for granted! Mostly I chose not to think about it, but if I let the matter enter my head, at least I now knew why people hated the Party. I didn't have to ask myself, "Why are people suspicious of me? Why don't we have any friends, other than those who are in a similar position? What happened to our communist ideals? Did they ever really exist?" If I asked myself these questions, I knew the answer: were we not all corrupt – not only our government? But if I ever had such doubts, I must have suppressed them for many years because they surfaced rarely and only on particular occasions, mostly connected with issues relating to Jews. I can't say that I gave any thought to the censorship, or to the oppression.

What I did observe was that the system by which party members in the Security forces and with access to material privileges had created a situation in which the scum of society and opportunists had penetrated the party, and more so the Security forces. It soon became clear that many party members were the same old Polish anti-Semites as before. Having to deal with these people was not only disappointing; it hurt.

There were episodes such as this. One night when I was on duty in hospital, a patient complained to me that a woman orderly was drunk. I found the woman in the duty room stinking of alcohol, lurching on her feet, mumbling incoherently, and obviously a danger to the well-being of the patients. A very coarse woman, big-boned and fat, she looked at me aggressively – "Whaddya wan' with me?" As physician on duty, responsible for the order in the ward, I asked her to leave her post, go home, and sleep. "I always knew you were a witch," she replied, "and I don' have to obey you." "Oh yes, you do, and you'd better do so unless you want me to call the doorman to put you out." But she was too drunk to argue. She collapsed on the bed and was asleep before anything could be done about it. So I left her there and went about my work. Nevertheless, she remembered the incident. It turned out that she was a party member in the hospital unit, and at the next meeting she accused me of "having pestered an honest member of the working classes without any cause." Her son, who served as an orderly to a Soviet general, was also present, although he had nothing to do with the hospital or our unit. The expressions on most of the faces as I described the incident were palpably and crudely anti-Semitic. I was the only Jew present, and the atmosphere was tense. So rather than requesting permission to call witnesses from among the patients or staff, I did not respond. Instead of reprimanding the woman, telling her that she should not have come to work in a state of intoxication, the party cell executive reprimanded me instead. And although it could never be said, it was clearly implied that it was dangerous to antagonize her because of her son's high connections.

Through this and similar episodes, I learned that there was no concern for justice or truth even within the Party, and that silence was required about the application of these principles. Not only did this situation disappoint and disillusion me, but it also demanded a constant mental vigilance, along with a double standard, which was both stressful and against my nature. However, until I left Poland, I remained a party member. So did Alina. We knew that she was being interrogated but nothing more. It was happening to many people then. I did not ask, and she didn't volunteer any details.

Socially, our lives were limited. I was too busy with my work, too tired to entertain. We met only our closest friends – Alina, Max and his wife, Mietek's sister and her husband. There was also another friend of his from the war and a few other couples, people who were in the Security, but all Jews. Really, nothing had changed. Sometimes we visited my mother and Karol, but they would never visit us in our flat. Neither did Mira and Jerzy, though we always kept in touch. Sometimes we visited them, and they played bridge with Mietek. Mira and Jerzy detested communism, but although they knew that I was a party member and that Mietek worked in the UB, it didn't interfere with our relationship. Mira had always taught her pupils to be good Polish patriots, and to her way of thinking, this was not compatible with being a communist. It caused her great distress that I, whom she regarded almost as her own child, had become a party member. But our disagreements were only on matters of ideology and never really came between us.

I think it was in 1950, because I was still in Szczecin, when the phone call came from Mira. She was crying and sounded desperate. "They've taken Jerzy ... he's in prison. With his duodenal ulcer, it'll be the end of him. He won't survive. It's the end." I tried to calm her, said that I'd come as soon as possible, and took a plane to Warsaw. I'd never seen Mira so distraught. I pieced together the story: Jerzy, who was always telling jokes, particularly anti-government ones, was telling a new one to a colleague with whom he was shar-

Stasia with Mira Sawa in 1945 or 1946

ing a taxi to go to work. The driver was a Security informer. That evening, when she was beginning to worry because he was late for dinner, Mira received a telephone call from someone she didn't know telling her that Jerzy had been arrested and that he'd probably get three years' hard labour. While she was telling the story and crying, I was sitting beside her, listening, trying to calm her, my mind going around. How could I help? How could I bring him back to her? Could "they" torture him? Kill him? How could I save him? At this moment of despair, she was probably subconsciously counting on me, with my "connections," to help. As my mind churned, one idea emerged – I had to go to Jacek. But would he help me? How could I approach him? I hadn't seen him since the time we met again at the rest house in Kudowa.

Leaving Mira with only the assurance that I would do my best, I went to a public telephone and called the UB Investigation Department. Giving my name to the person who answered, I asked to speak to Colonel Rożański. "What do you want to talk to him about?" "It's a personal matter." A few moments later I heard Jacek's voice. "What's the problem, Stasia?" "Jacek, I have to see you." I must have sounded desperate, because he didn't question me any further, but just said I should come immediately. "Do you have your identification papers or party card on you?" I did. "All right, Stasia. I'll give the order at the gate to let you pass." At the time, it seemed to me almost miraculous that I was to be let into the inner sanctum of the Bezpieka because, as far as I knew, the public was never allowed in. Unless, of course, they were going to be interrogated. For most people, the building was a place of fear, but I couldn't let myself indulge in any apprehensions.

The gates closed behind me. The guard at the entrance took my identification papers and party card, examined them slowly, his eyes expressionless as he looked back and forth from my face to the photographs on the documents. Keeping them, he spoke into a telephone and then told me to go across the courtyard to a door. I rang a bell. Another guard opened the door, and I followed him up wide stairs and along echoing corridors. He knocked on a heavy door and then opened it into a large room with a high window, the walls blank. Jacek was sitting behind a large desk. He greeted me, offered me a chair opposite him, his manner, as always, charming, calm, and informal. "So, Stasia, why do you want to see me?" "It's about the case of Jerzy Sawa." "And why should this case concern you?" His dark eyes seemed to penetrate my thoughts, as though he could read the secrets of my soul. I could see Jerzy in the Gestapo prison, his eyes alert while the Gestapo officer interrogated me. "Take your time," said Jacek. "Tell me everything."

He didn't interrupt while I spoke. I told him my story, who Jerzy Sawa was for me, how he had saved my Peter's life, how he and Mira had gone to the Gestapo prison and risked their lives for mine. I swore that he was not an enemy of the state, that he simply joked for the sake of a joke – all of which was true. I begged Jacek, pleaded with him, to help Jerzy because he was ill and didn't deserve punishment. When I'd finished, he asked me a few more questions, details I'd left out, how I was so sure that Jerzy didn't belong to some organization that was working against the government, and whether I would agree to take responsibility "before the Party" if he were freed and then "something happened" – he didn't specify what the "something" could be. I agreed eagerly, but Jacek made no promises. All he said was that he "would look into the matter," which in itself was a lot and gave me hope.

I had the feeling that if Jacek were to help Jerzy, it would be because I had told him that Jerzy had saved Jewish lives and that it was the Jew in him that was reacting. Mietek says it cost Jacek nothing to help Jerzy and that Jerzy would probably have been released anyway. But the point is that three days later Jerzy was free.

There was a vulgar expression in Poland – *zydokomuna* ("Jewish-communist conspiracy" or maybe "commie Jew"). After the war we were hated not only as Jews but as members of the Party, and the Polish people connected the two. The truth is that in those first years many Jews were involved in the apparatus of oppression, and Jacek Rożański is remarkable only because we knew him. I cannot make up my mind whether I share Mietek's or Peter's opinion about this. Mietek thinks that Jews did it because they were true communists and so took on themselves the jobs that Poles could not or would not do. According to him, there was nothing wrong with this attitude because they considered themselves Polish citizens and wanted to help as much as they could in the building of a communist Poland. As for anti-Semitism, he says it is simply in the Polish blood. Peter, on the contrary, feels that Jews absolutely should not have become involved in the Security forces, either in the oppression or in any part of its machinery. I am not sure, but it seems to me that my feelings are now closer to Peter's than to my husband's, and that if Poland had to have Jaceks, they should have all been Poles – Catholic Poles, not Jewish Poles.

Although at first I had accepted my position as one of the privileged class without giving it any conscious thought, a sense of discomfiture had been growing. I began to see things from the other side, and I had to acknowledge to myself that what was going on was wrong. I started to criticize myself and the system that had created the situation. The turning point for me was the so-called

Doctors' Plot in the Soviet Union in the last months of Stalin's life, when several eminent Moscow physicians, mostly Jews, were accused of trying to poison their patients in the Politburo. I could not make myself believe that it was true, and I had a big argument with Mietek about it. "What's the matter with you?" he said. "If they've been arrested, it means they were guilty." I told him that as far as I was concerned, the whole thing sounded suspicious. Mietek got really cross and shouted at me, "Don't you believe the Party?" "No, I don't!" And I wouldn't budge. My reaction had only one meaning – that although I still believed in the communist ideology, at the same time I knew that "the revolution was eating her own children" and that my faith in the party apparatus, already shaken, was now beginning to dissolve. Mietek was so furious that he refused to talk to me for three weeks.

I now found myself questioning everything. "Brainwashed" was not part of my vocabulary then, but it was as though a film started to lift from my eyes. I never stopped believing in the idea, but I saw the lies, the distortions of the truth that were being spread in its name. In 1956 the Hungarian popular uprising had been crushed brutally by the Soviets, and we were told it was an attempted fascist coup. There were rumours that it might also happen in Poland because unrest was growing among the ordinary workers, and the Soviet government was suspicious that the new – you could say, "more popular" – government under Gomułka would not be able to maintain control.

Then came the shock with Jacek. He was arrested and imprisoned for abusing his authority, for torturing prisoners to get confessions. Mietek believed that Jacek was guilty, that he was a sadist, but I couldn't. I knew Jacek, and I couldn't imagine him doing these terrible things. Peter has told me that he once met one of Jacek's victims and that when he visited Jacek in prison, he denied nothing. I really can't be sure how much of what Peter says is true because he confabulates. I have never been able to shake the suspicion that maybe Jacek was used as a scapegoat because he was Jewish. Whatever the truth, he paid for his obedience.

Although I was among the privileged and was never threatened or verbally abused – on the contrary, for a long time I was feared because of Mietek working in the "oppression" – I now felt very uneasy about the system and about what I could see was the growing open anti-Semitism. I could see *"Zydokomuna"* in the eyes inspecting Mietek when we were out together in the street or on a tram, eyes looking at his officer's uniform and at him and recognizing him as a Jew, eyes that were saying, "What is this Jew doing in our Polish army?" I recognized the look from the war. Eyes do not lie.

I had supported the new system, strongly believing that it could bring the principles of Marxist doctrine into life, that once capitalism was no more, the "brotherhood of man" would rule and racial prejudice would be no more. I couldn't have anticipated that the virus of anti-Semitism would survive after the horrible war, when millions of Jews had died on Polish soil. When I acknowledged to myself that it was still there and that communism had not got through to people, that nothing had changed, I was dreadfully disappointed and disillusioned. The seeds had been sewn with the rebuff of my attempt to see Stefa Kunowska brought to justice and when my cousin Irena killed herself. The hopes that I'd had of seeing a system based on justice and equality take root after the horrible years of degradation and butchery faded. My enthusiasm for the new regime, for the new Poland, for my own freely chosen party, vanished. Slowly but surely I came to the conclusion that we must leave Poland, because they simply do not want us there and they never will, and we should no longer accept the humiliation. When we left, it was not from communism that I was escaping but from anti-Semitism.

In 1957 Mietek's sister went to Israel as a tourist. "Life there is very difficult," she said when she came back, "but we have to go, all of us." As she was speaking, tears rolled down her face. The new Gomułka government was allowing Jews to emigrate to Israel. This was not out of some new-found enlightenment; it was an excuse to get rid of us. There were rumours of anti-Semitic "incidents," although there was never any concrete proof. Perhaps the Polish government was spreading the stories; perhaps, as we later heard in Israel from communist friends, it was the Israeli government spreading the rumours in order to encourage immigration. Mietek was very upset at my insistence that we emigrate. The idea of leaving Poland was painfully difficult for him. He is a very honourable man, and he felt ashamed – how could he desert the Party and the trusted position he had been given? He had friends in the Central Committee of the Party; he was an officer who had advanced with

Mira and Jerzy Sawa in 1959 (the photo sent with the message quoted on 223)

the army from Russia; he had been in the Kościuszko division, the division that took Berlin. How could he leave? But my mind was made up. I brought home the emigration papers and told him that, if he wanted, he could stay, but I was going. When he told his superior at the Bezpieka medical administration that h7 was handing in his resignation because his wife wanted to emigrate to Israel, the man laughed. "What? That 'goya'!" – he'd known me from before the war, when the term was applied to assimilated Jews. In fact, I didn't want to go to Israel. My idea was to go to Canada, the United States, or a western European country. But Mietek was absolutely firm: if he had to leave, it would be only for "the land of my ancestors." During those last weeks, I often saw Mietek in tears. It is the only time I have seen him cry – not when we left Israel, not when his sister and brother-in-law died, not even when Max died.

My chief at the hospital couldn't understand why I would leave, telling me that he was going to recommend me as co-department head. As for Mira, she was devastated when I told her. "Why are you doing this? You are Polish. Israel isn't for you. You'll never be happy there. Poland is your country. It's your fatherland, and your place is here." I tried to explain that I didn't want to live any more with the Stefa Kunowskas, that nothing had changed or would change. "Yes, there are Kunowskas," she said, "but there are also Sawas." She was in profound distress.

Before we left, Mira and Jerzy gave me a photograph of themselves. On the back they wrote, "Stashenka, when you think about Poland, remember that as long as we live, you have in your homeland eternal and loving friends who will never forget you and will always love you and remember you as the person closest to them. Yours, Mira and Jurek."

Emigrants normally had to renounce their Polish citizenship, but through Karol's influence, we were given special passports, valid for two years in case we wanted to come back. Also – and it must have been at my mother's urging – Karol arranged that I should have a special consular stamp on mine, which meant that I was still a Polish citizen. Karol, now an old man, wasn't powerful in the obvious sense, but he was one of the best-known people in Poland, and he had connections everywhere in the country. Even though the relationship between my mother and myself had improved after my suicide attempt, I still felt I was peripheral to her life, and I don't know what distressed her most – the thought of my going away from her or my willingness to leave Poland, her beloved country, which was central to her existence. She was also appalled at the idea that, of all places, her daughter would go to Israel.

The Earth and the Thought

The pungent smells of the East, the heat, the dust, the oriental ambience, the Hasids in their long coats and sidelocks, the odours of falafel and hummus, of everything fried in olive oil, that permeated the grubby, dingy, airless hotel and the surrounding area of Tel Aviv – all of it appalled and repelled me.

The conflict over our destination continued to Paris, but Mietek was unshakeable in his determination, and I didn't want to leave him; nor did I have the courage to go on alone. The moment we arrived in Israel, he was at home. To my surprise, he could speak Hebrew. And his sister and brother-in-law and Max and his wife soon arrived. He also found work in his speciality, whereas I discovered that in mine women couldn't get hospital appointments and that I would get work only in a clinic. From that time my professional life stagnated, and I lost interest in my work. It became no more than mere routine.

Stasia in Israel in 1959

I felt that I had made a terrible mistake. I didn't like anything about a country in which I felt alien, whose language I didn't know, and which was going to deny me any professional satisfaction. I told Mietek I wanted to go back. "In that case," he replied, "our paths will separate." I went to the Polish Embassy, where Bida, the elderly ambassador, was a friend of Karol's. He could speak Yiddish because he'd been brought up on a Jewish street, playing with the children there. When I told him I wanted to return, he shook his head. "Think it over again. You know and I know that anti-Semitism hasn't died out in Poland, and it won't die out for a long time. I really wouldn't advise you to go back. Give it time." Anyway, I stayed, though Peter wouldn't try to adapt, and he returned to Poland after less than two years. But Mietek's words remained with me, and they affected my feelings towards him.

For a while during those first war-free years, I accepted Israel as my home. We bought a small house in Acre, and we lived modestly, with a small circle of close friends in different cities, people we already knew, including Max and his wife, Mietek's sister and her family, one of Mietek's companions from the Kościuszko division, and an old school friend I'd met one day on the beach. There was even a period when I had a real sense of belonging. I became aware

Stasia in Israel in 1957

of it when I boarded a ship in Naples to go back to Israel after a trip to Europe. Surrounded by the familiar voices speaking Hebrew, I suddenly had the feeling that I was among my own, that I was going home. But unlike Mietek, who took out Israeli citizenship the moment we arrived and never went back to Poland, even for a visit, I held onto my Polish passport until 1968, when Poland severed diplomatic relations with Israel after the Six Day War. It was then that, together with other veterans, we gave the passports and our war medals – Mietek had a lot – to the Israeli authorities to be sent back to Poland.

My mother had visited us some time before that, when Karol was still alive. She took care not to get an Israeli visa on her passport, and on her return to Poland, she told people that she'd been in France. The Polish government required its citizens visiting Israel to register with their embassy, so we took her there. We saw Bida, who was still the ambassador, and spent a few minutes in his office. I wasn't aware of it at the time, but my mother didn't introduce Mietek as my husband. Mietek was convinced that she simply could not publicly acknowledge that she had a Jewish son-in-law. He was disgusted, though he said nothing to her about it, and he refused to see her off at the aiport a couple of days later. I know that she implanted some of this self-hatred in me. I never deny being a Jew, but it is something that does not particularly appeal to me. It's the same way, and to an even greater extent, with Peter.

The first time I returned to Poland was after Karol became ill and wanted to see me. I went to the embassy for an entry visa and showed my special passport to the new ambassador, a young man whom I could sense was anti-Semitic. He told me that it was useless – "It means nothing. You have no right to go to Poland." Karol again had to use his influence at the foreign office, and a telegram was sent to Tel Aviv ordering that I immediately be granted a visa. The next time I returned was for Karol's state funeral. Side by side, her face hidden behind a black veil and rigid with self-control, she and I walked in the cortège behind the bier on the black carriage, pulled by black horses, through the closed-off streets lined with hundreds of people, the men taking off their hats as the procession went by.

Karol was the personification of my mother's ideals, her worship of the Polish culture, everything she aspired to. Although she was lonely after his death, she refused to move to Israel to live with us. On one occasion, on the telephone, we had a conversation about the past in which I reproached her for her treatment of my father. Upset, she replied slowly: "You don't understand. Don't think I didn't love your father. He was my first love. I would like to explain many things to you, but I'll have to be in the right frame of mind to talk about them. The next time we're together, I think I'll be able to do it." We arranged to meet for a holiday in Romania in 1968, and she was so excited about this trip, writing to me about "a thousand things I want to tell you" and about "opening your eyes to many facts that you don't know." But that year the Warsaw Pact troops invaded Czechoslovakia to frustrate the Dubček government's democratic reforms, and at first I postponed and then cancelled the trip for fear the unrest would spread. She was very disappointed. In the late autumn of 1969 she had a minor accident with a car. When I telephoned, she was obviously pleased to hear my voice. She said that she was all right and I was not to worry, but she wanted me to visit her because there was so much she wanted to talk about, so many unsaid things.

But we never had what might have been our moment of understanding, of reconciliation. A few days after that conversation, we were in Haifa when Mietek answered the telephone. It was Jerzy telling him that my mother was in hospital after a major heart attack. Racked with a sense of guilt, I began crying and couldn't stop. I wanted to go to her side immediately. For this I needed an entry visa, but since Poland had severed diplomatic relations with Israel, the Finnish embassy was handling visa applications. In turmoil, I forgot that it was the day after Christmas, and when I arrived at the embassy in Tel Aviv, there was a sign on the door that the offices were closed for the next eight days. On my way back to Haifa I made the decision to travel without a visa and trust that they would understand. Mietek didn't like it. He called the Israeli Ministry of Foreign Affairs and was told that they couldn't be responsible for me if I went without the proper documentation. The first air connection I could get was on a flight leaving two days later, but by then Jerzy had called again to say that my mother had died. I told him to send me a telegram signed by the Warsaw police to this effect because I was coming for the funeral.

Through the frost and grime on the airport window, the blurred faces of Alina and the old people, Jerzy and Mira Sawa, waiting for me in the freezing cold of a Warsaw winter night. It was the end of December, and I was being refused permission to enter Poland because I had no visa, only the telegram, sent to me in Israel by Jerzy, stating that my mother had died and that the funeral was being delayed until my arrival. The airplane arrived at the shabby, old-fashioned airport in the middle of the night; the other passengers disappeared; only I was left, trying to persuade the officials to let me in. My mother's desire to mask her origins had created a ludicrous situation: I couldn't prove that I was her daughter. Her name was Irena Grywińska-Adwentowicz, née Stange, and officially she was a non-Jew, while I, with an Israeli passport and married to Mietek, am Stanisława Ałapin-Rubiłowicz, née Grynbaum. To prove my identity, I gave the officer a list of names of people who could attest to my being who I am.

Only staff and passengers were allowed inside the building, and I kept gesturing through the window to Jerzy and Mira, elderly and frail, to go home. Each time they shook their heads, though finally they took shelter in an unheated waiting room. Seven hours passed, and daylight was tinting the grey Warsaw sky when permission was granted for me to stay in Poland for three days. One of the names I had given them was Nina Andrycz, the wife of the prime minister, Józef Cyrankiewicz; she was an actress and a friend of my mother. It was possibly her word that they took as guarantee of my identity – an Israeli daughter of Irena Grywińska, the famous actress and theatrical director of pure Polish blood.

I started to cry again when I went with Alina and Jerzy and Mira into my mother's apartment, everything still redolent of her presence, everything in her perfect taste. She had lived here for twenty years, at first with Karol; since his death, alone. I began the process of opening and emptying the contents of her writing table, wardrobes, chests of drawers; of going through her personal possessions. I occupied my mother's room, lying on her bed, my cosmetics beside hers on her dressing table. Alina slept in Karol's room, left unchanged since his death a decade before. Exhausted but unable to sleep, I was overwhelmed with memories, doubts, and guilt.

Could it be that I had been unfair to my mother because of how I felt about my father? I saw her rarely after they separated. Nevertheless, it was only in her that I confided about my first love affair, when I was seventeen, with Jan. Yet there was always a feeling of distance between us. She was extraordinarily clever, intelligent, and very well read; she knew Russian and German so perfectly that she translated plays from these languages for professional use; and she was the most beautiful of women. But she put herself on a pedestal, distancing herself from "ordinary" people – among them her own daughter.

Alina stayed with me in the flat, helping me to do everything and to keep me steady. She held her own feelings to herself more than ever. Alina was one of the few of us who had remained in Poland after most Jewish communists were thrown out the year before. She didn't talk about the situation; she just shrugged her shoulders when I brought it up. I thought she'd never leave, just as she had refused to leave when Alexei Berdayev – she always loved him – wanted her to join him after the war in the United States and I'd urged her to go, but she didn't want to take the risk of being dependent on him and in such a distant, different country. If it were me, I would have gone.

My cousin Zenia came to the flat with Aunt Genia, the widow of my father's brother, Uncle Franek. Aunt Genia had returned to Warsaw after the war, but her son, Stefan, had left Poland years ago. Zenia was my only blood relative left in the country. It was now a quarter of a century since Zenia and I had hid together in the old bitch's flat and watched the "bedbugs" burn in the ghetto uprising. Both she and Aunt Genia never returned to their real names; they kept their wartime "Aryan" identities. They wanted to stay in Poland, but not as Jews. Many remained under this camouflage. If they married, even their partner may not have known their origins; so even today it is impossible to know exactly how many Jews are living there, because there were many like my aunt and my cousin. In time they get used to it, forget who they are, and don't tell their children. My old school friend Lena is doing the same kind of thing in England. When she and I met again in 1957, the first time we'd seen each other since that night when war was declared, there was a distance between us – the distance of our feelings of guilt as survivors, the distance of unspoken words. Lena refused to talk of the past and of her murdered family, that poor but loving and very Jewish family from which she'd wanted to distance herself when we were girls. Now she wants only to be English, to behave and think in the "English way," to have only English friends, to be thought of as English.

The Warsaw newspapers carried my mother's obituaries:

IRENA GRYWIŃSKA-ADWENTOWICZOWA
Actress, director, and theatre manager of renown, passed away on 26th December. She was associated after the war with the stage in Łódź, Kraków, and Warsaw. She was decorated for her artistic achievements with the Officers' Cross Order of the Renaissance of Poland and with the medal of Ten Years of the People's Poland. The Polish stage has lost a talented actress, and the world of acting has lost a great woman of the theatre.

The Ministry of Culture and Arts.

The Directorial Board of the Classical and Diversity Theatres announce with sorrow the death of the actress IRENA GRYWIŃSKA-ADWENTOWICZ.

There was a lengthy article about her in the magazine *Theatre*. It says that the greatest influence on her artistic career had been her meeting with and then marriage to Karol.

I found a biographical note written in my mother's hand. It gives her date of birth as 1898 – in fact, she was born in 1894 – and it doesn't give her Jewish-sounding maiden name. It says that after her father's death, when she was three, her mother left for Dresden, Germany, and remarried, and she was brought up by her grandparents in Poland. She writes that after high school she was sent to Dresden to learn foreign languages, including German. She then took stage training in Poland, her first contract being in Łódź in 1923. A list follows of her pre-war appearances in Warsaw, Łódź, and Lwów, "often under direction of K. Adwentowicz." The note refers to Karol being in Pawiak prison for several months during the war and to her working as a housekeeper in the country for the last two years of the war – the period at Albinów. The long list of the parts she played both before and after the war, often with or under Karol's direction, includes Nora in Ibsen's *A Doll's House*, Hilda in his *The Master Builder*, the title role in *Anna Karenina*, Regina Giddens in Lillian Hellman's *The Little Foxes*, and Mrs Bernburg in *Girls in Uniform* by Christine Winsloe; she also took leading parts in several of Molière's plays. She makes no reference to her first marriage with my wonderful, beloved father, nor to me, her daughter and only child.

The funeral was scheduled for the week after I arrived – in Poland one had to queue even to be buried. My permit was for three days only, and as I wanted to stay for another couple of days after the funeral to recover and to make sure all her belongings were properly distributed, I had to go to a government office to get an extension of my visa. The official adamantly refused to prolong the permit past the moment of the burial, insisting that I should go directly from the cemetery to the airport. "Very well," I said finally, "then I'll stay without a permit." "That will be a misdemeanour and violation of the law. You could easily be sent to prison." "You know something?" I said. "After having survived Hitler, I'm not afraid of anything you can threaten me with." He went off to consult with his superior, and when he came back, he had the extra extension.

When she retired – unwillingly – from the stage, I had asked my mother to come and live with us in Israel. "What are you talking about?" she wrote back. "I cannot leave. I must be buried beside Karol." She had told me, Aunt Genia, and the Sawas, as well as some of her colleagues from the theatre, that she had paid a gravedigger to keep a place beside him in the Communal Cemetery. I knew that this was one of the reasons why, in later years, she wouldn't stay away from the country for long periods. When I found the receipt in her writing desk, I went with Władysław, a taxi driver, to look for the man. I'd hired the taxi by the day so that I could get around to do all the things I had to do as expeditiously as possible. It was cold, the queues for the buses and trams seemed longer than ever, and my dollars were worth a lot of zlotys. Because I was now living outside the country, Władysław spoke to me freely. The communist establishment was "them" and "they"; the rest of the population, "us" and "we." He grimaced with disgust when he pointed out the special stores where the Security and the upper echelons could buy whatever they need. "They are stuffing themselves with sausages, but we can't get anything." I didn't tell him that I used to be one of "them."

Władysław was a nice man, very considerate. At the cemetery we were told that the gravedigger had retired, so we went to the address on the receipt, but the man's wife told us that he was dead and that she knew nothing of his dealings. We had to return to the cemetery, and I paid gravediggers to open the ground beside Karol, whose remains lie in the section reserved for Poland's "Immortals." We stood for hours as they laboured at the frozen earth, until their pickaxes hit another coffin, too close to the surface for another to be placed on top of it. I had to agree to a place in the general area, far away from Karol. There was nothing else I could do.

A few of my mother's colleagues from the theatre visited the flat with their condolences. They didn't know that I was living in Israel; my mother had told them that her daughter lived in Paris. I didn't enlighten them. My mother was respected as an actress and a director but had few close friends among them, and I know that she was not much liked – as a director, she was very authoritarian and always kept herself at a distance. When one of her neighbours came in, she commented, "The lady was Jewish, wasn't she?" Everyone knew.

Aunt Theja, my mother's half-sister, telephoned from California. She told me that Grandmother Schwartz had wanted to be buried in a Jewish cemetery, but when she died, my mother had her put into the Communal Cemetery in Kraków, under her wartime, Polish name, and a cross placed on the stone. During a visit to Poland, Theja had had the cross removed.

I kept only a few things from the flat – some books and Karol's gold watch for Peter, and for me, my mother's large collection of photographs, mostly of herself. I took a list of the items to the Central Bureau of Customs to get official permission to remove them from the country. When the officer in charge saw my family name, he asked whether I was connected to Bolek. He happened to be one of his former patients and signed the papers without even looking at them.

My mother's jewellery had been stolen. She'd had some good pieces, but when I found her jewellery box, nearly everything of value had disappeared. Aunt Genia told me that my mother, who even as an old woman was beautiful and fastidious about her appearance, still used to wear it. The only person who had access to the flat was a neighbour to whom she gave the key when she was taken to hospital, but I couldn't prove anything, and anyway, there would have been nothing I could do about it.

Most of her furniture went to the Old Artists' Home, and a painting by the famous artist Wyczółkowski was donated to the National Museum in her memory. I gave Mira and Jerzy the TV that Theja had sent to my mother only a few months before. Władysław took it to their flat one night. Everything else was also distributed quietly after nightfall – we didn't want to draw attention to what I was doing. It had to be done that way because my mother left no will, and it would have taken a lengthy and costly court process even to establish that I was her daughter.

Aunt Genia told me that when my mother had the heart attack, she was taken to a general hospital, where she was never seen by a cardiologist and was left neglected and untreated in a corridor. The thought of you having died alone and unattended is intolerable, you, the most beautiful, all-knowing, and adored of women. Was it guilt that caused me to grieve so inconsolably for you, to lie sleepless in the flat where you spent your last lonely years? Was it guilt for having reproached you for events that took place half a century before? Or was it the sudden memory of my father's words when we met in that terrible place, surrounded by horror: "Take care of your mother. Never, never abandon her. Promise me that." Now I have the feeling that I was not true to his wish and my promise and that I failed you and him.

Lying in her coffin, my mother was still beautiful, her face unlined. I broke down at her funeral, irritating Alina, who told me to control myself. There were only fifty or sixty people present, actors, actresses, theatre staff, my mother's teachers from a school of languages where she'd been learning English and Esperanto. Aunt Genia was there, and so was a young actress Peter had been in love with before he left, also the granddaughter of old Zawadzka, our housekeeper when I was a child. And of course, Jerzy and Mira. Jerzy was outraged at the absence of a religious ceremony. When the coffin was being lowered into the ground, he suddenly shouted, "Irena, you are being buried like a pagan! No priest to pray for the peace of your soul!" Making the sign of the cross, he fell to his knees at the side of her grave, praying aloud.

Two days later, when I was leaving Polish soil for the last time, I was harassed at the airport by a stupid customs officer, a girl who looked and behaved like a peasant of the coarsest type. Out of some kind of viciousness, she ignored the signed document listing the items in my suitcase and threw everything on the floor, checking every item, even putting a finger through one of my mother's photographs, saying that people had been known to smuggle diamonds in this way. It delayed the airplane for two hours. I finally lost my temper and accused her of anti-Semitism. She shouted back, "Don't you dare talk to me like that!" I was furious with her and everything she represented.

Growing up, I had wanted so strongly to be part of Polish society that I had rejected my Jewishness, because the two were palpably incompatible. If nothing else, the war years had forced on me a strong sense of belonging. This was reinforced when I married Mietek, who although a non-believer, had a strong feeling of being part of the Jewish people. But paradoxically, in Israel, after a short period when I felt that I had found my place, my alienation returned, and my sense of belonging evaporated. I felt trapped in a vicious circle of permanent conflict, agonizing over the endless toll of death not only of Jews but of Palestinians, whose treatment as unwanted, second-class citizens awoke familiar echoes. The Arabs wanted us dead or gone, but the Jews, who had made the desert bloom, planted forests on the sand dunes, built modern cities, and established a high level of university education, health care, scholarship, science, and agriculture – they also had their right to live there.

During the Six Day War in 1967 and then in 1973, during the Yom Kippur War, I was half out of my mind with the horror of the deaths, of our children returning home blind or maimed, and of the terrible screams of the bereaved mothers – many of them had already lost their first families in the Holocaust. And this against the background of hateful intolerance on the part of the extreme Orthodox, the endless bitter political disputations, in which personal ambitions were mixed with religious and racial prejudices. I somehow felt myself guilty for all the deaths and for all the injustices, and in a state of constant conflict between myself and the order of things. Finally, I couldn't take it any more. When I retired, I said I was going to Canada, where Peter had settled, to be near him and his family, and to spend my last years quietly in a peaceful, tolerant democracy, in a country that doesn't make me feel ashamed.

Seeing my life as I do, as a failure, a waste, and a defeat, I ascribe the cause before all else to the war. But it also lies within myself, in my search for something that existed only in my imagination – some idyllic, perfect love. Somebody has to pay for unfulfilled dreams, and both my husbands, as well as I, had to pay for mine.

Bolek left Poland in 1969. He went to London and worked in a psychiatric hospital. Peter says that his father, who lived and breathed Warsaw, hadn't intended to remain in Britain, but the Polish government wouldn't let him return. He has found references to many articles that Bolek wrote for psychiatric publications in Britain as well as in Poland. Bolek and I got into the habit of writing to each other on our birthdays, and on the few occasions when Mietek and I were in London, we would meet in one of the Polish restaurants, where Bolek was known. I know that he regretted the divorce and that he never found a common language with either of his other wives. I so enjoyed seeing and talking to him. I would have liked to speak to him alone, to talk to him about everything, and to tell him … But we were never alone.

Peter visited him several times and told me that Bolek had become part of the Polish émigré community, the people who had fought in the war under the Polish Government-in-Exile lead by General Sikorski, with the Anders Army and the Home Army partisans or with the Royal Air Force, and who had left Poland or not gone back after the communists took over. Bolek took Peter to his club, The White Eagle, in Knightsbridge near Hyde Park, where the members and waiters spoke in an old-fashioned manner and used terms of address with formal titles – Pan General this or that, Pan Count, or Pan Professor – and the women by their husbands' titles – Pani Admiral, Pani Minister, and so on – which, said Peter, amused Bolek. Peter says his father was in contact with Solidarity and hoped to go back if they took power. But he had a stroke before it happened. When he was dying in 1985, I longed to go to him. Although Bolek could not speak, he could hear, and there were several things I wanted to say to him. Mietek opposed the idea so adamantly that I gave in, but Peter went to London, and he arranged for Bolek's daughter by his second marriage to go from Poland to his bedside – the first time that father and daughter had met.

Bolek had a formal, traditional Christian funeral as accorded to real Poles. Other veterans were in the church in their war medals, and he was given the full military honours due to an officer of the Home Army partisans. So one could say that Bolek had finally achieved complete assimilation, complete acceptance into the old Polish heroic tradition.

Later that year I went to visit his widow in London. She was an alcoholic, and I was shocked to see the dreary little house in a dreary area of London where he had lived. There was nothing of human presence in it, nothing personal and certainly nothing of Bolek left there. It was shabby and ugly, smelling of grime and cats. Years earlier, some time in the 1950s, before Mietek and I left Poland, she and I had come across each other in the street in Warsaw. We went for a coffee, and she told me that Bolek had said to her that he had been in love only once – with me.

Now there is no one who remembers the girl in the red beret, the nights of talk, the little cabin by the sea at Jastarnia, your shouting that the fascists have taken your wife's purse just as they have taken Abyssinia, the little boy being taken from the ghetto courthouse – or my infidelities, our reconciliations, our separations.

Mietek didn't want to leave Israel. He came here to Canada to please me, as I had gone to Israel to please him. It is true that all these years he has been a good, loyal husband and friend, and it is true that I cannot imagine how, without him, I would have survived all these years of this, my second life. Yet most of the time now there is silence between us. He spends much of the day horizontal, asleep or watching TV, cynical about all politics, uninterested in anything, even the chaos in the countries of what was the Soviet Union. He is often in a state of what he calls "interior immigration."

How did we – people like Mietek, Alina, and me – ever believe all the lies? How could we have been brainwashed? Today, reading freely about Stalin, how can I forget that both Alina and I cried at his death, the death of the person whom we didn't know had murdered forty million of his own people? I believed in justice for all, that communism was the greatest idea ever conceived. I still cannot completely rid myself of it. Alina and I argue constantly in our letters. She was annoyed by my admiration for Gorbachev, whom she cannot forgive for still being a communist, and for my own unchanged opinions. Her health is not good, and she is in constant pain. I have known her for so long. She's always to be relied upon, and she stood by me during many of the times when I lost my balance, when my feet could not find firm ground. We exchange long letters, endless debates about politics, each accusing the other of intolerance to the other's opinions. Alina criticizes my sympathy for Castro, my belief in socialism. She is outraged by my drawing analogies between the United States and Soviet systems. She cannot see how I can be so uninterested in contemporary Polish events, and I tell her that not even my devotion to poets and writers such as Mickiewicz and Słowacki, who formed my very soul, can erase the images of a finger-pointing boy and of Stefa Kunowska as they denounced me to the Nazis. In truth, socialism, in the form we knew it, is bankrupt. As Mietek puts it, "At this point, history has proven her right."

Alina is also disgusted that I am still equivocal about Jacek. But I cannot be objective about him. And now Peter has heard that sometime in the early 1980s, when Jacek was walking in a park in Warsaw, he was murdered. That is all we know.

When the time comes, I will be long gone, but I know that the day must come when the dreams of generations of revolutionary fighters for freedom from oppression will be made real, when there will be peaceful coexistence, when there will be no more wars, no more starving children, no more arms race. I will never accept the idea that the revolution is dead because it has devoured its own children. The Soviet Union cannot be blamed for all the evils that have been laid at its door. They tried to build a better world, and their way of doing it proved wrong, but this does not mean that the door is closed to trying it again and again. The idea of social justice will never die because it is too great. It is immortal.

⁂

As we were leaving my mother's grave, the young actress took a handful of the icy-hard earth and gave it to me. The photographs of my mother, her letters, her obituaries, and the handful of soil are the only physical manifestations that I have of her presence and of Poland.

All that remains now is the earth and the thought. I cannot bear to watch television or hear the news from Bosnia, where they are hunting down men, women, and children and slaughtering them for the crime of being Muslim or Croat or Serb. Condemned to live this second life of the Holocaust survivor, with all the horror in constant pursuit, I attempt to escape by filling in my last years studying languages and taking an arts degree at university; with painting (I have learned the technique of making icons); and with writing letters and reading, more at ease with characters in novels than I am with real people. Which was possibly always the case. Sometimes I attend an Anglican church, where I've been welcomed – I was, after all, baptized during the war. These activities are all like narcotics that act only for a limited period of time, and then the thoughts and memories return. At my age, reminiscences have lost most of their significance, but during the restless nights, as I look at them closer and closer, I think that Professor H. not only destroyed my marriage to Bolek but undermined my second marriage too, because he corrupted me and made me expect as my due the kind of attention that is probably impossible in any marriage. When I was in Warsaw for Karol's funeral, H. came all the way from Łódź in the vain hope that I would spend the night with him. He lived until he was ninety years old. Like Bolek, he too had converted to Christianity.

Recently I described to my older granddaughter, a psychology student, the theoretical situation of a young child whose conscious memory had been awakened by a scene of violent emotions and by death, a man killing himself, her mother hysterical, her father rejected. How, I asked her, did she think this would affect the child. After some thought, my granddaughter replied that in her opinion this child would, as a grown woman, find it difficult to have normal adult relationships with men and that she would be suicidal.

For myself, I have had enough of this long journey, this extremely tiresome search for meaning and love. I have concluded that in life the rational and the irrational are so intertwined that they cannot be unknotted. Probably, I should neither have married nor had children, because, in truth, the only person I ever really loved was my father, and the only child was myself. Last night I watched a movie on television about a woman's life. She was loved by three men, and she loved a fourth for whom she waited all her life. But when she finally encountered him again in her old age, he did not even remember her. I too only loved illusions – illusions that blew away and burst like soap bubbles, leaving nothing behind. The show comes to an end; the stage is empty; the audience has left. Alone in the last row is a clown with my face.

> Evening is drawing into night.
> Everything is empty and hopeless.
> I am the wandering soul of all my ancestors.
> Lost in the world of those who never knew.
> Lost in the dense fog.
> In all the cities of oblivion.

Postscript

Stasia and Mietek would often say, "Nobody can know what it was like unless they were there at the time." That is obviously true, and it is the reason that this story of interwoven odysseys has been told through the voices of those who were indeed there at that time. I would add that I am thankful I can only imagine, but cannot know, what it was like.

During a ten-day visit to Poland in 1992, I tried to get at least some small sense of the place and the people among whom these lives had unfolded. The opportunity arose when Peter was a guest lecturer at Warsaw and Kraków universities, giving courses on entrepreneurship, a skill in demand in a reborn capitalist economy. It was now a couple of years since the unexpected collapse of the Soviet regime shook the world, ended the Cold War, and thrust the responsibilities of independence upon its satellite states. For two decades before the collapse, a genuine trade-union movement, Solidarity, had been exposing the fundamental lie at the foundation of what was theoretically a workers' state. But the turbulent events that took place on Polish soil after the death of Stasia's mother at the end of 1969 play no part in this story, coinciding as it did with the period when virtually all Poland's remaining Jews were being pressured out of the country.

The Warsaw that I visited would have been immediately recognizable to Stasia and Bolek Ałapin a half-century earlier, when they were young and before the city was reduced nearly to rubble by the retreating German army. In an extraordinary act of national will and commitment, the Polish people re-created the centre of their capital, complete with its palaces, medieval castles and squares, cobblestoned alleyways and streets, with their nineteenth-century European-style facades. On the reconstructed walls are many, so very many, plaques commemorating executions by the Nazis of civilians and partisans or their deaths in the fighting.

Peter was staying in a small attic flat, centrally located, belonging to two old friends. Shelves and cupboards were crammed with hoarded basic provisions – boxes of soap powder, toilet soap, toothpaste, toilet paper, matches, towels, and canned goods – the learned response to a half-century of unreliable production and distribution of consumer goods. The wife, Ewa, an actress, had been Irena's protege; it was she who took the lump of soil from Irena's grave and handed it to Stasia. She and her widowed mother had become close to Irena in her last, rather lonely years. Ewa and her musician husband were trying to adapt to new working conditions now that the state was no longer the sponsor of the arts. I went into theatres where Irena and Karol had performed and where Irena had directed.

In the courtyard of the apartment block at Narbuta 8, in the pleasant district where in 1951 Stasia, Mietek, and Peter had lived on the same floor as the Rożańskis, Peter inspected the names above the doorbells. He was annoyed to find one of "them" – the old *nomenklatura*, a woman who had been a propogandist on the radio, still in possession of one of the better flats in the city. According to Władisław Szpilman, author of *The Pianist*, the block, which had escaped destruction in the German retreat, had been built during the war by forced labour to house ss officers.

Over a doorway in the downtown area was the sign "Adria," now the in-place for hot rock music, at the same location as the nightclub where Bolek was arrested for shouting his protest at the Italian occupation of Abyssinia. One night Peter took me to an old-fashioned, one-roomed flat to meet his father's second wife, a writer and artist. Like Alina in Copenhagen, she had a small trunk filled with photographs, letters, papers, and documents. It was to her, in the city of Łódź, that Bolek had gone when he parted from Stasia shortly after his return from the Soviet prison camp. A pretty, plump old lady, she described how he then walked out on her when she refused to abort a pregnancy and how, before her baby was born, she would listen in vain for his footsteps in the snow outside their wooden cabin. Their daughter, Wilga, met her father only once, in London just before he died, the meeting arranged by Peter, to whom she bears a clear resemblance.

One morning in the bright coffee room of a hotel near the American embassy, I noticed a group of distinguished elderly gentlemen, discreet medals on their jackets and an air and style reminiscent of the old British RAF. Veterans of the famed Division 303, the Polish airmen whose skill and heroism played a vital role in the Battle of Britain, they were joined by a handlebar moustached younger British airman. "We like to keep in contact with them," he said.

The wartime ghetto area has not been rebuilt, but one relatively undamaged structure had been repaired – the courthouse with the two entrances, front and rear, onto parallel roads, from which Peter was smuggled as a small child.

The past seemed to be constantly, often oppressively, present, possibly because it was the context in which I was looking at everything around me. I became aware of where my feet were treading, of an inescapable sense of a people who had been there and, except as a museum display, was no longer there.

And here's a strange irony: the culture of the disappeared people was becoming trendy. At one of the city's many theatres, a pre-war, cabaret-style musical by the left-wing Jewish poet and playwright Julian Tuvim was being peformed. The leading actress played the Jewish roles and sang in Yiddish; parts like this had become her speciality, though, of course, she is not Jewish. In a modernistic jewellery shop, an expensively dressed man was looking through the catalogue from a major exhibition of Jewish cultural artifacts he had attended in Berlin. A kosher restaurant, in a fashionable downtown area, has a non-Jewish proprietor.

At dawn on Easter Monday, an old friend of Peter's, from the days when he was into "Mickey Mousing," took us on the long drive south to Albinów, along nearly empty roads through shabby but visually charming provincial towns and villages, their appearance scarcely altered for more than a hundred years. In the old square at Opartow, on the wall outside a dingy building that we were told had been the Nazi HQ, was a plaque celebrating the release of a group of prisoners by partisans. One could tell, said Peter's friend, that it was installed during the communist regime because the partisan group was unidentified and Poland's white eagle symbol lacked its pre-war crown. In Iwaniska, worshippers were coming out of the church that Stasia used to attend.

The house that Jan and Zofia Pikulski built at Albinów in the 1930s, surprisingly small and stark, was now owned by a pleasant and energetic young farm family. The husband was the son of the girl who had helped in the kitchen during the war; the young couple had looked after Madam Pikulski in her declining years, and she left them the property. They knew of Peter, his mother and grandmother, and some of the story of the wartime years. A feast quickly appeared for the unexpected visitors – sausage, cheese, pickles, and bread, all homemade. In the simple kitchen was the old bread oven, now unused, its chimney set into the wall and under the stairs, returned to its original use as a storeroom, the tiny room from whose window Stasia saw the SS bursting out of the forest in the dawn light.

And the forest itself – solid oaks and beeches, along with the ubiquitous pine and birch of central and eastern Europe. On its perimeter remain earth bunkers made, I was told, by the Red Army. Whether the path to Iwaniska is still there, I forgot to ask.

Before we left, the husband brought out a medal from Yad Vashem in Israel, given in honour of gentiles who had risked their lives to save Jews during the war. It had been awarded to Jan Pikulski at Stasia's recommendation, but the communist government had refused him a passport to go to Israel to accept it in person. To Peter's deep satisfaction, it was agreed that he could buy it. Then on to the nearby farm belonging to the young man's parents, the barn still standing where Stasia hid when the Nazi soldiers were visiting Albinów, his mother greeting Peter warmly, remembering Irena, his great-grandmother, and himself as a child. Much talk and more hospitality. Before we left, the tall, angular old man brought out and mounted a splendid bay horse, clearly no ordinary farm animal, its saddle crafted with the accoutrements of the gentry. The horse was a descendant of Pan Pikulski's horses, and the saddle had been his. "I try to keep his tradition," said the old man. With his peaked cap, the rider and mount re-created the timeless picture of an *uhlan*, a Polish cavalryman.

Afterwards to Iwaniska to put candles on the Pikulskis' grave, an old lady coming over to us to say they were "good people who had saved many lives." Before Jan Pikulski's death, a documentary was made about Albinów during the war and about the couple's later work educating local children. In it an actress read a poetic letter from Stasia to the producer about Jan Pikulski and Albinów, along with the words she wrote in the visitors' book before she and Mietek left Poland in 1957.

For myself, I had a sense of relief when I left the country, the dust weighing heavy on my shoes and overwhelmed by a visit to Auschwitz. The past was too present; there seemed to be too many derelict freight wagons shuttled onto sidings along the railway tracks to Kraków and to Berlin. A weight lifted when the train ferry left Rostock on Germany's Baltic coast, heading towards Denmark and Alina.

Our last day together chanced to coincide with a ceremony in a Jewish cemetery on the outskirts of Copenhagen, where a memorial had been created for Polish victims of the Holocaust. Some of the people gathered there had been part of the same exodus as Alina. Their children, she told me afterwards, were all anticommunist like Peter. There were Hebrew prayers for the dead and a short speech by the Polish ambassador, who, together with his aide-de-camp, represented the new Polish state. One sensed a mutual lack of ease – people seoerated yet joined by too much history.

I have asked myself whether, in Alina, Stasia, and Mietek's circumstances, I would have remained in Poland after the war. But brought up in such a different society, a pluralist democracy, and with such different influences and experiences, I simply cannot know.

⊰⊱

Peter's wife, Zosia, left Poland for Canada in 1968. She was born after the war to parents who were Jewish, although she was ignorant of this until she was thirteen, a not uncommon circumstance. "The thinking was that if you are going to live in Poland, you cannot live as a Jew." The family had taken her mother's surname, Wielgosz, because it sounded more Polish than her father's, Roszenfeld. She and her brother were baptized, confirmed, and taken to church, and they lived like their neighbours in a provincial town – except that her parents were excessively protective. For example, Zosia was not allowed to learn to skate, swim, or ski. Her mother was a teacher and school librarian, and her father a photographer. They rarely spoke of the past, yet, says Zosia, "though they tried to cover it up, the Jewishness was trying to come through, so when I found out, it wasn't a shock. I'd seen my grandfather praying, wearing a tallis, though I didn't think about it. He didn't bother to hide anything, but he didn't try to pass anything on. When he died, he was buried in a Jewish cemetery in another city so that nobody would know, but I'm sure they did. We had a good life, but if I think about it, it was twisted." While attending Warsaw University, Zosia stayed with an aunt and her husband. "He was very Jewish-looking, so I didn't want friends to visit me because they'd know that I was Jewish, and my closest friends were not. A lot of the students were anti-Semitic and pro-communist – to be successful you had to join the Party." Zosia came to Canada because of what she felt was Poland's pervasive anti-Semitism and because "I wanted a normal quiet life, not a confusing double life."

I met Zosia's father a couple of times in the mid-1980s. A jolly, sweet-natured man, he had survived a German forced-labour camp because he was given the job of official photographer to the Nazi administrators. On both occasions when I met him, he told me the same story: "Hey, I tell you something funny. I was in a camp, yes? My boss was this big Nazi, I took photographs for him. So one day he says to me, 'Leon, you don't have to worry. When the time comes, I won't let anyone else kill you. I'll do it myself.' Funny guys, those Germans." And he laughed and shook his head.

Zosia knows about some of her father's experiences. He escaped from the camp; dogs sent after him missed his scent when he was hiding in a wheat field. He managed to join his parents, brother, sisters, and brother-in-law, who were being hidden by a Ukrainian family in their attic. When one of his sisters became pregnant, she and her husband left because the crying of a baby could have revealed their presence. They were never heard of again. The others remained there until the area was liberated by the Red Army. Zosia was named for her dead aunt, whose older daughter, like Peter, survived the war in a convent.

Of her mother's war years, Zosia learned only that they were spent in the Ukraine with Aryan papers. "No more. She wouldn't talk about it, but she did say it had helped that she didn't look Jewish." Before Zosia's father, his mind failing, went to a nursing home, he lived in a small apartment overlooking Halifax's harbour. Sometimes he would go out and root around in the rubbish at construction sites for pieces of wood. Along with pieces of automobile mud flaps, he took them back to the apartment, where he would whittle out clogs and make shoe lasts. The neighbours complained about him pacing up and down in the clogs during the night. Up and down, up and down.

⁂

I met Mietek's old friend Max in the summer of 1991, when he was in Canada on a visit and they came to stay at my country home for a few days. Max was a delightful man in his early seventies, short and stocky with bright blue eyes, emanating mental and physical energy. Mietek, usually so uncommunicative and politely distant from whatever was going on around him, came to life. They talked and joked incessantly, ideas, learned comments, and historical chit-chat flying back and forth between them, their conversation ranging everywhere and over everything, with erudition and wit in four languages – Polish, Russian, Hebrew, and English. Once I happened to react to a comment of Mietek's about his health by saying, "Carpe diem." "Ah, Horace," he said and, without a pause, recited the whole passage and then translated it. Amazed, I asked when he had last studied Latin. Not since he left school. It was then that he told the story of the schoolteacher, who finding in this Jewish boy a kindred spirit in her love of the language, put aside her anti-Semitism.

By chance, also vacationing in the area was an elderly Jewish couple from the United States who had been active communists most of their lives, with the attendant harassment during the anti-communist frenzy of the early Cold War years. I brought them together with Mietek and Max, but their experiences had been so profoundly different that they seemed to have little in common, apart from a once-shared ideology. The demeanour of the elderly Americans was hesitant and quiet, without any spark, reflecting their years spent "underground" in a triumphalist, capitalist society, whereas Mietek and Max exuded self-confidence – two old guys who had fought in the 1st Kościuszko division with the victorious Red Army and who had been part of the establishment in a communist state. It was only after Max had returned to Israel that I learned from Peter that he had been the medical director of the Bezpieka prison hospital. His description of how this came about and of his encounter with Jacek Rożański was in reluctant response to a letter I sent him. Max died unexpectedly a year later.

When Jacek Rożański was released from prison, he found employment in the state mint and worked there until his retirement. The last years of his life were lived in isolation from the world, in contact only with his family and some of his friends. In the absence of public information about him, while he was still alive, he was sometimes written about as though he were dead. Some people thought he had died in the 1960s; others that he had gone to Israel on his release. Peter heard he had been murdered in a Warsaw park in the early 1980s. Much of the information given here about his early life was found in *Borejsza i Rożański*, a book about him and his brother by a Polish writer, Barbara Fijałkowska, written during the 1980s but published only after the fall of the regime. She had found him and persuaded him to talk to her in his apartment and in hospital over a period of a year from 1980 to 1981.

Rożański, she wrote, did not want to be the subject of a biography but agreed to give his version of the historical era in which he had played a role. He wanted people to forget him but to remember his brother, a propogandist and writer. She observed no change in his ideological viewpoint or any remorse for his actions, but she noted that he analyzed and thought through his arguments, taking the attitude that communism could not be built without people like him.

Fijałkowska sensed in him cynicism and anger against himself and his old colleagues. He knew that he had been used to do the dirty work, but, she said, he believed it had been necessary "to clean out the enemy" and that he had been well qualified to do this job. However, "when he also was treated as an enemy and disposed of," she surmised that he had understood "that he had taken part in a big swindle and been made a fool of." What he had done had been in the name of a cause, but this cause had then shown itself to serve the interests only of a group of people "whom he in the depth of his heart despised" and who had evaded punishment for their wrongdoings. It was this, she contended, that had prevented his "re-education." One thinks of Luna Brystigier.

After reading Fijałkowska's book and the newly published records of Rożański's trials, Peter's uncertainty about him returned. "Nothing is simple about Jacek. He was consistent: what he said in 1980 was exactly the same as he said to me when I visited him in prison in the late sixties and to my mother in Kudowa in the late 1940s. Fijałkowska confirms my own mixed feelings about him: one knows the horrible things that he did; nevertheless, some kind of respect and sympathy lingers because of his intellectual honesty, and I knew him as a very pleasant man, with presence and charm. That is why Stasia and I are so ambivalent about him. There is nothing new in his moral relativism. Look at what the French did in Algeria, and what the United States has been doing."

When Roman Werfel, a leading party ideologist in the post-war era, was interviewed in the early 1980s, he referred to Rożański's "symbolic name" and commented, "Perhaps he was a psychopath. I knew him quite well. Devilishly clever, very two-faced, a Dr Jekyll and Mr Hyde." "There's one principle you have to stick to in beating," Werfel added. "Johnny has to be beaten by Johnny and not by Moishe."* This was the case: beatings and murders by the Security forces were to continue until the fall of the regime. In Arthur Koestler's *Darkness at Noon* the old Bolshevik, waiting his execution, concludes that what had made his generation of revolutionaries run amok was the precept of "the end justifying the means." They had, he says, sailed "without ethical ballast."

Shortly before Jacek Rożański died, from cancer, in August 1981, his old friend Anka visited him from Australia. It was in her home that Stasia had first met him before the war. Anka, who fought in the ghetto uprising, had left Poland in the 1950s. His wife, Bela, survived him by seven years. They are both buried in the Jewish cemetery in Warsaw, where Lusia, Bolek's cousin, erected a memorial for the unburied members of her family killed during the war.

---

* The interview is in Toranska's *Oni: Stalin's Polish Puppets*.

Stasia said that the only time she had seen Mietek weep was before they left Poland. I also once saw Mietek in tears. When he was recovering from his first heart attack, he told me about a school friend, Beila Gołombiewska, a very clever girl who had always been at the top of the class with him and who had entered medical school at the same time. When the Germans invaded, she went home to her parents in Lida and then, with her physician father, joined a Jewish partisan group in the forests. There casually one day she and her boyfriend were murdered, possibly by another partisan group, possibly by bandits. "They wanted the leather jackets they were wearing. It was for their jackets ... just for their jackets."

In early 2001, when it was clear that he did not have long to live, Mietek also told me about Leib Czertok, his closest childhood friend. Leib had a sister – "I was crazy about her." His father had sent Leib, a musician, to study in England in 1938. "When war broke out, he joined the Polish emigrant army – they accepted Jews on an equal footing – and Leib, who was good-natured and a musician, was a popular officer." Leib's parents and sister survived the war through the help of the Japanese consul in Wilno who obtained Japanese passports for them and many other Jews, and evacuated them to Shanghai.* Leib was killed when his unit took part took part in the disastrous British-Polish parachute landing at Arnhem in the Netherlands in September 1944. Decades later, Mietek arranged to meet Leib's sister in Boston. "She was in her fifties then, but to me she was still beautiful." There were whys I did not ask.

A couple of weeks before his death, he suddenly said to me, "It is hard to live in a country which wants of you only your duties as a citizen, your legal and civic responsibilities, but which denies you your rights. It is hard to be treated as a foreigner in your own country." And a while later, "And how do you think of somebody who has abandoned his ideology?"

A book called *The Scapegoats*, by Josef Banas, tells the story of the last exodus of Jewish communists from Poland, during the Moczar and Gomułka years of the late 1960s. At the end Banas

---

* This was probably Chinue Sugihara, who saved the lives of an estimated six thousand Jews in that region.

writes, "The movement which had given meaning to their lives now expelled them ... their hopes had proven empty, their image of the world and themselves in it false, and their lives, as they had lived them, tragically wrong – their world fell apart."

That book was among others from Alina's library sent to Peter after her death in June 2001. For years, she had never been free of the pain that had started on the day she was called as a witness at Leon Gecow's trial. Leaving a note explaining that it was simply because she was tired of pain, she had quietly taken her own life with an overdose of medication.

The spring of 1964. Under the blue sky and glaring sun of Tel Aviv. Stasia is in a fashionable café on Allenby Street, drinking coffee and eating a chocolate éclair. It is her day off from the clinic in Acre, where she works and lives. A slim, attractive woman, her hair coloured the same soft, discreet blonde that she will keep into her seventhy-fifth year, fair-haired like a Polish woman. She is wearing a simple but smart sleeveless linen dress; her mother would approve of it, and her mother's approval in matters of appearance has always been important to her.

The eclair bulges with cream, the chocolate coating thick and rich. Her longing for rich cakes and desserts unabated since the ghetto, she forks it slowly into her mouth. In a few months she will be engulfed by the voices, sounds, and images of the time of horror. With an overwhelming sense of a wasted life and, with the onset of middle age, fearful of the loss of her sexual attractiveness, she will sink under the depression that is constantly waiting to submerge her, and she will again try, and nearly succeed in, taking her life. But now she waits for a friend.

As usual, she has chosen a corner table from which, while waiting, she can look out at the street and at the other people in the restaurant. She is often repelled by what she considers the brashness of many Israelis, but today it does not particularly bother her, although she finds some of the women vulgar, dressed ostentatiously, with too much jewellery, their heavy makeup threatening to melt in the heat. She assesses them as petite bourgeoise, the sort who do not work.

Stasia has an ambivalent relationship with Israel, accepted as one of its own but uneasy with this status. She marvels at what has been created here in so short a time and yet is appalled at the intolerance and hatred that Jews and Arabs display to one another. The only way to fight for what she believes in would be to join the Communist Party. But with it she has her own unsettled accounts. She has a sense that someone's eyes are on her but cannot see anyone watching her.

The coffee house is noisy, people talking loudly, gesticulating. A place like this would not be her usual choice, but it is what her friend wanted. Anyway, the cakes are delicious. She thinks that later she may try one of the tarts, sweet, rich almond pastry heaped with fresh strawberries and served with liqueur-flavoured cream. Out of the corner of her eye she notices a middle-aged couple beside her holding hands. The woman is a brassy blonde, with black eyelashes thick with mascara; she find the couple rather ludicrous. Later the sight will remain incongruously and irrelevantly in her memory.

An old man has stopped by her table. "You are the daughter of Boleslav Grynbaum, aren't you?" The voices around her have faded. His suntanned scalp shows through sparse white hair. She cannot place him in the past. He is looking at her through dark eyes behind heavy glasses set on a bulbous nose. After a few seconds of silence, she asks him to sit down, and he takes a seat opposite her but does not introduce himself.

When she speaks, her voice is distant, haughty. "Where do you know me from? I don't think I know you. Who are you?" The old man is not discouraged. He answers slowly, deliberately. "Actually, I even remember you as a little girl. Stasia Grynbaum. Your face hasn't changed much." Then he leans forward. "I knew your father. And I saw him dying."

The colour has disappeared from the scene around her; she is surrounded with darkness; blood pounds in her temples. Wordlessly, she holds onto the table with both hands, afraid she will fall from her chair. "Calm down, child, calm down," says the old man's voice flatly. She wants to shout, to scream; she wants someone to hold her close. But there has been no one to hold her like that since the day she knew he was dead.

The old man continues. "He wasn't tortured, and he wasn't killed. He died of a heart attack, when there were only a few of us left in the workshop. I was with him to the end. He didn't suffer long. And how it was then – they left him there; no funeral, naturally; no burial. The Nazis didn't allow Jews to be buried. They just let them lie there. They were in a rush then. They already had no time."

She hears her voice whispering, "Stop now, please. You've told me enough. Thank you for having remembered me." She stands up, trembling, fumbling for money in her purse. She does not ask the old man his name, where he lives, his connection with her father, how he had survived.

Somehow she is outside, in the hot, dry wind on the street, hurrying towards the glittering, warm, turquoise sea, walking alongside the rush of the waves, walking until she can go no further, until the stars are sparkling in the blue-black night.

In her old age, in another land, she lies sleepless, watching a procession, listening to the voices. Her mother enters her boudoir with a man. As the door closes behind them, old Zawadzka gives a knowing smile. Through the opened door into his room, she sees her father sitting at a desk with a revolver in his hand. Grisha Malinovsky turns back from the door and reaches up to the top of the armoire for his forgotten revolver. Bolek is standing beside her as they look through a window at a small boy, his hand held by a woman who leads him out past a soldier holding a rifle and down a street. Children's voices chant in a wailing singsong as she steps around a body, covered with newspaper, lying in a street. A heap of tiny shoes. The stench of formaldehyde. "Jewess! Jewess! Hold the Jewess!" shouts a boy; other eyes look away, indifferent. Stefa Kunowska, her white skin flushed, points towards the doorway, talking vehemently to the concierge, making sure that he understands what she wants. At the end of a long corridor, a door opens into a large bare room where Jacek sits behind a desk. All around is dark. Burdened with the weight of a child in her arms, she struggles to move her feet, calling for help, but nobody comes. A man's body lies on the threshold of a door, blood on his head. An hysterical woman screams on a bedroom floor, violently rejecting a man's attempt to calm her. A child is watching.

In old age she lies sleepless. Watching. Listening. Waiting.

Selected Bibliography

Ascherson, Neal. *The Struggles for Poland*. London: Pan Books, 1988.
Banas, Josef. *The Scapegoats: The Exodus of the Remnants of Polish Jewry*. London: Weidenfeld and Nicolson, 1979.
Bednarski, Eric. "The Soviet Destruction of the Polish Home Army: 1944–45." MA major research paper, York University, 2001.
Behind the Scene of the Party and Bezpieka. Document 225542. Stanford: Hoover Institute on War, Revolution and Peace, Stanford University, n.d. Contains the reminiscences of Józef Światło.
Davies, Norman. *God's Playground: A History of Poland*. Volume 2. Oxford: Oxford University Press, 1981.
Fijałkowska, Barbara. *Borejsza i Rożański: Przyczynek do dziejow stalinizmu w Polsce*. Olsztyn: Wyzsja Szkoła Pedagogiczna, 1955.
Fuks, Marian, Zygmunt Hoffman, Maurycy Horn, and Jerzy Tomaszewski. *The Polish Jewry: History and Culture*. Warsaw: Interpress Publishers, 1982.
Gibney, Frank. *The Frozen Revolution: Poland: A Study in Communist Decay*. New York: Farrar, Straus and Cudahy, 1959.
Koestler, Arthur. *Darkness at Noon*. London: Jonathan Cape, 1940.
Korbonski, Stefan. *The Jews and the Poles in World War II*. New York: Hippocrene Books, 1989.
– *The Polish Underground State: A Guide to the Underground, 1939–1945*. New York: Hippocrene Books, 1981.
Marat, Stanisław, and Jacek Snopkiewicz. *Ludzie Bezpieki*. Warsaw: Wydawnictwa, ALFA, 1990.
Piotrowski, Mirosław. *Ludzie Bezpieki: W Walce z Narodem i Kośkołem*. Lublin: Klub Inteligenczi Katolickiej, 2000.

Polonsky, Antony. *Politics in Independent Poland, 1921-1939: The Crisis of Constitutional Government*. Oxford: Clarendon Press, 1972.

Schatz, Jaff. *The Generation: The Rise and Fall of the Jewish Communists of Poland*. Berkeley: University of California Press, 1991.

Starr, Richard F. *Poland, 1944-1962: The Sovietization of a Captive People*. Westport, Conn.: Greenwood Press, 1975.

Sword, Keith. *Deportation and Exile: Poles in the Soviet Union,1939-48*. New York: St. Martin's Press, 1994.

Syrop, Konrad. *Poland: Between the Hammer and the Anvil*. London: Robert Hale, 1968.

Szczypiorski, Andrzej. *The Polish Ordeal: The View from Within*. London: Croom Helm, 1982.

Tomaszewski, Irene, and Tecia Werbowski. *Zegota: The Council for Aid to Jews in Occupied Poland,1942-45*. Montreal: Price-Patterson, 1999.

Toranska, Teresa. *Oni: Stalin's Polish Puppets*. London: Collins Harvill, 1987.

Zywulska, Krystyna. *I Came Back*. New York: Roy Publishers, 1951.